IMAGES
of America

Between the Rivers
Manhattan
1880–1920

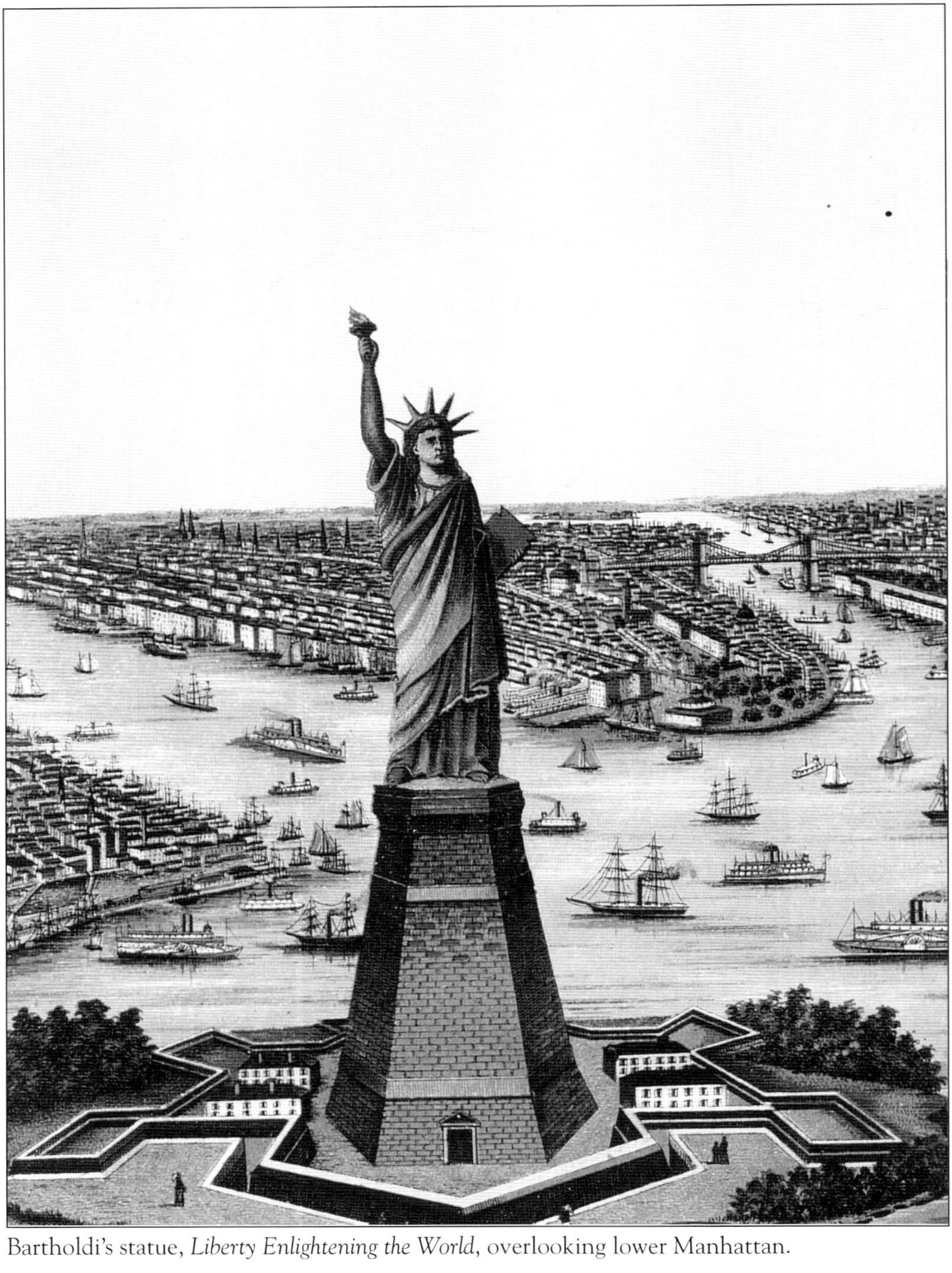

Bartholdi's statue, *Liberty Enlightening the World*, overlooking lower Manhattan.

Cover Image: Lower Broadway looking north.

IMAGES
of America

BETWEEN THE RIVERS MANHATTAN 1880–1920

Jeff Hirsh

ARCADIA
PUBLISHING

ISBN 978-0-7385-3548-7

Published by Arcadia Publishing
Charleston, South Carolina

Printed in the United States of America

Library of Congress Catalog Card Number: 2004100637

For all general information contact Arcadia Publishing at:
Telephone 843-853-2070
Fax 843-853-0044
E-mail sales@arcadiapublishing.com
For customer service and orders:
Toll-Free 1-888-313-2665

Visit us on the Internet at www.arcadiapublishing.com

This book is dedicated to my father, a true man of letters,
and to his daughter-in-law, my true girl of postcards.

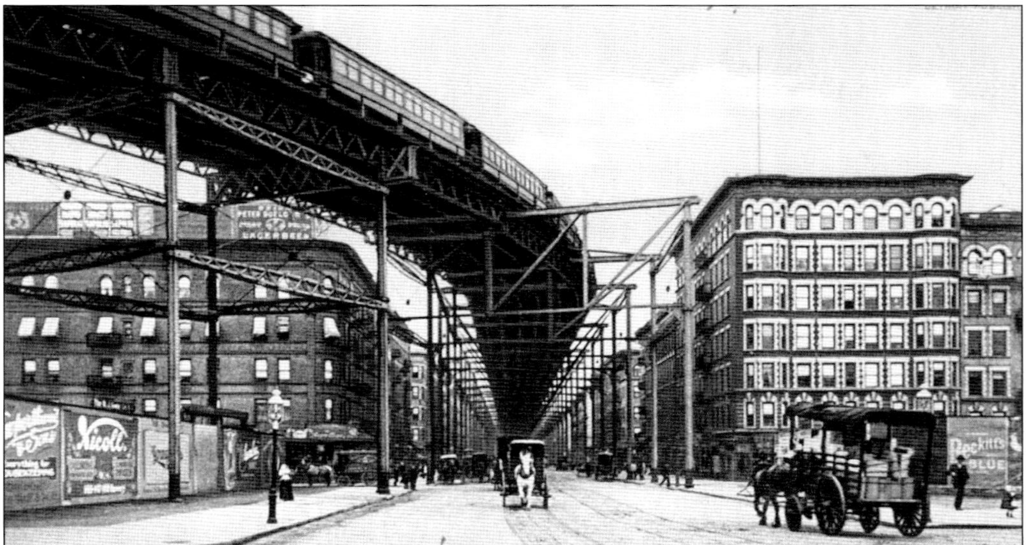

The elevated at Eighth Avenue and 110th Street, early 1900s.

Contents

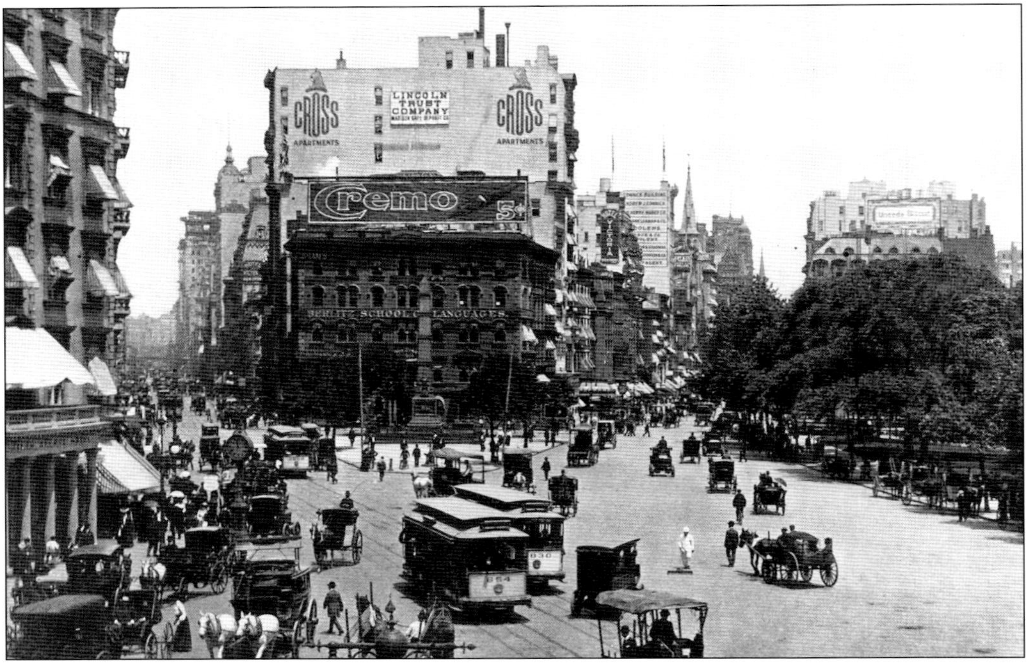

Madison Square, looking north, early 1900s. The building on the far left is the Fifth Avenue Hotel.

ACKNOWLEDGMENTS

My thanks to the many generous individuals who made this book possible with their suggestions and by sharing information and images with me. In particular, I am indebted to the library staff of the New York Historical Society, my friends Dorothy and Carlton Bloodgood, Garth Davidson of Garth Davidson Gallery, and to my wife for her patience, inspired help, and for making available the extensive image archives of Roslyn Manor Antique Postcards on Greeting Cards.

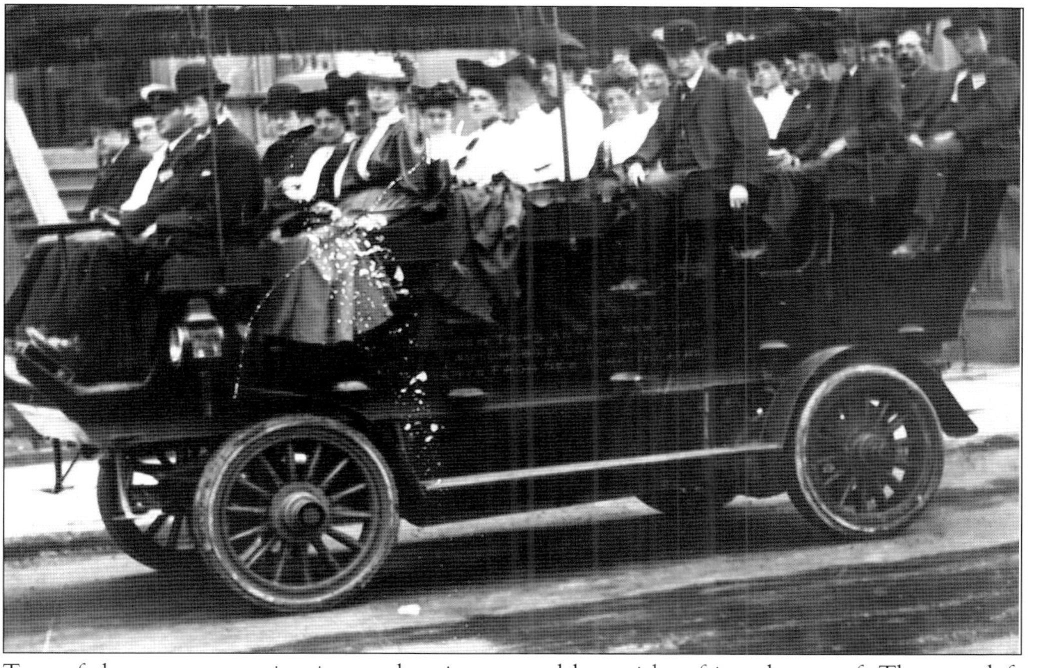

Turn-of-the-century tourists in an electric-powered bus with a fringed sunroof. The tour left from Forty-Second Street and Broadway opposite the Astor Hotel.

INTRODUCTION

Join us for a walking tour of Manhattan in the years between 1880 and the 1920s. These were glorious decades in the island's history. The town was evolving from a bustling seaport into a world financial center.

Manhattan rapidly became America's preeminent East Coast steamship port. During the years depicted in this book, steamships grew in size and became ever more luxurious. They brought with them the very rich and, in far greater numbers, the very poor.

The former made the voyage on the palatial reaches of the upper decks. In Manhattan, they were the catalyst that spawned the gilded era of its hotels and restaurants.

The latter made the travel deep below decks. From the damp, dark reaches of the steamers poured a flood of immigrant labor and talent that enriched Manhattan's industries.

The flow of rich and poor generated a vast well of material drawn upon by writers and artists who chronicled the end of the 19th and beginning of the 20th centuries.

In the 1880s, no building stood as tall as the spire of architect Richard Upjohn's Trinity Church. Horses pulled the trolleys. Steam-powered elevated trains gradually sliced north from the battery to upper Manhattan.-

In 1883, John Augustus Roebling's Brooklyn Bridge was opened. The outlines of this incredible engineering feat could be seen rising above the island's eastern skyline. In a few years, it was joined by the Statue of Liberty guarding the southern horizon.

The 1890s began the defining decades of the skyscraper. The technology was born in Chicago but soared to new heights in Manhattan as it was done to excess. By the turn of the century, there were more skyscrapers on the island than anywhere else in the world.

Corporate America was growing fast and needed to house a swelling army of clerks and managers within the narrow confines of lower Manhattan.

The evolution of skeletal steel construction technology in the 1880s and 1890s ended reliance on load-bearing walls. A succession of technological advances, from electric lights and telephones to safe elevators, made skyscrapers feasible. Thousands of office workers now did their jobs on relatively small "footprints" of land.

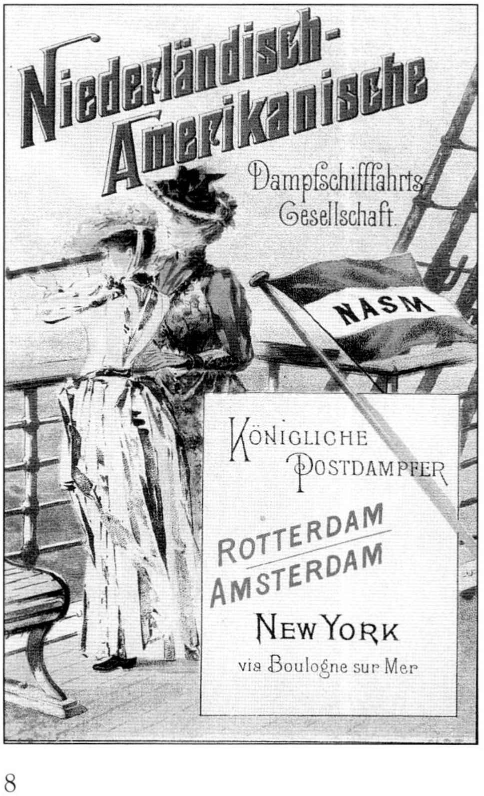

Travellers aboard an Atlantic steamer, 1880s.

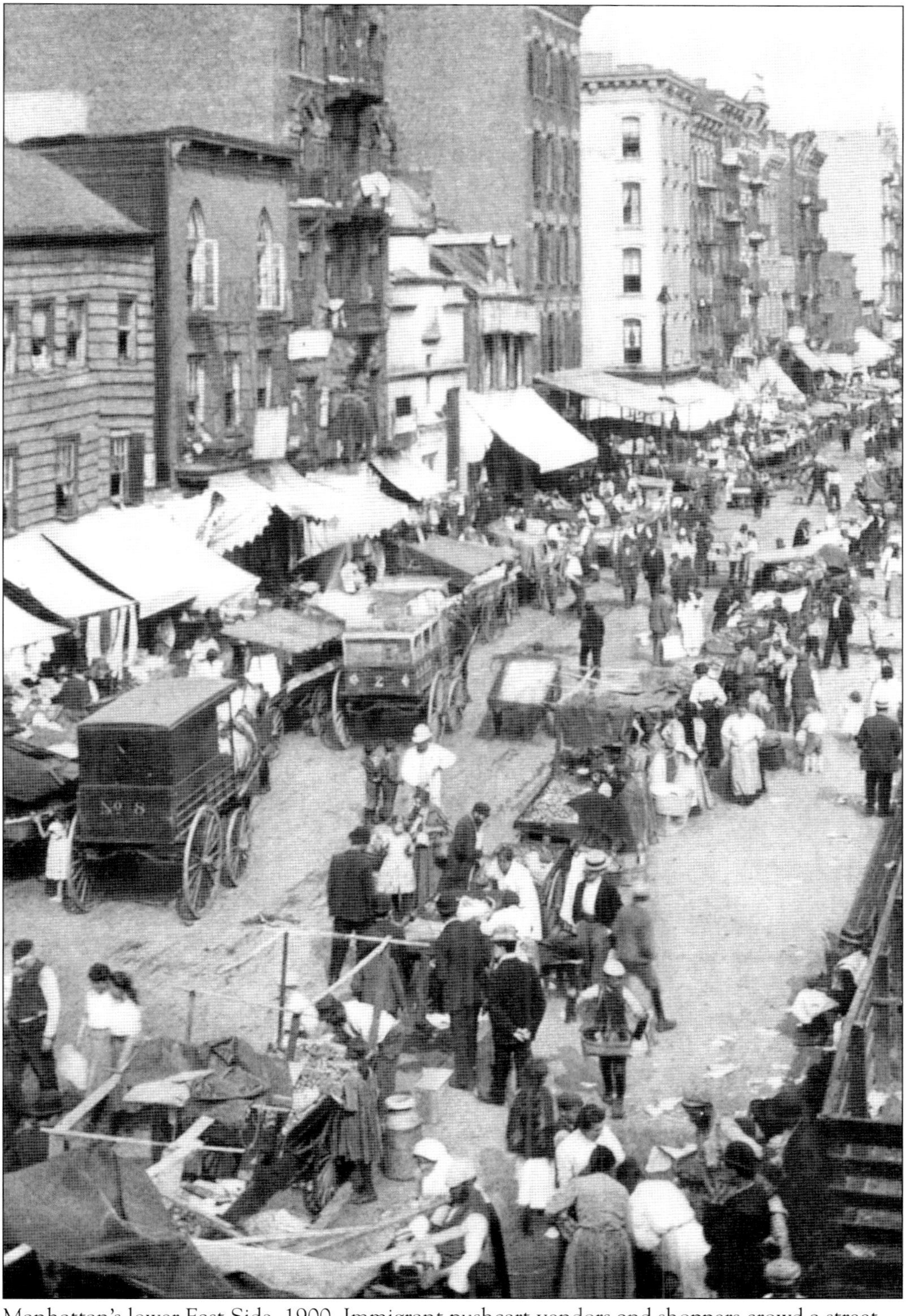

Manhattan's lower East Side, 1900. Immigrant pushcart vendors and shoppers crowd a street.

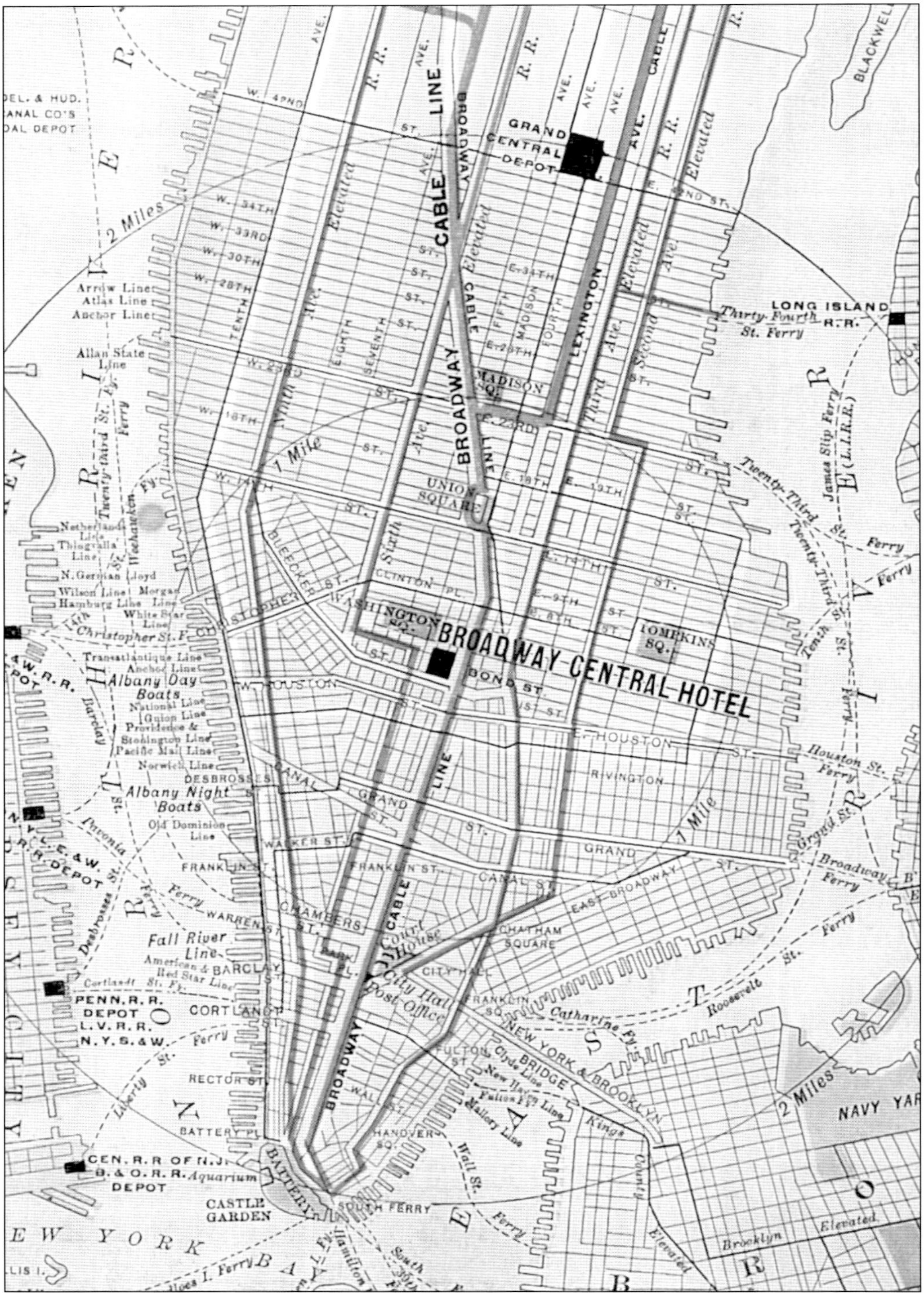

A map of Manhattan showing steamer docks, ferries, elevated and cable car lines, and other important features of the city south of Central Park.

One

BETWEEN THE RIVERS

Geography has been kind to Manhattan Island. The thin sliver between the rivers is lined by long strings of piers on both the eastern and the western banks.

In the days of sail, Manhattan was a bustling seaport. With the coming of steam, the opening of the Erie Canal, and the development of the railroad terminus, Manhattan gained access to markets across the continent and became America's import/export hub.

Vast quantities of raw materials flowed through Manhattan from all over the world. Industry flourished as huge streams of immigrants arrived, offering an abundance of cheap labor and specialized skills and crafts. Manhattan and its neighboring cities were transformed into a regional industrial powerhouse.

As steamships became larger and more luxurious, the wealthy moved through the city in record numbers, spurring a growing demand for luxury hotels, restaurants, and consumer goods.

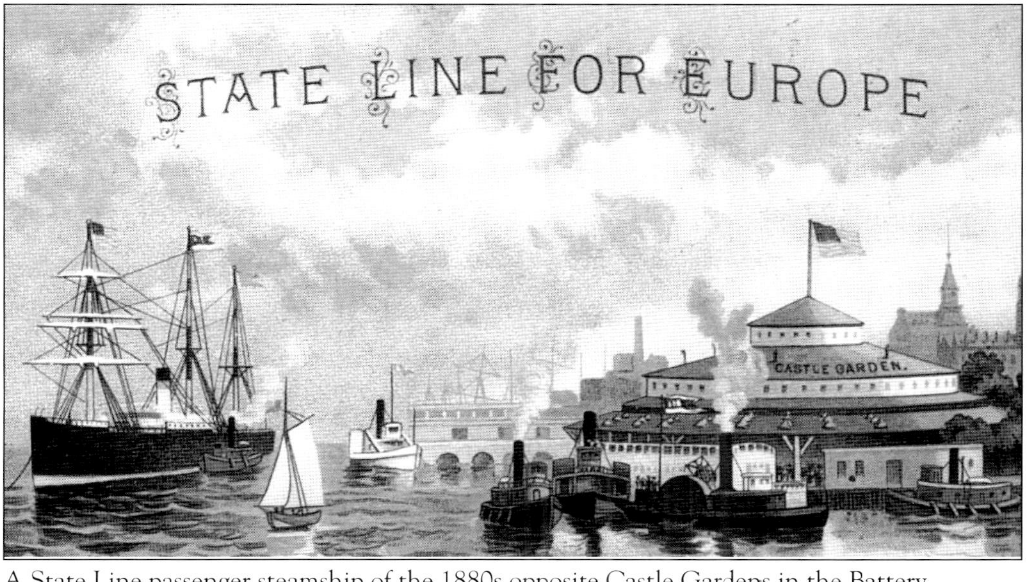

A State Line passenger steamship of the 1880s opposite Castle Gardens in the Battery.

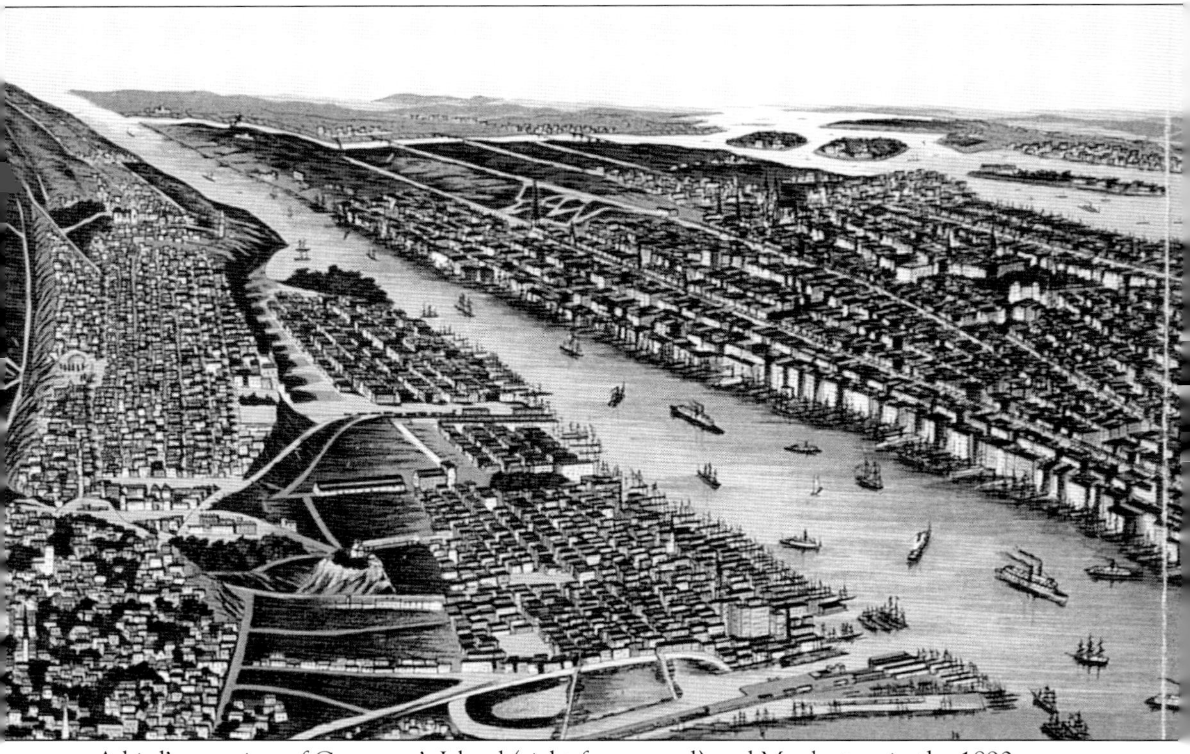

A bird's-eye view of Governor's Island (right foreground) and Manhattan in the 1890s.

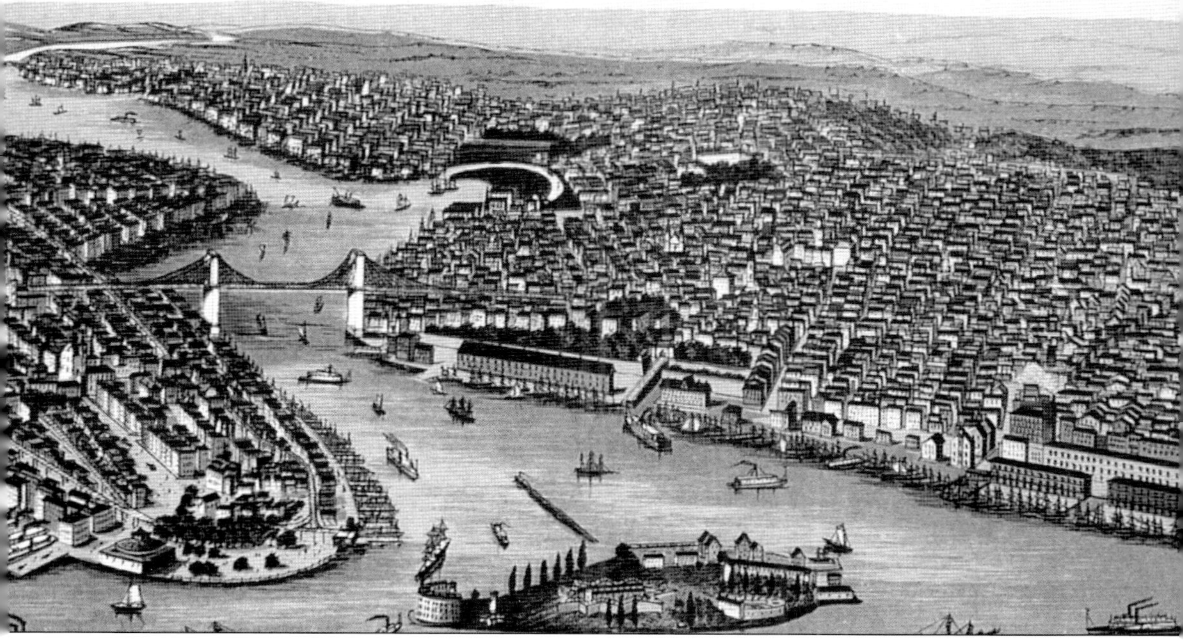

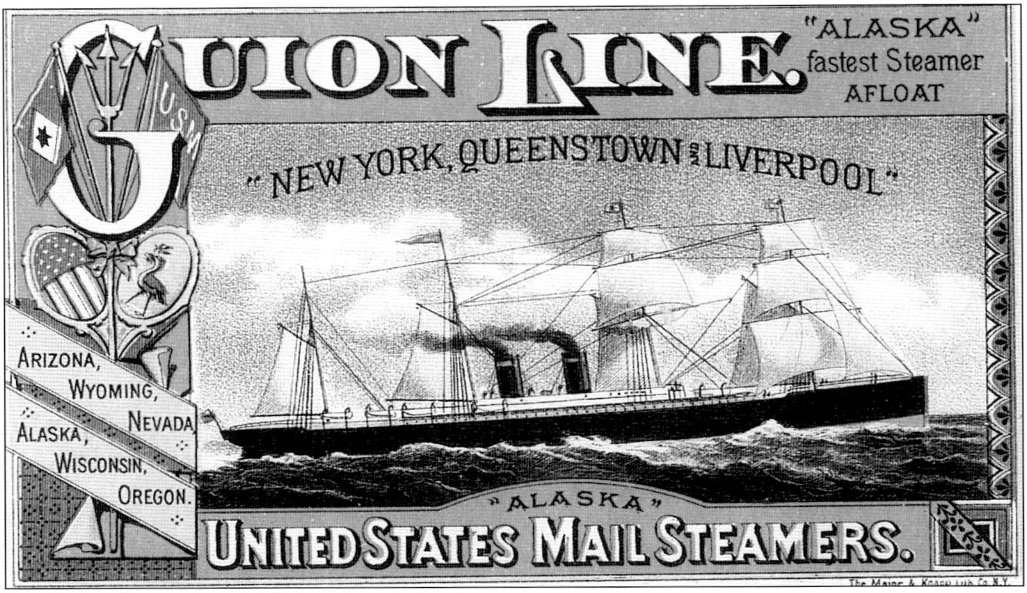

Typical steamships that called at the port of New York in the 1880s, depicted on trade cards. (*Above*) Guion Line's *Alaska*. (*Below*) Cunard Line's *Servia*.

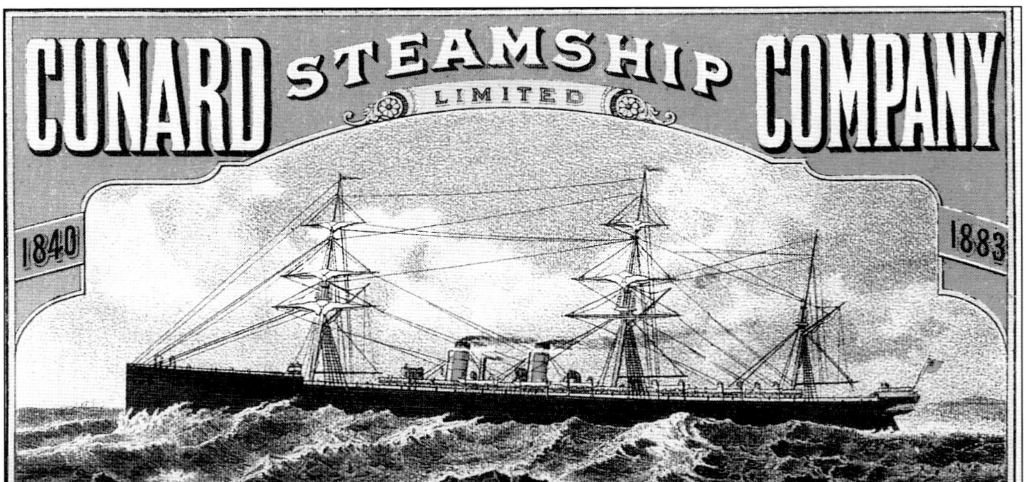

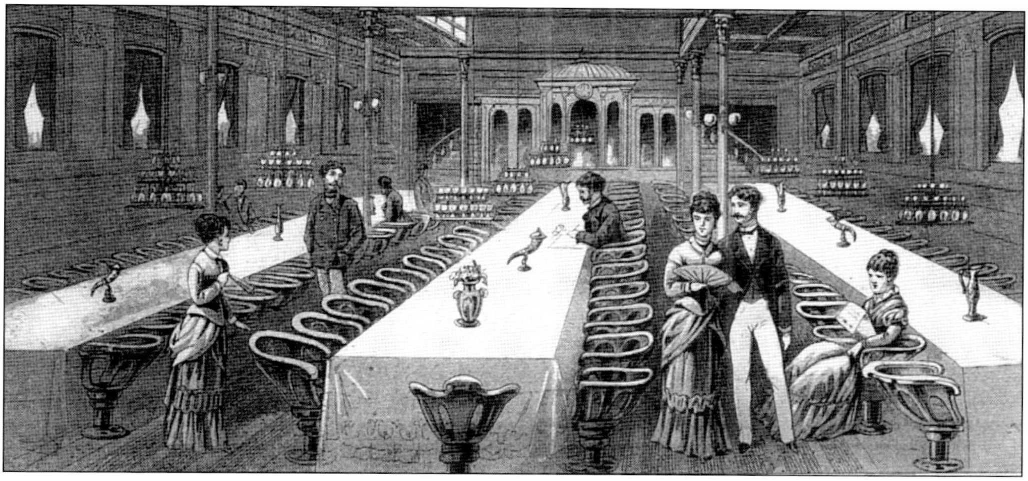

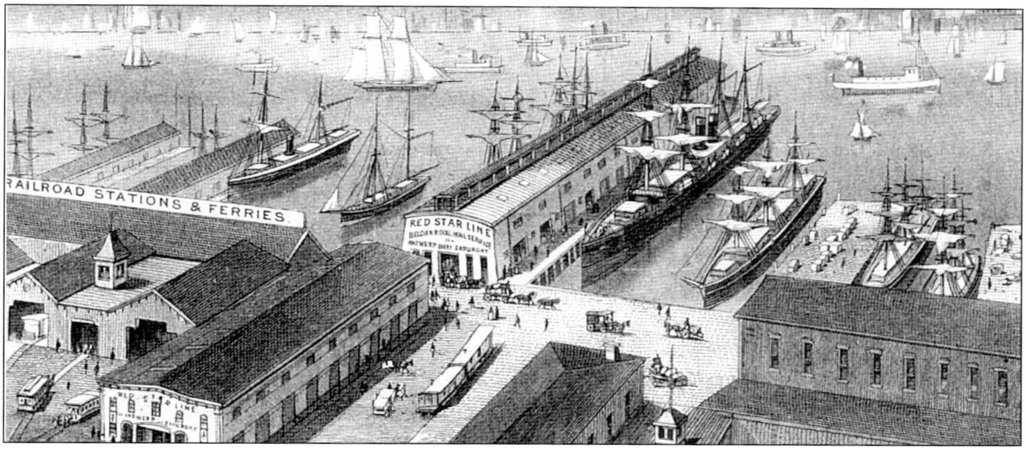

(*Top*) The dining room of one of its steamships. (*Middle*) Red Star Line's docks. (*Right*) A Red Star Line advertisement of its transatlantic service in a 1883 folder.

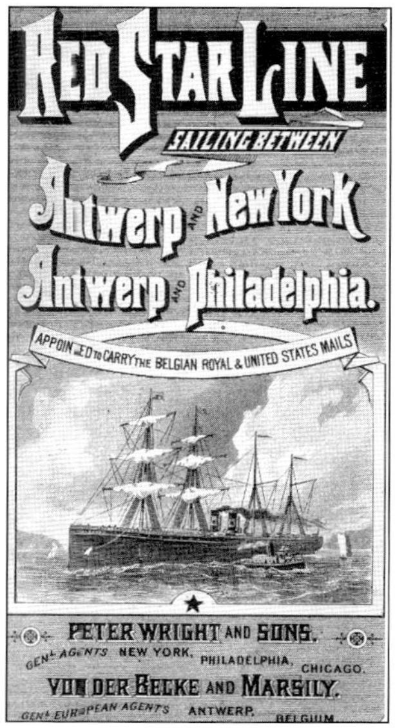

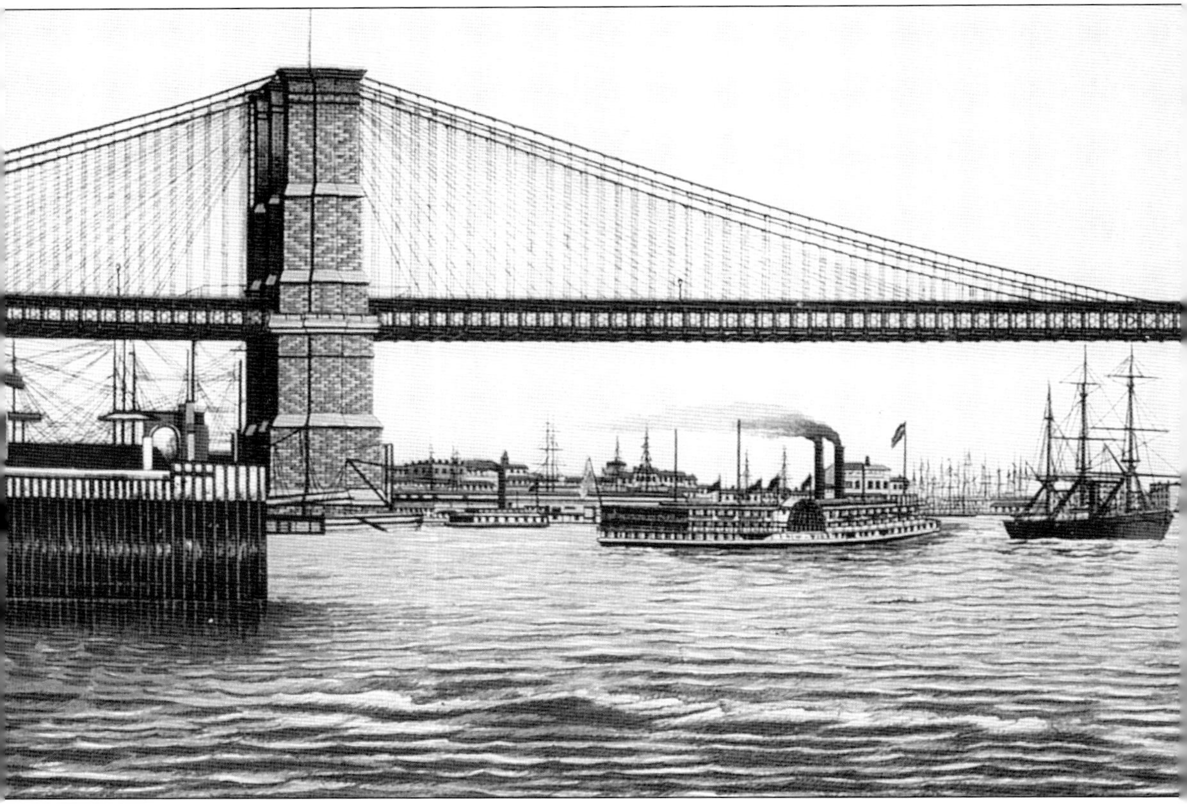

The Brooklyn Bridge about a decade after its opening.

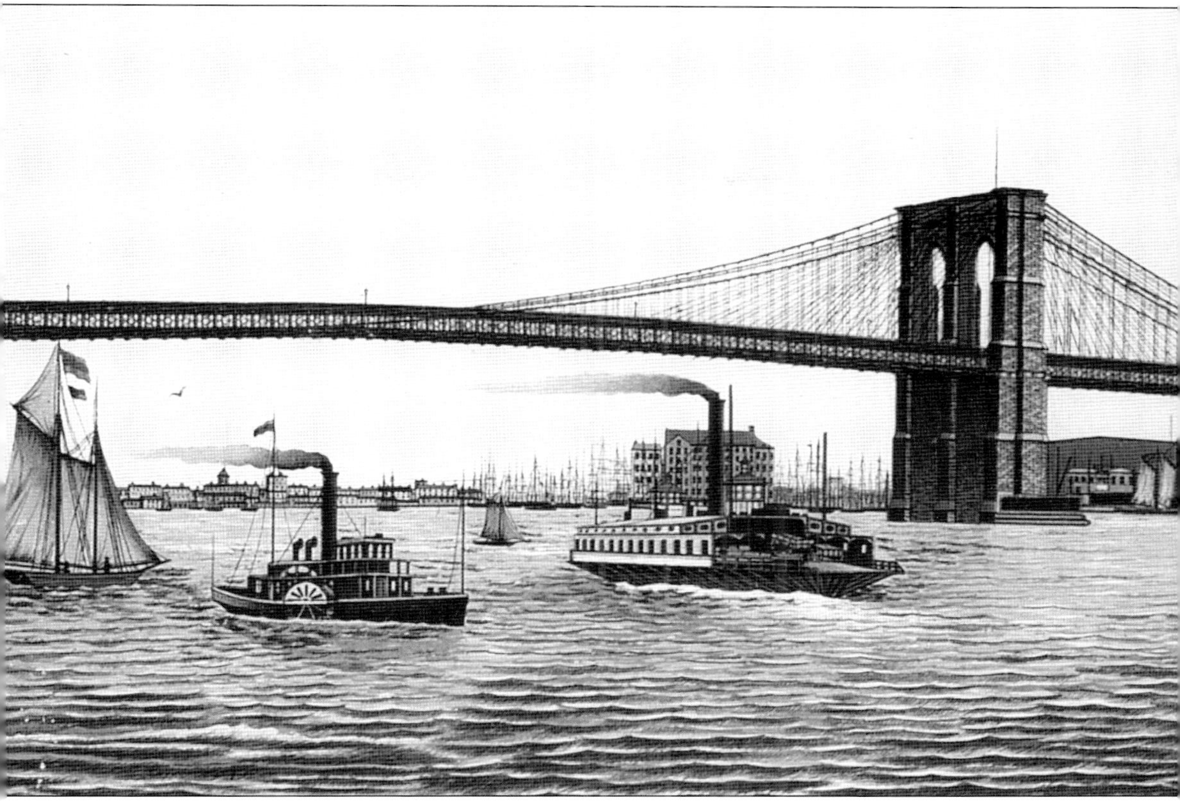

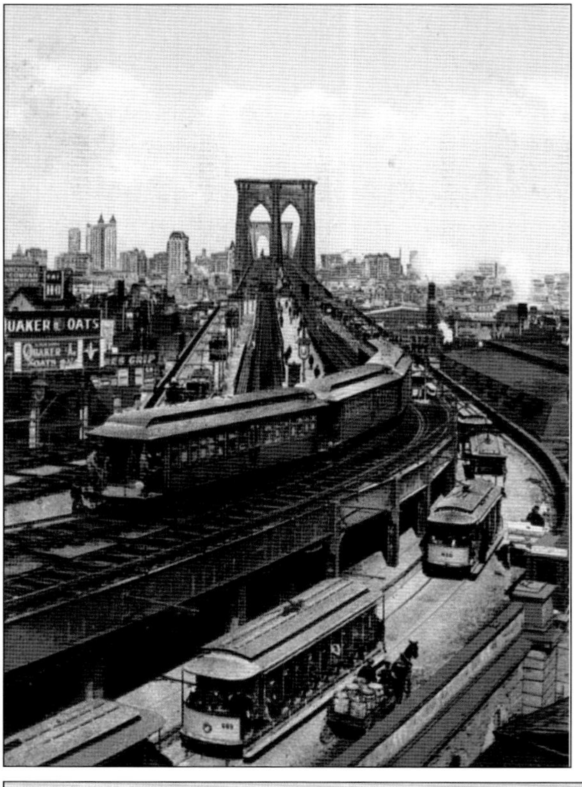

(*Left*) Trains, trolleys, and horse carts on the Brooklyn Bridge. (*Below*) The Manhattan Bridge.

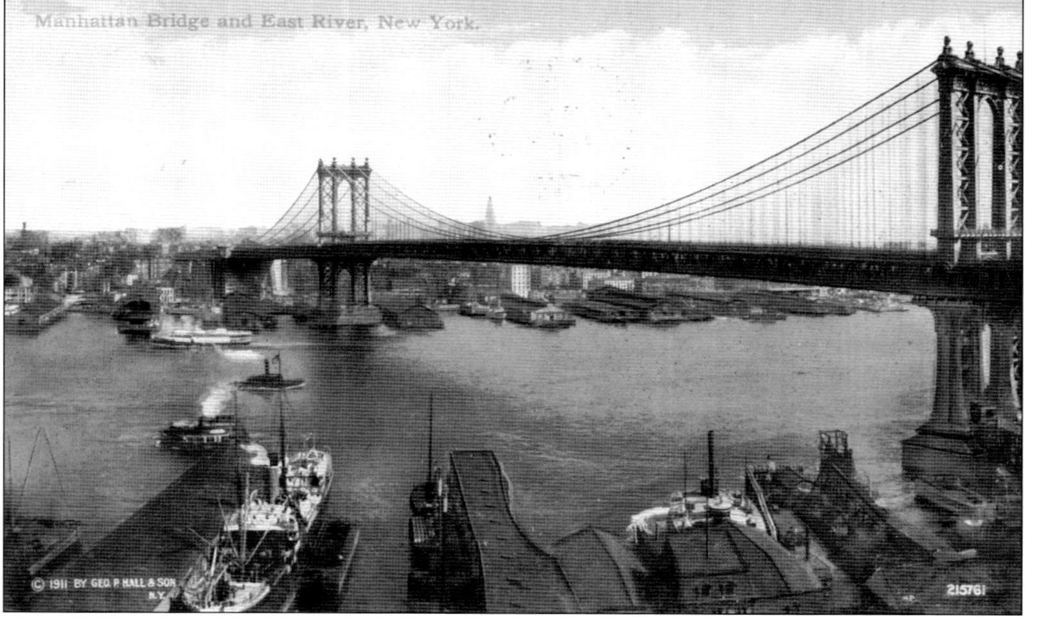

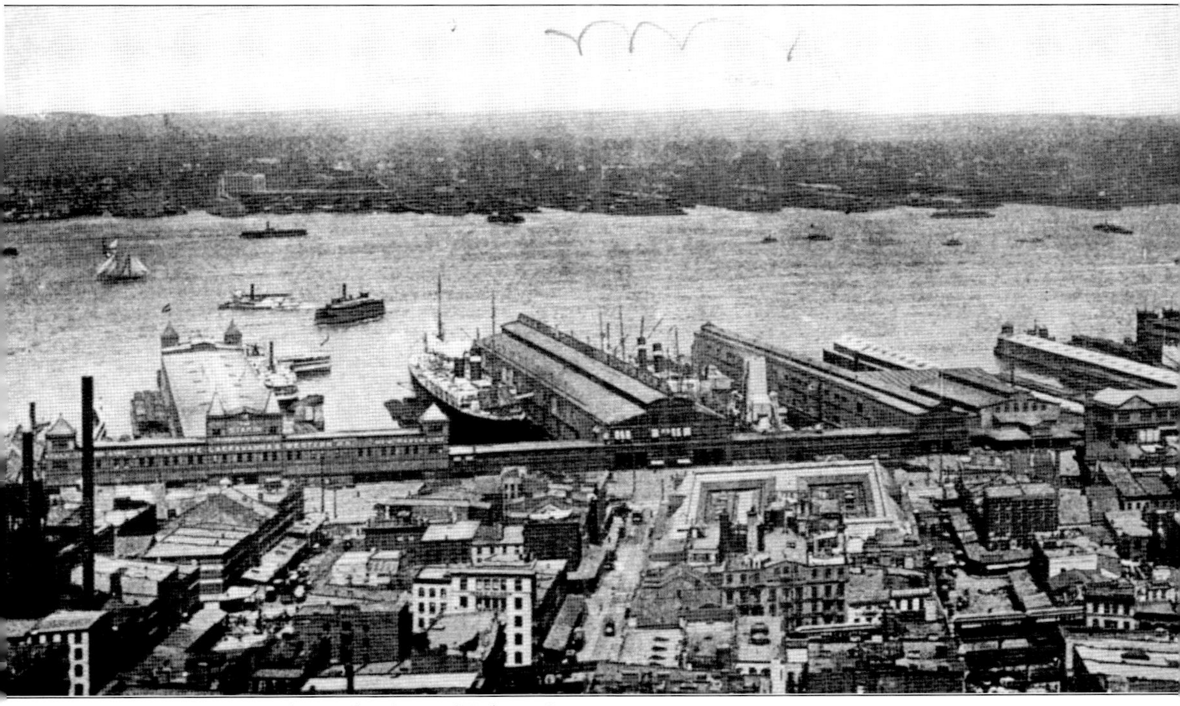

American Line Docks at the foot of Fulton Street.

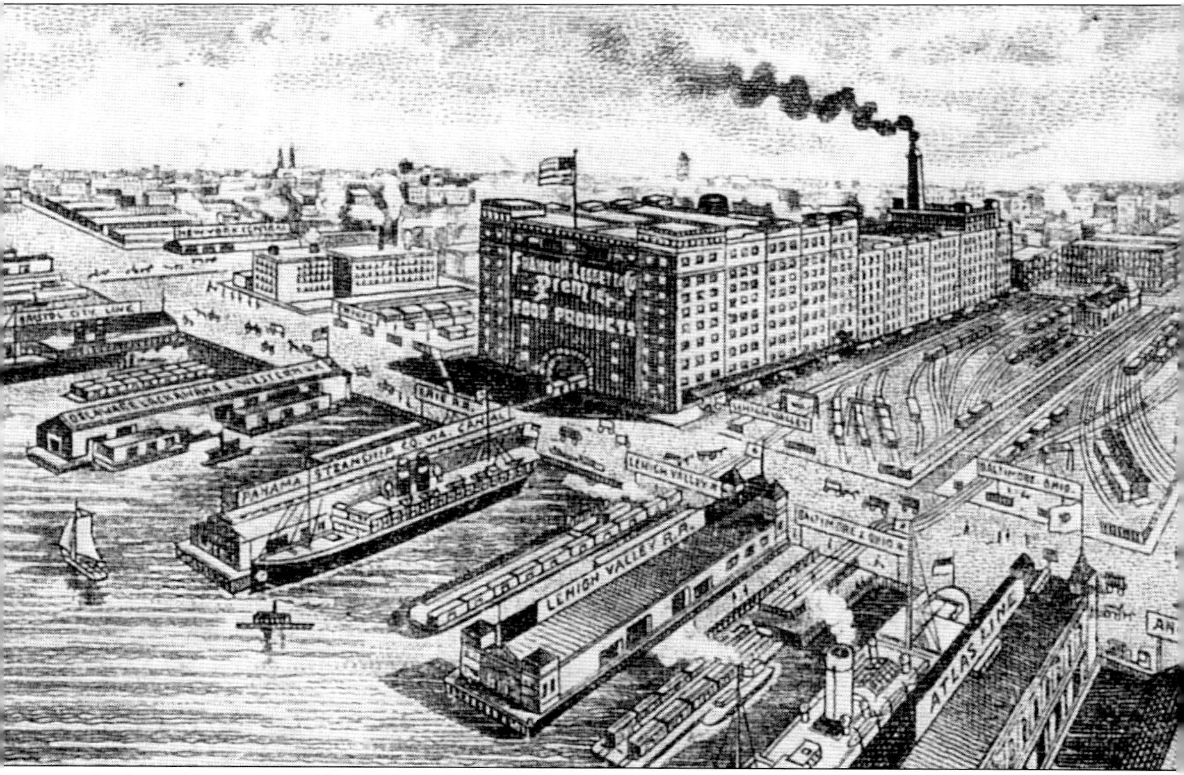

Light industry in Manhattan. The Francis H. Leggett & Company food-products plant flourished on the Hudson River between Twenty-Sixth and Twenty-Seventh Streets.

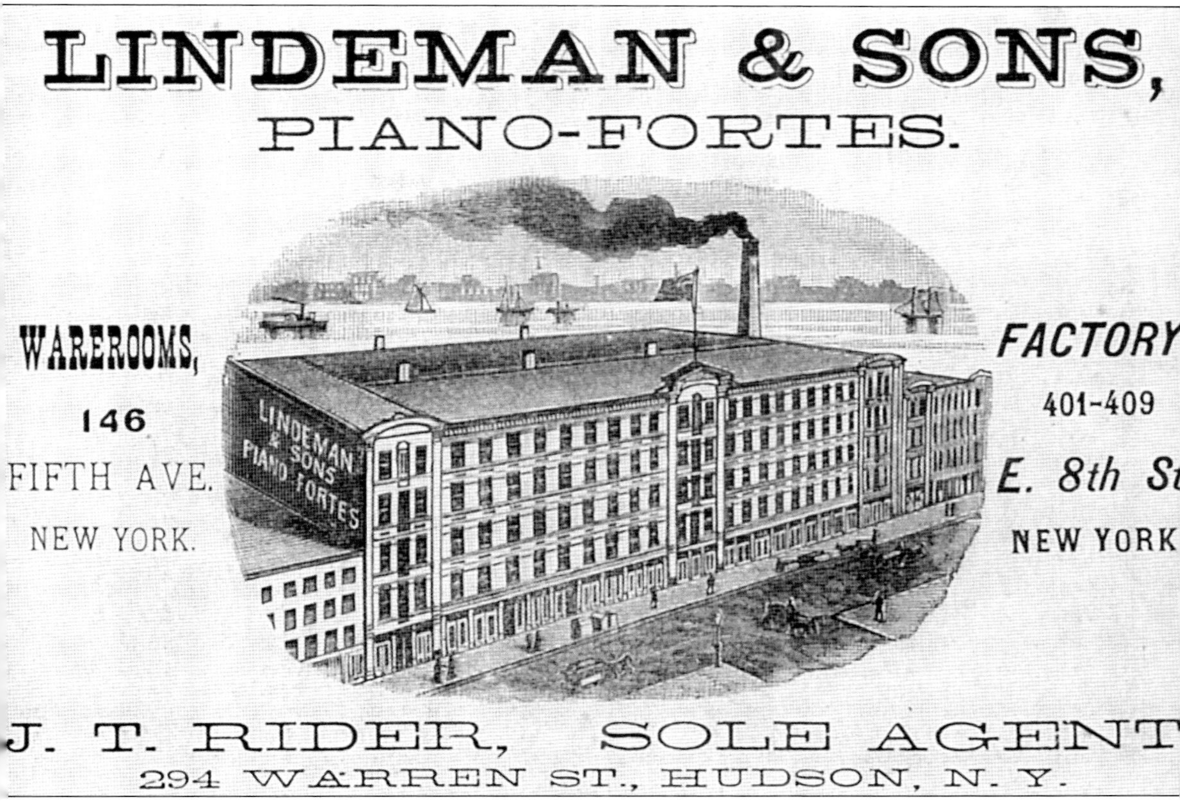

The Lindeman & Sons piano-forte plant near the East River on Eighth Street.

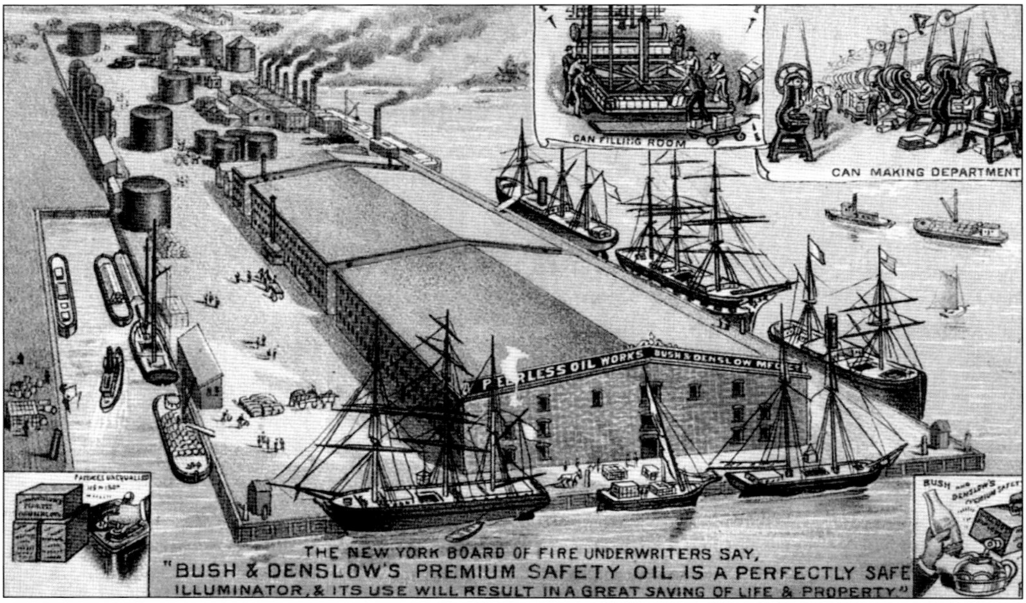

(*Above*) The Bush and Denslow safety oil plant. (*Below*) Hecker's flour and cereal mill on the East River at the foot of Corlears Street.

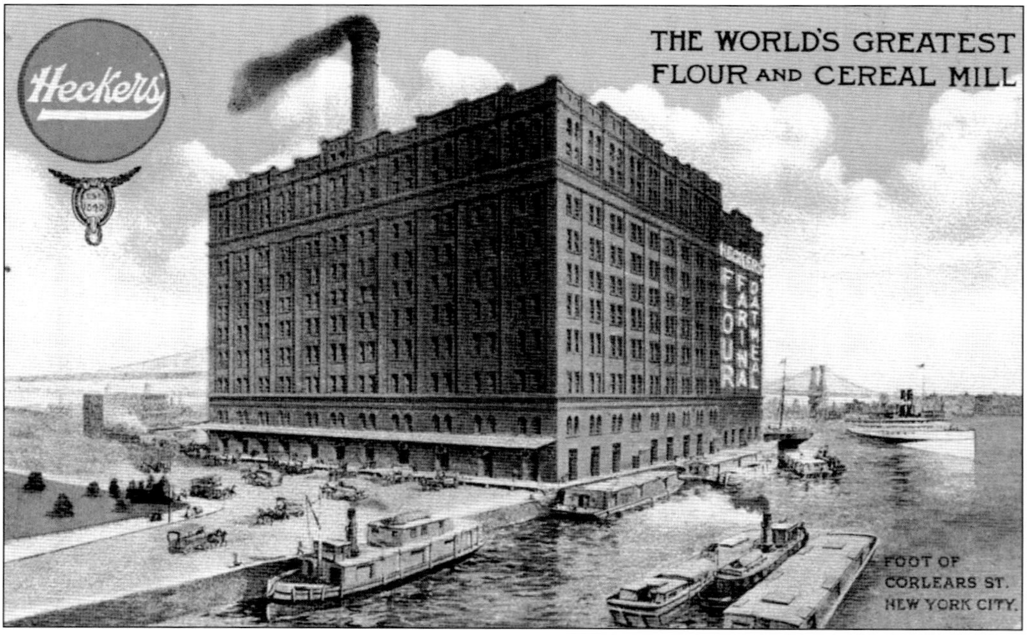

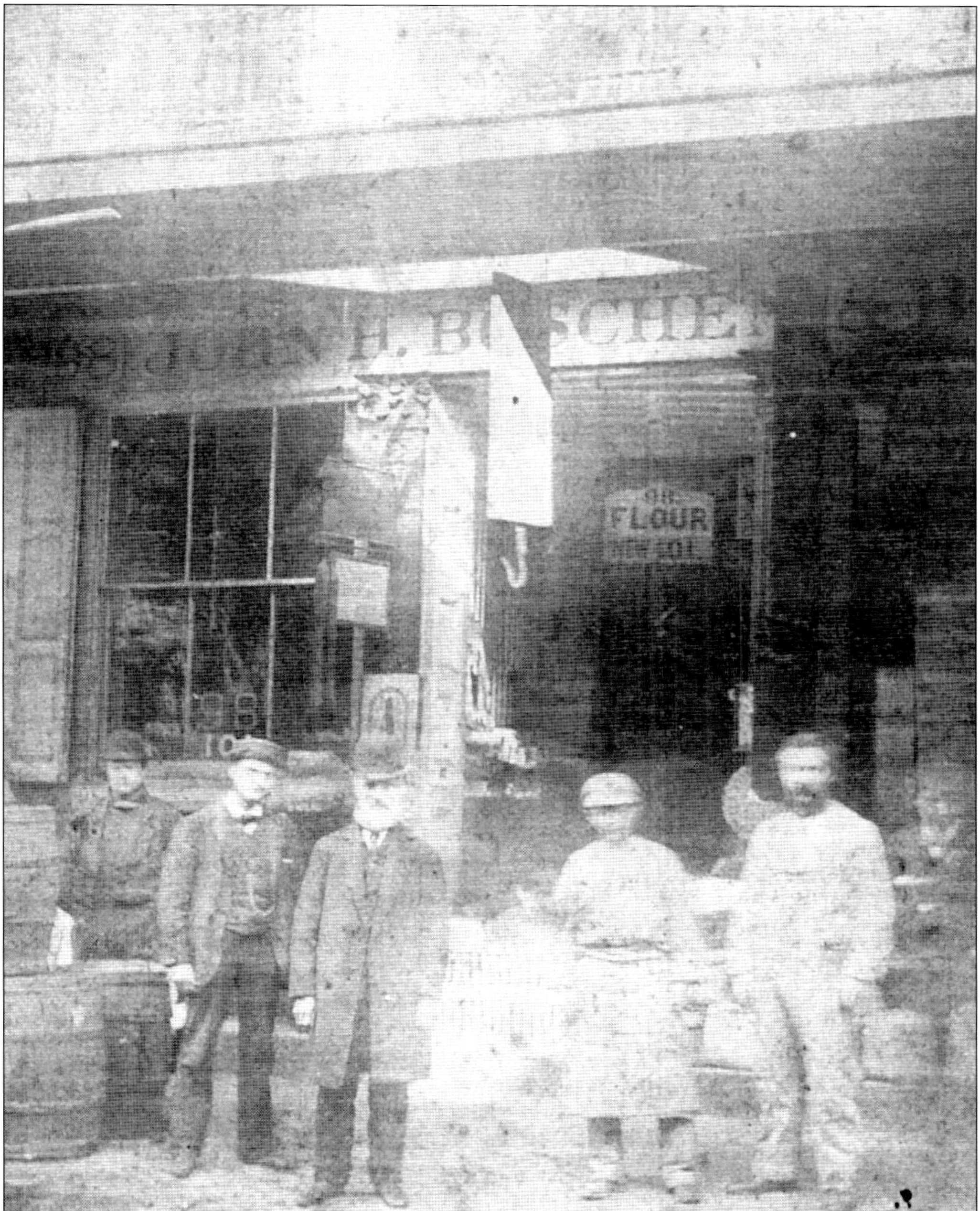

The John H. Boschen provision shop at 101 Barclay Street in 1881. The older man in the foreground is John H. Boschen. This image was photographed by G.W. Heppner.

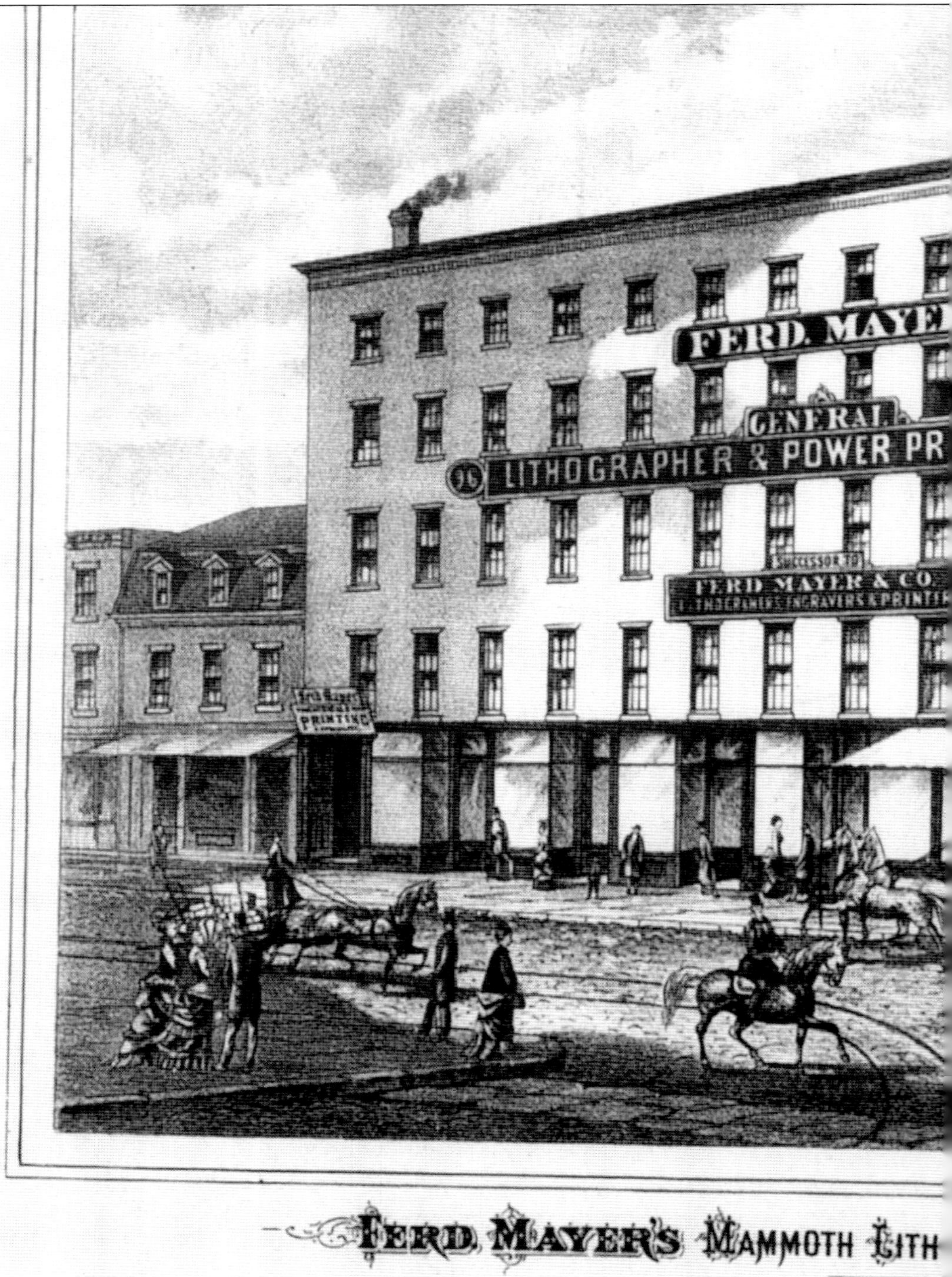

The Ferd Mayer lithography and printing establishment. In the late 19th century Manhattan's

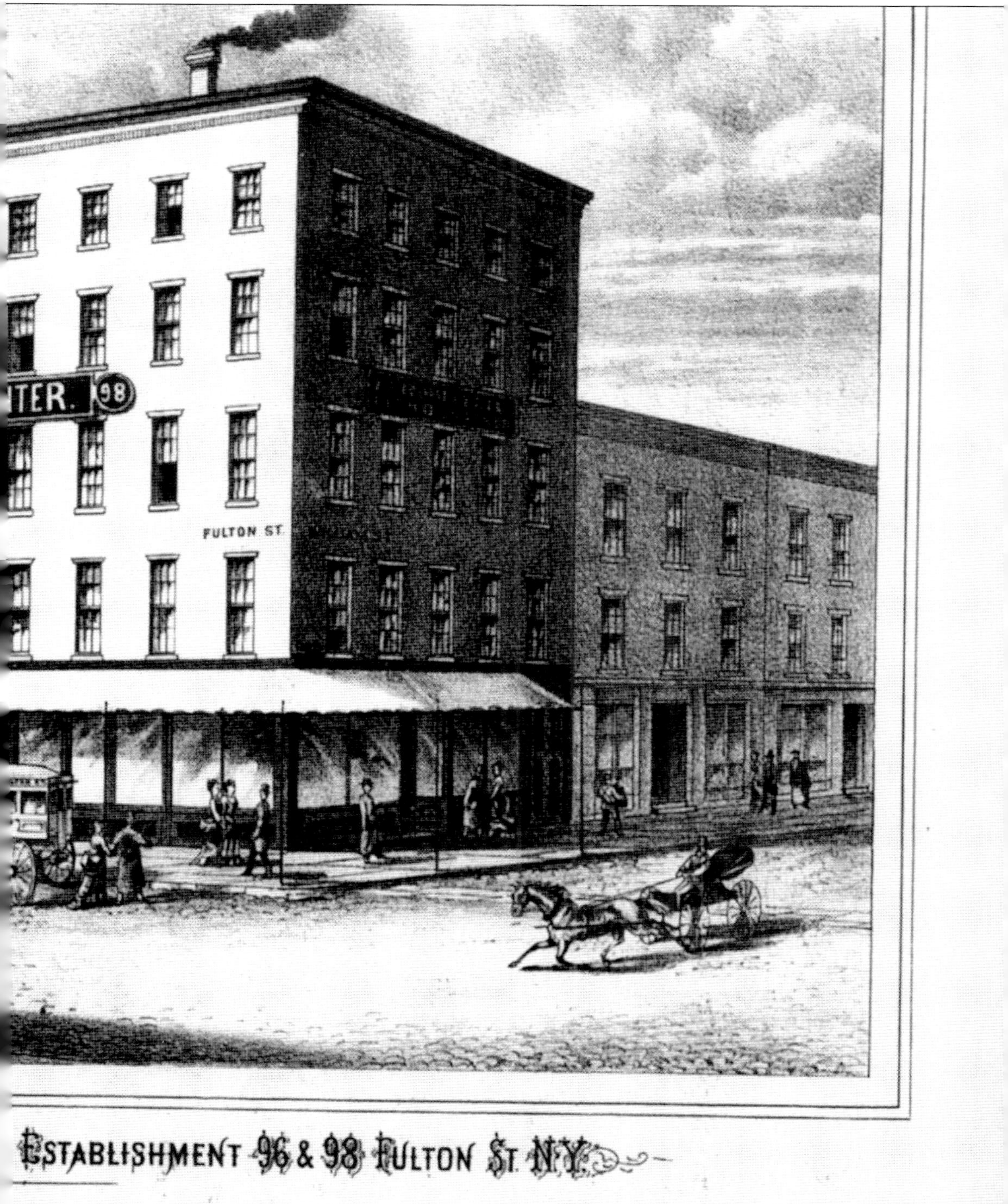

proximity to transportation caused it to be an important center for printing and lithography.

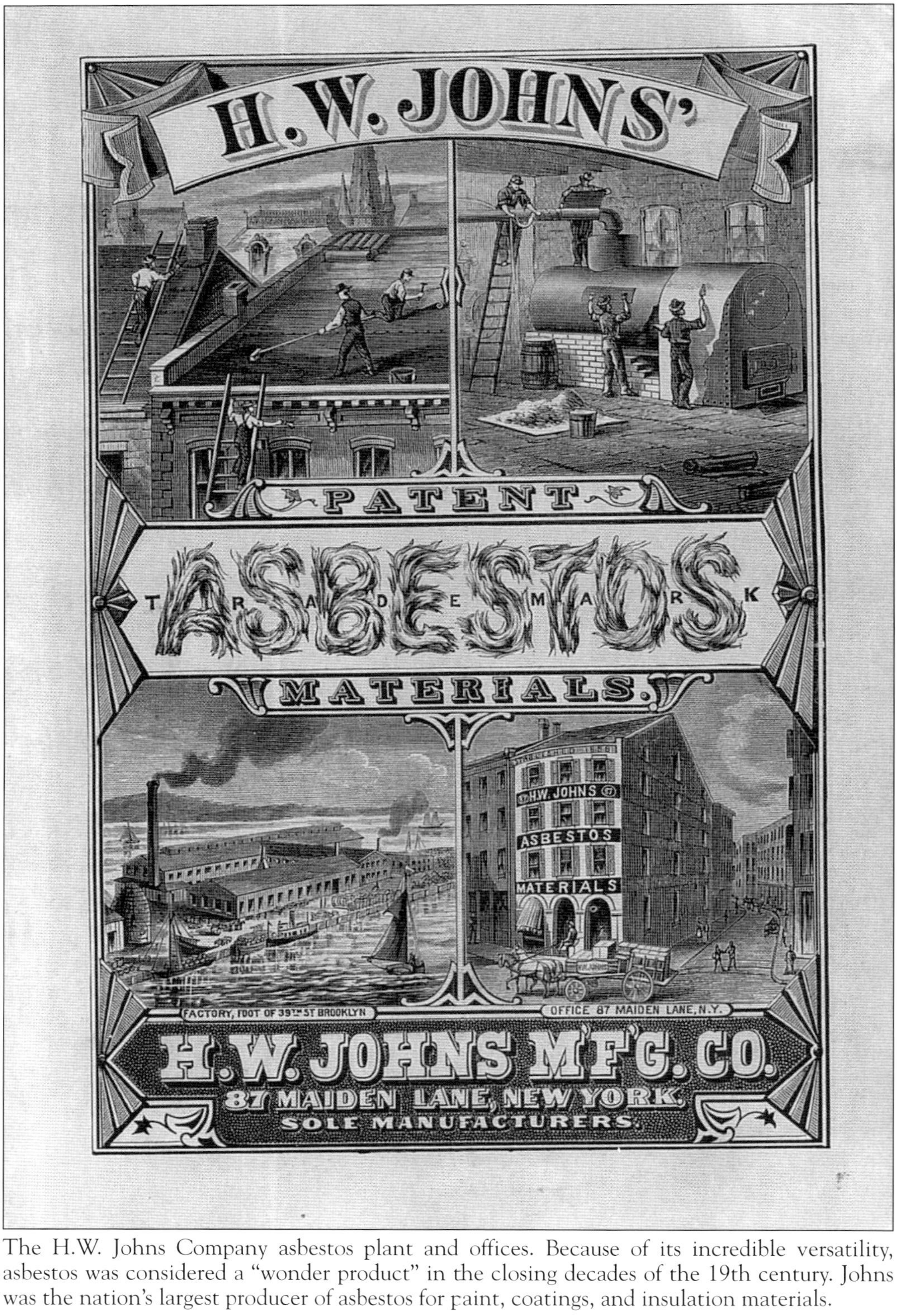

The H.W. Johns Company asbestos plant and offices. Because of its incredible versatility, asbestos was considered a "wonder product" in the closing decades of the 19th century. Johns was the nation's largest producer of asbestos for paint, coatings, and insulation materials.

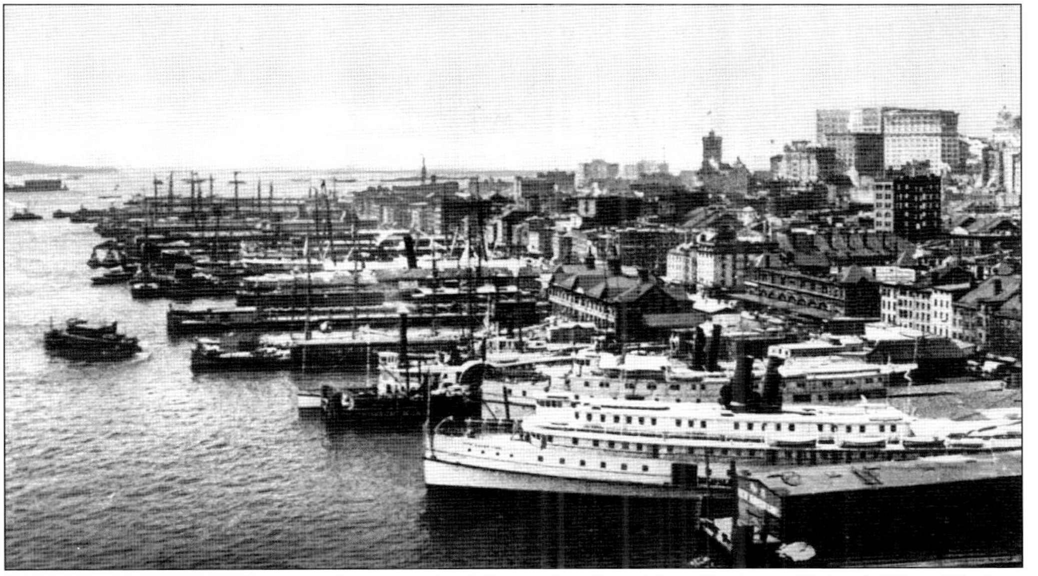

(*Above*) East River wharves photographed from the Brooklyn Bridge. (*Below*) The Chelsea Docks, about 1910.

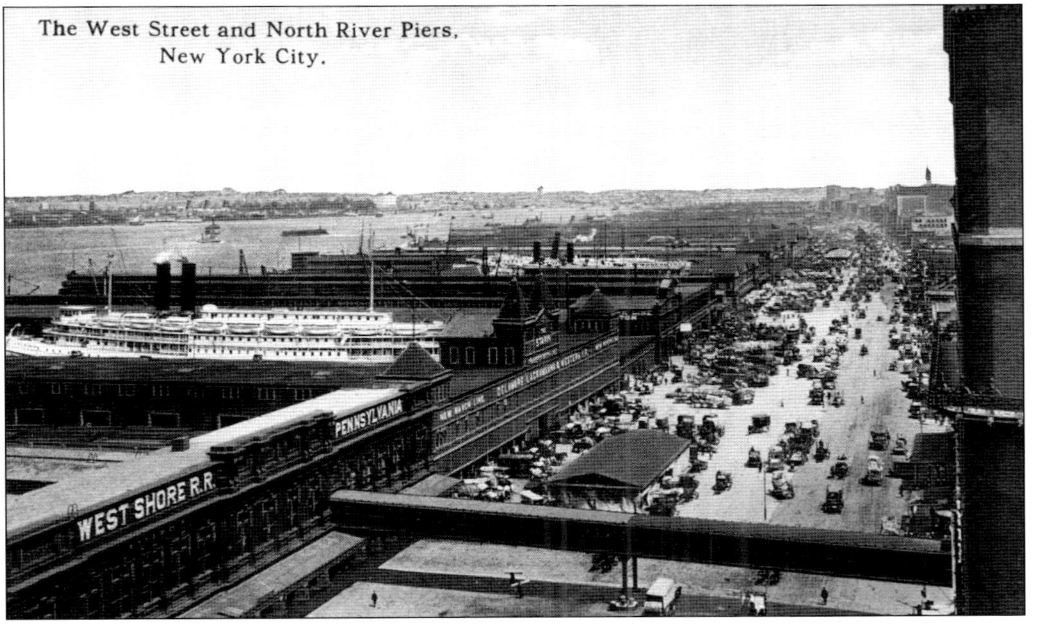

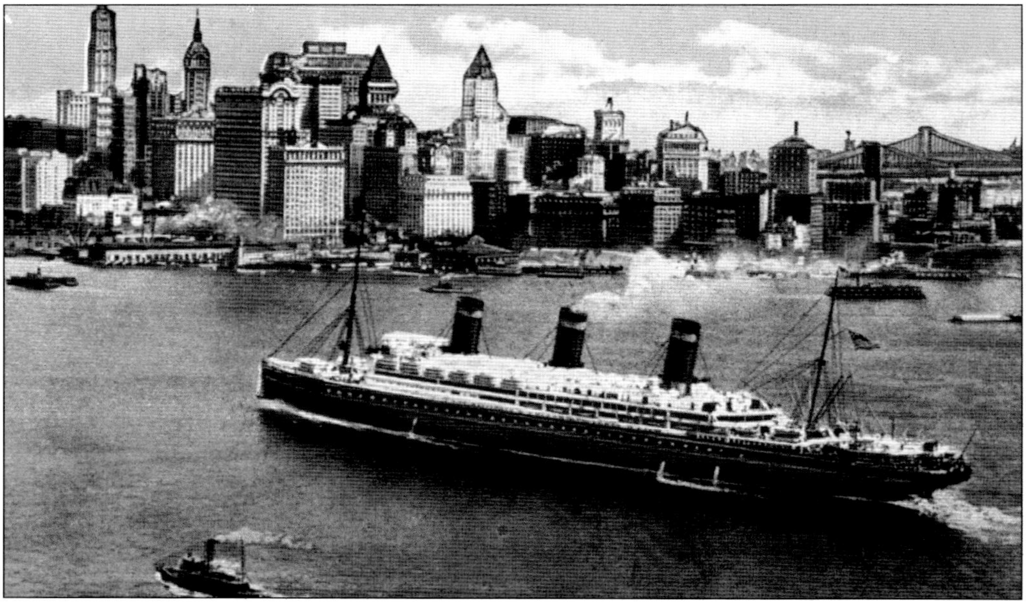

(*Above*) The 950-foot *S.S. Leviathan*. With accommodations for 3,700 passengers, it was the world's largest and probably the most luxurious steamship when it was launched in 1913. (*Below*) New York Harbor from the foot of Manhattan. The aquarium, formerly Castle Gardens, is on the lower left.

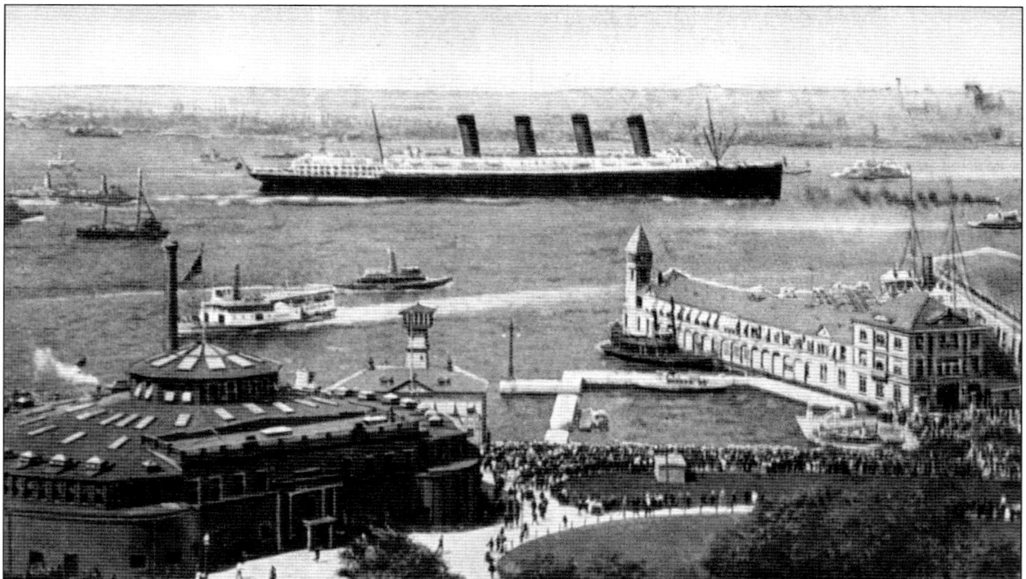

Two

SHOPPING

From the 1880s through the 1920s, the focus of fashionable shopping migrated steadily northward in tandem with the mansions of the wealthy.

Fine clothing stores and other shops along Broadway, from below Houston to the lower teens, were abandoned in favor of even more opulent cast-iron palaces along the Ladies' Mile. This shopping district, along Broadway and Sixth Avenue, stretched from Fourteenth to Twenty-Third Street. It was anchored by such famous names as R.H. Macy, Arnold Constable, and Lord & Taylor. In 1895, Chicago retailer Siegel-Cooper opened Manhattan's largest and most lavish store.

The chief target of these retailers was the wealthy, who were building mansions nearby along Fifth Avenue. By the outbreak of World War I, the Ladies' Mile had faded into obscurity. As the rich continued to move uptown, the stores followed to Herald Square and along Thirty-Fourth Street and further north in the fifties on Fifth Avenue.

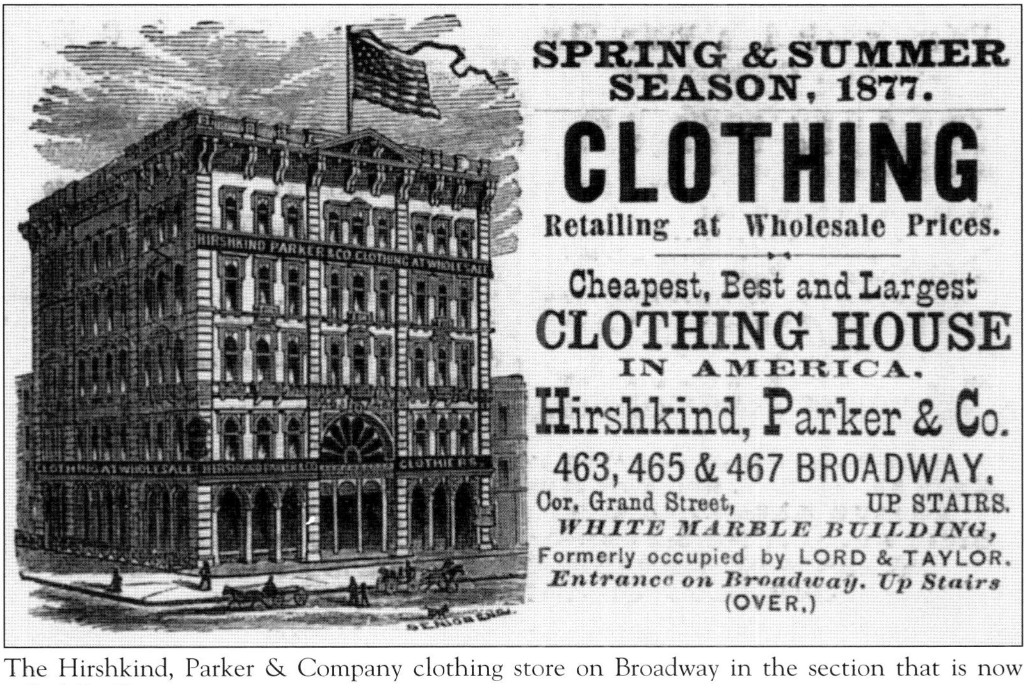

The Hirshkind, Parker & Company clothing store on Broadway in the section that is now called So-Ho.

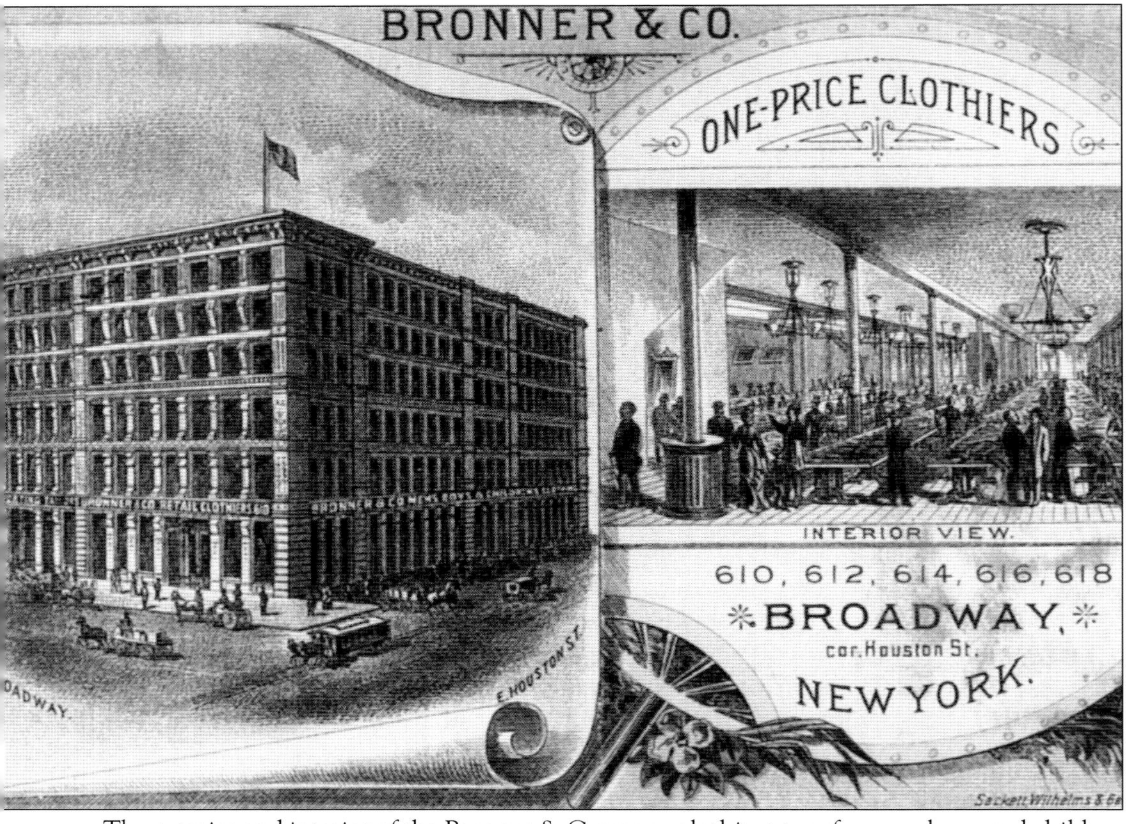

The exterior and interior of the Bronner & Company clothing store for men, boys, and children in the 1880s at Broadway & Houston Street.

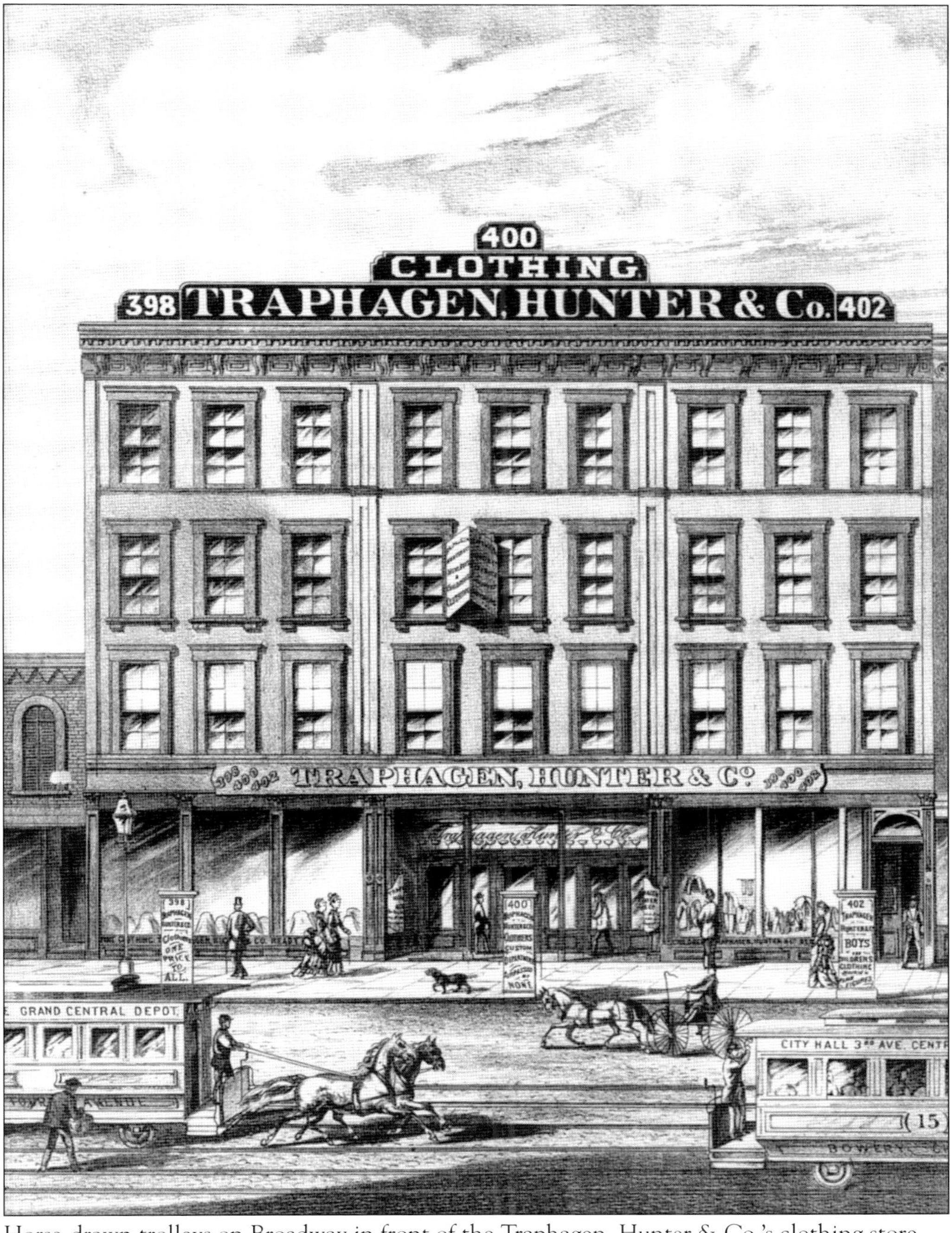

Horse-drawn trolleys on Broadway in front of the Traphagen, Hunter & Co.'s clothing store.

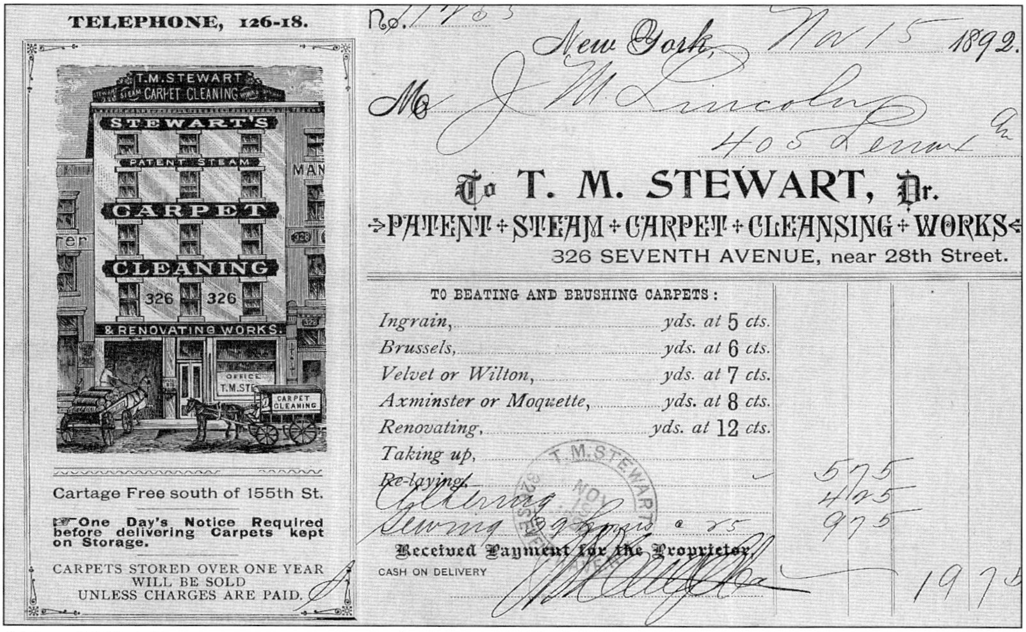

TELEPHONE, 126-18.

T.M. STEWART CARPET CLEANING

STEWART'S PATENT STEAM CARPET CLEANING 326 326 & RENOVATING WORKS.

Cartage Free south of 155th St.

One Day's Notice Required before delivering Carpets kept on Storage.

CARPETS STORED OVER ONE YEAR WILL BE SOLD UNLESS CHARGES ARE PAID.

New York, 1892.

To T. M. STEWART, Dr.

PATENT STEAM CARPET CLEANSING WORKS

326 SEVENTH AVENUE, near 28th Street.

TO BEATING AND BRUSHING CARPETS:

Ingrain, ... *yds. at* 5 *cts.*

Brussels, ... *yds. at* 6 *cts.*

Velvet or Wilton, ... *yds. at* 7 *cts.*

Axminster or Moquette, ... *yds. at* 8 *cts.*

Renovating, ... *yds. at* 12 *cts.*

Taking up,

Re-laying,

Received Payment for the Proprietor,

CASH ON DELIVERY

(*Above*) T.M. Stewart's steam carpet cleaning establishment. (*Below*) Stern Brother's Department Store on West Twenty-Third Street.

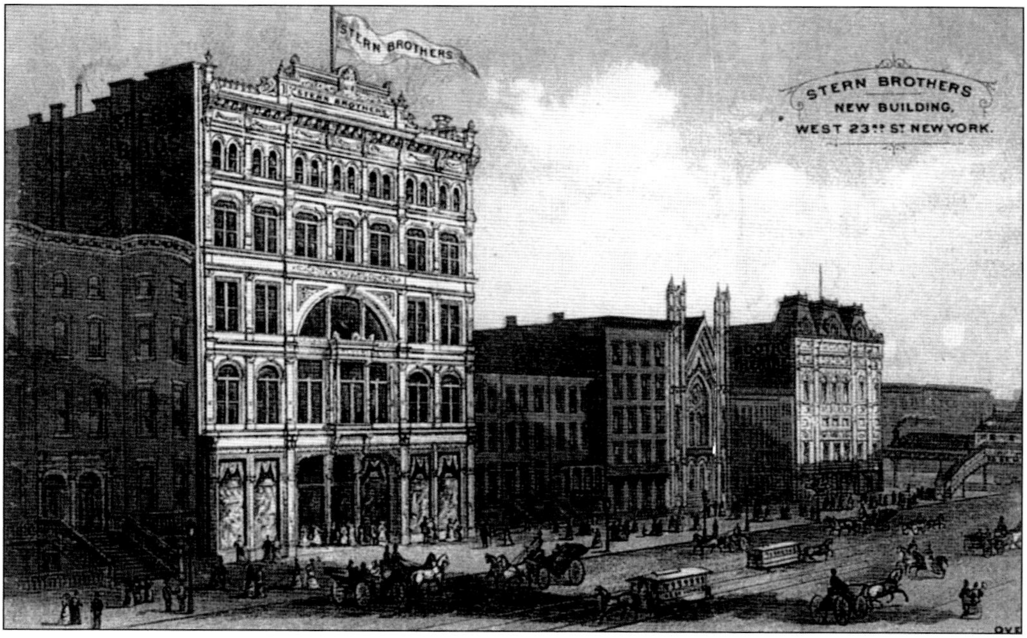

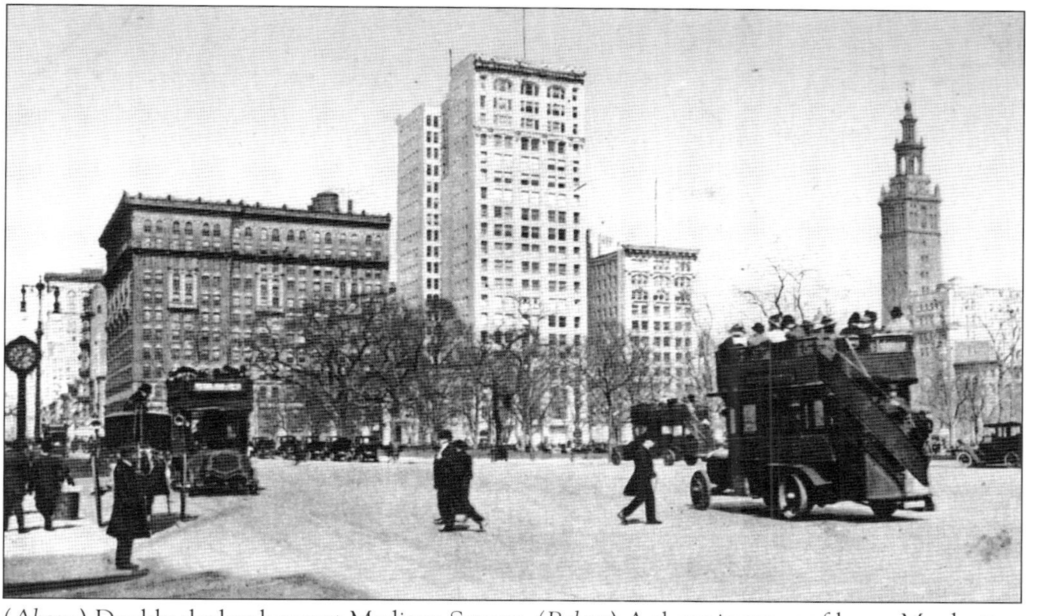

(*Above*) Double-decker buses at Madison Square. (*Below*) A shopping tour of lower Manhattan just after the turn of the century.

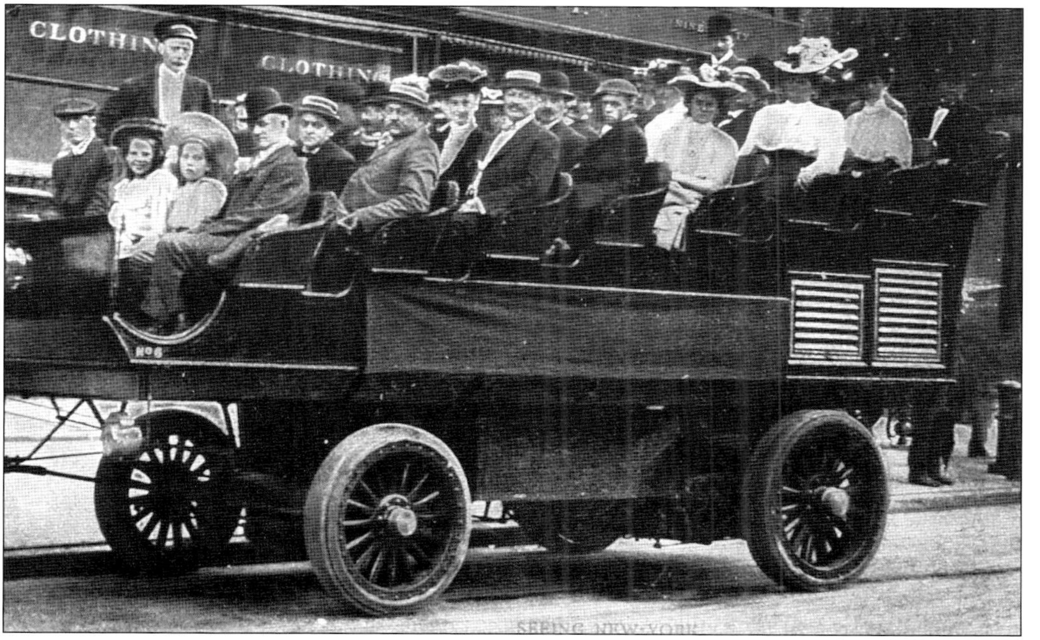

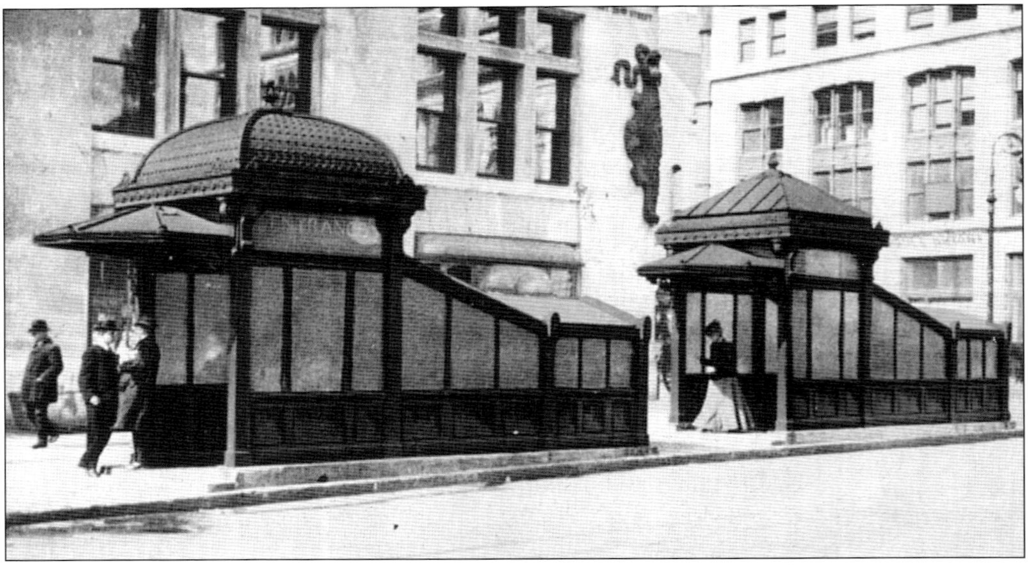

(*Above*) A subway entrance in the first years of the 20th century. (*Below*) The Transportation Center, opposite City Hall Park. This is where trolley, elevated, and subway lines converged. Excellent public transportation helped make Manhattan convenient for shoppers.

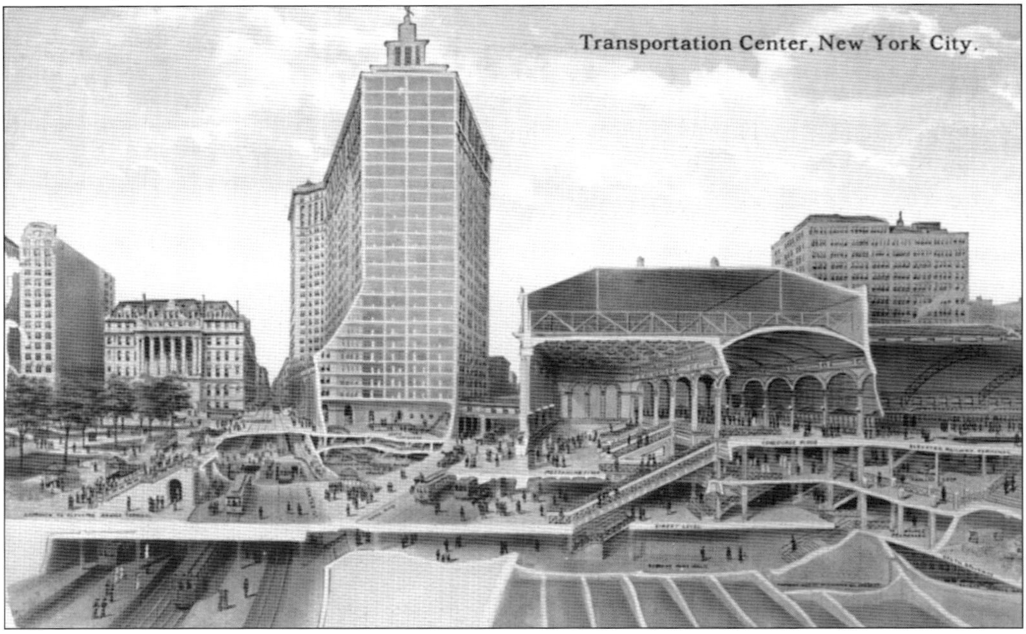

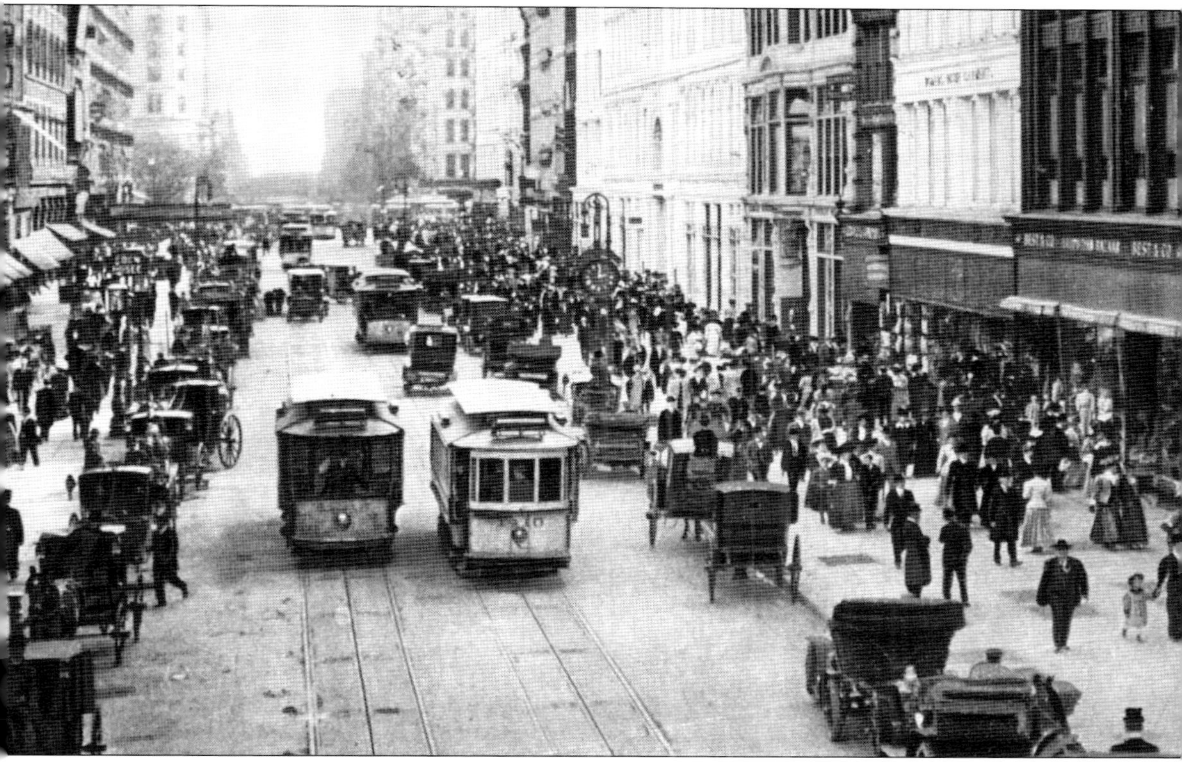

Shoppers and traffic on Twenty-Third Street around 1910.

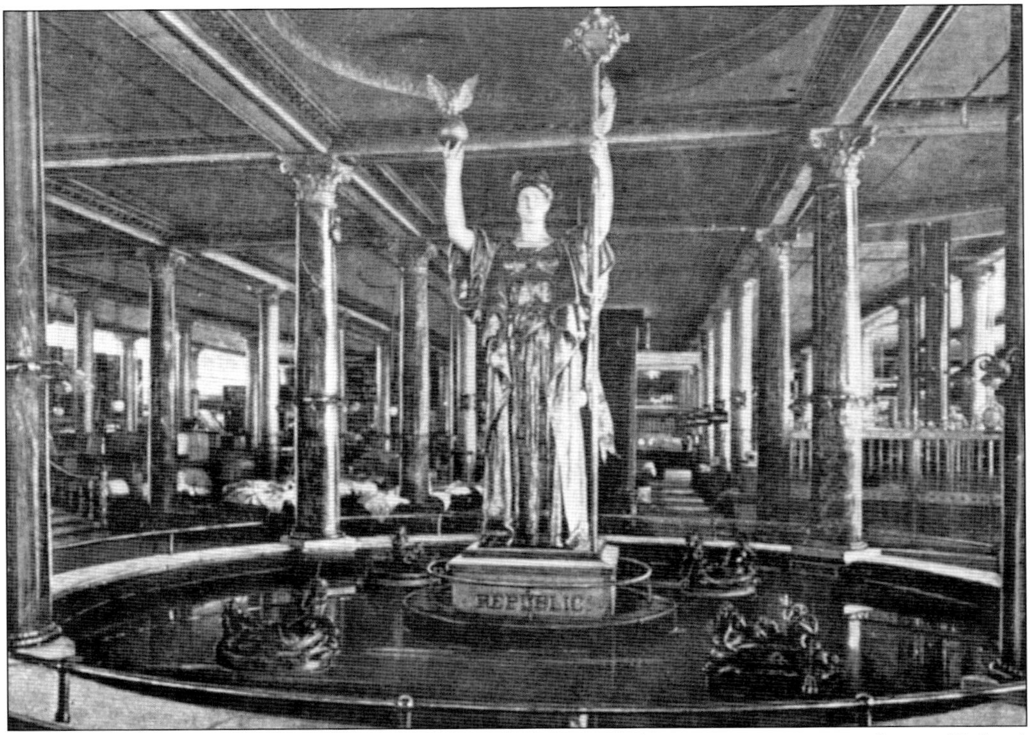

(*Above*) The fountain, a favorite meeting place at the Siegel-Cooper Department Store. (*Below*) The Siegel-Cooper Department Store. This store occupied a full block between Eighteenth and Nineteenth on Sixth Avenue.

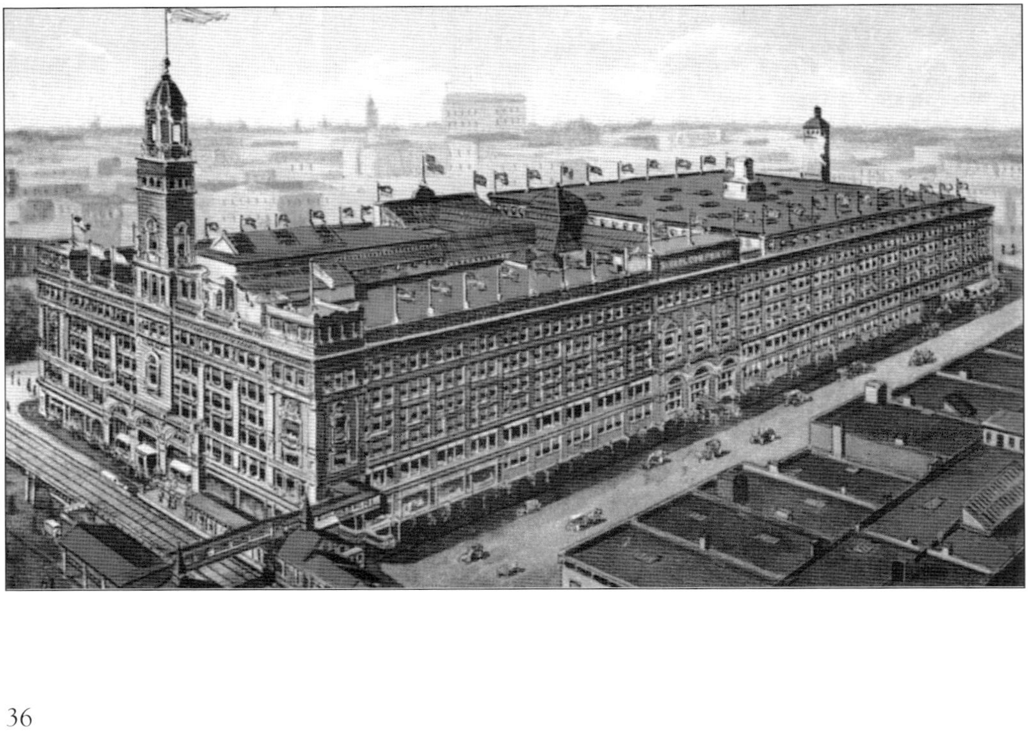

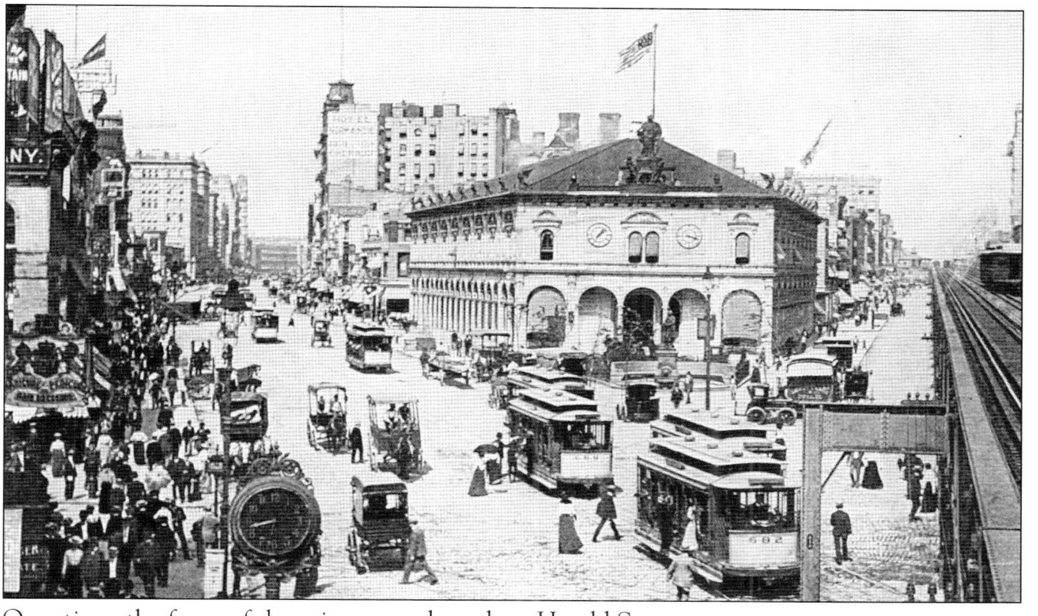

Over time, the focus of shopping moved north to Herald Square.

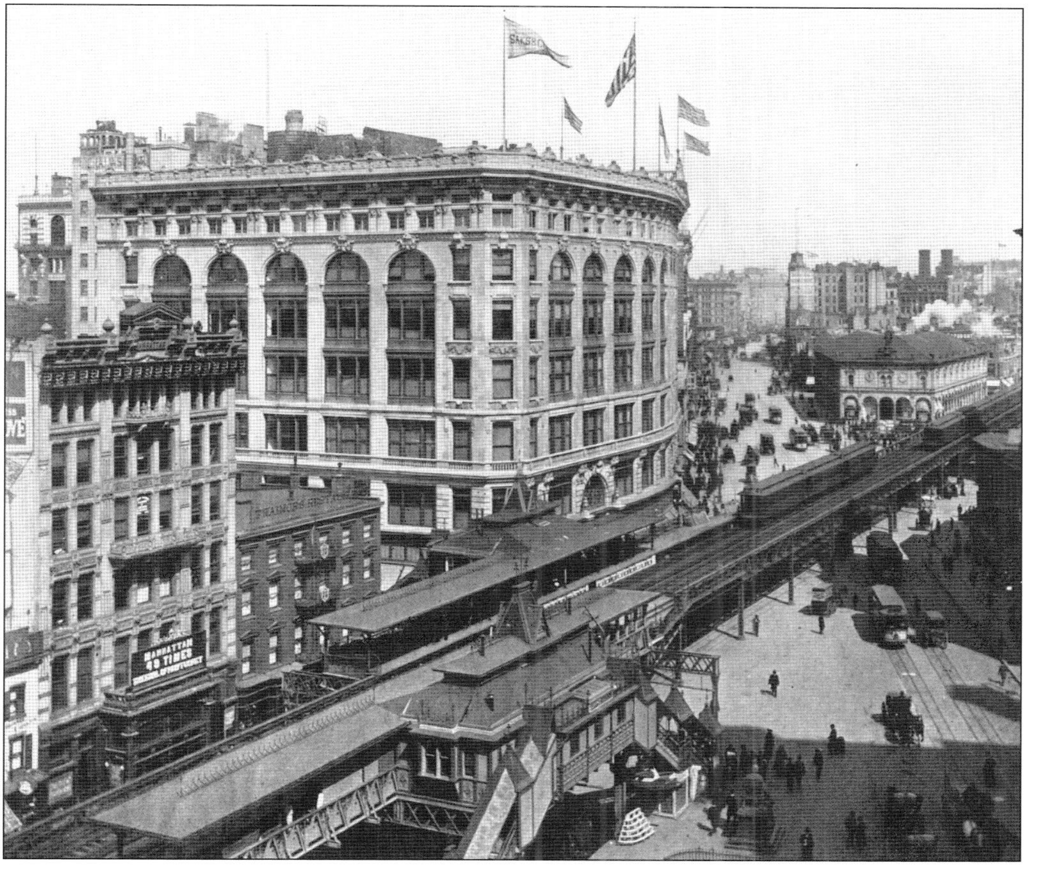

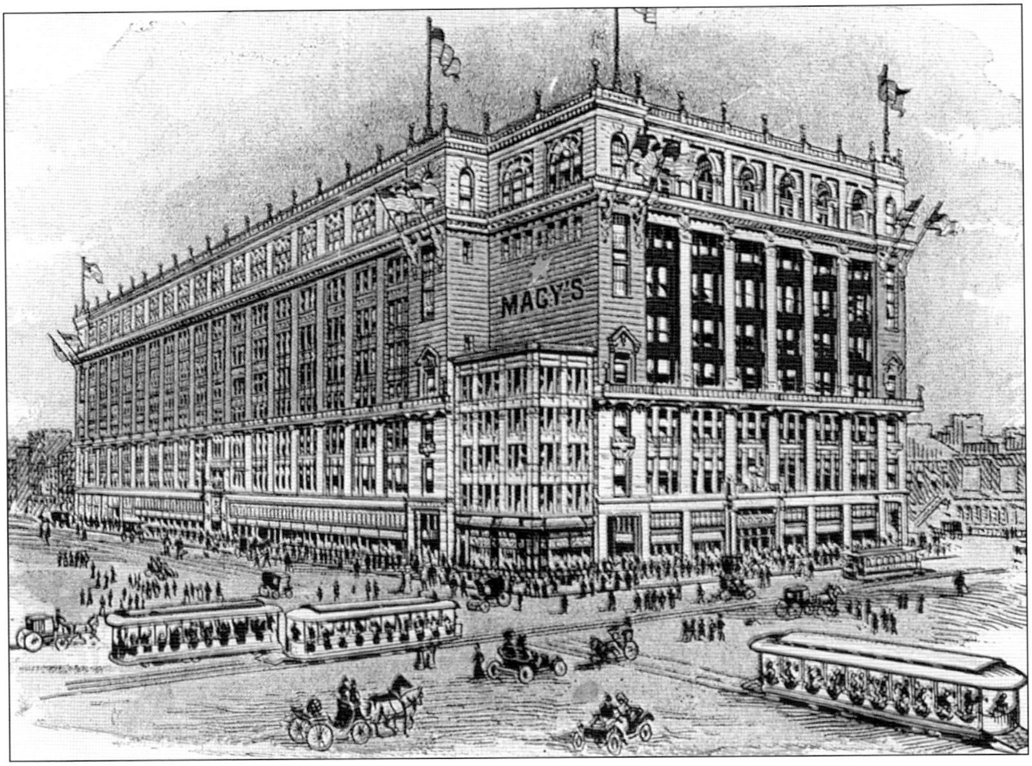

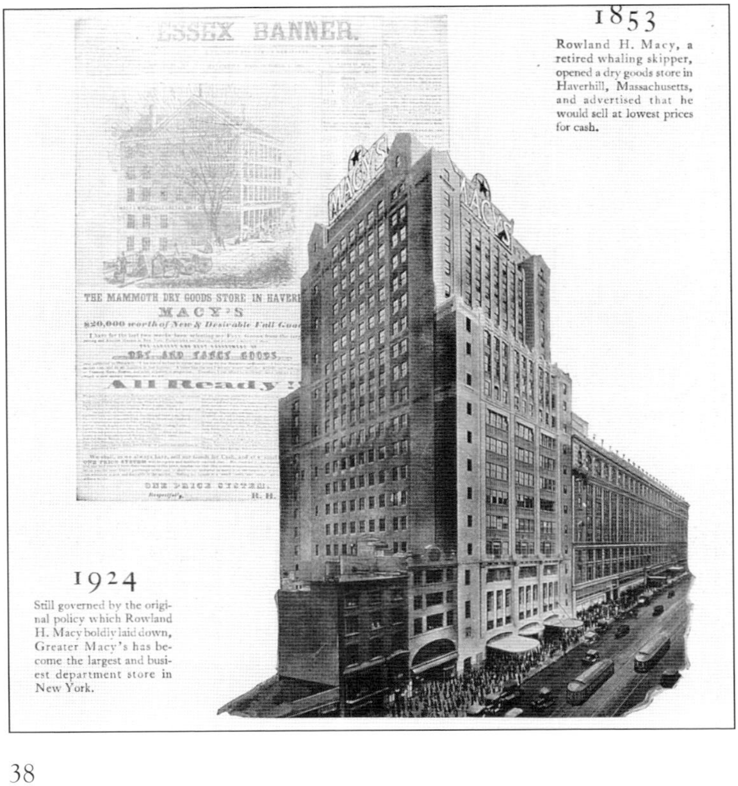

(*Above*) R.H. Macy, the first store on Herald Square. (*Left*) Macy's new store opened in the early 1920s.

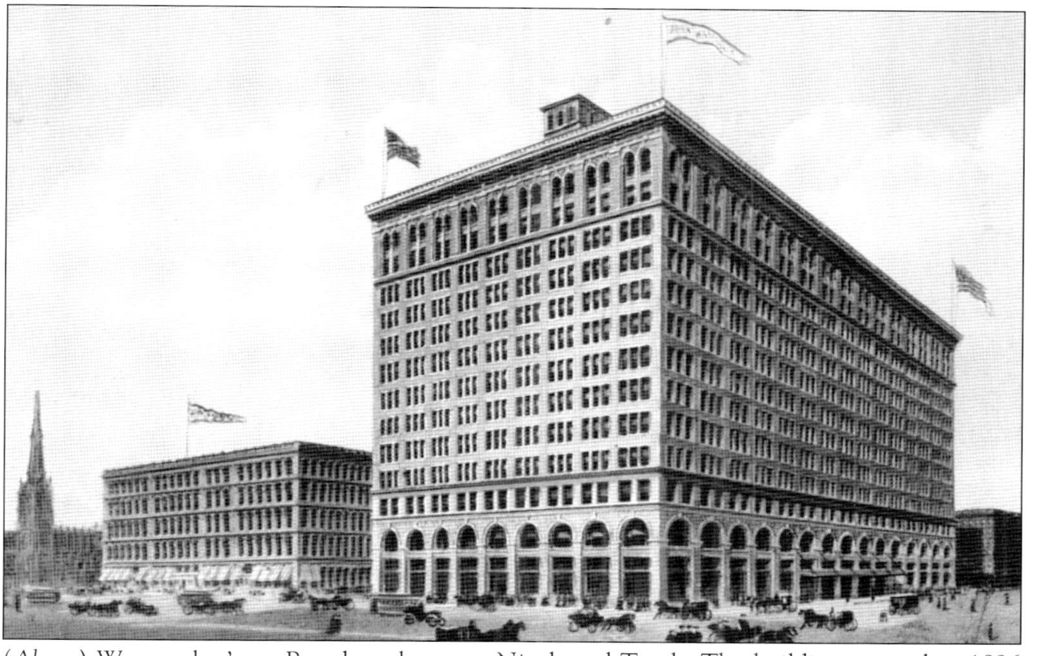

(*Above*) Wanamaker's on Broadway between Ninth and Tenth. The building opened in 1896 and was destroyed by fire in 1956. (*Below*) Gimbel Brothers, Herald Square, built in 1910.

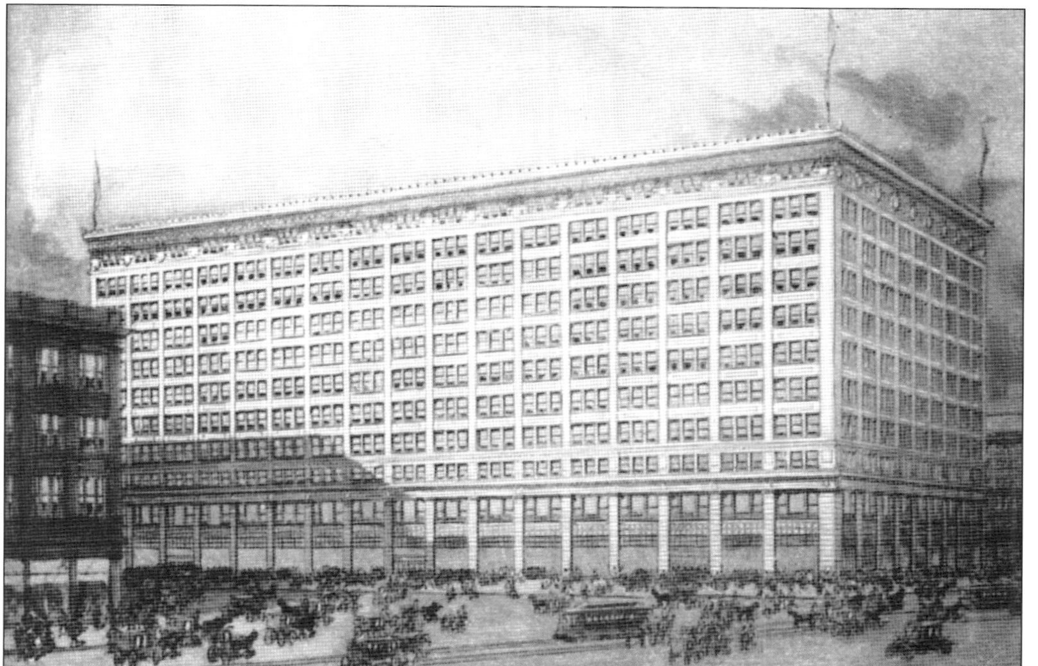

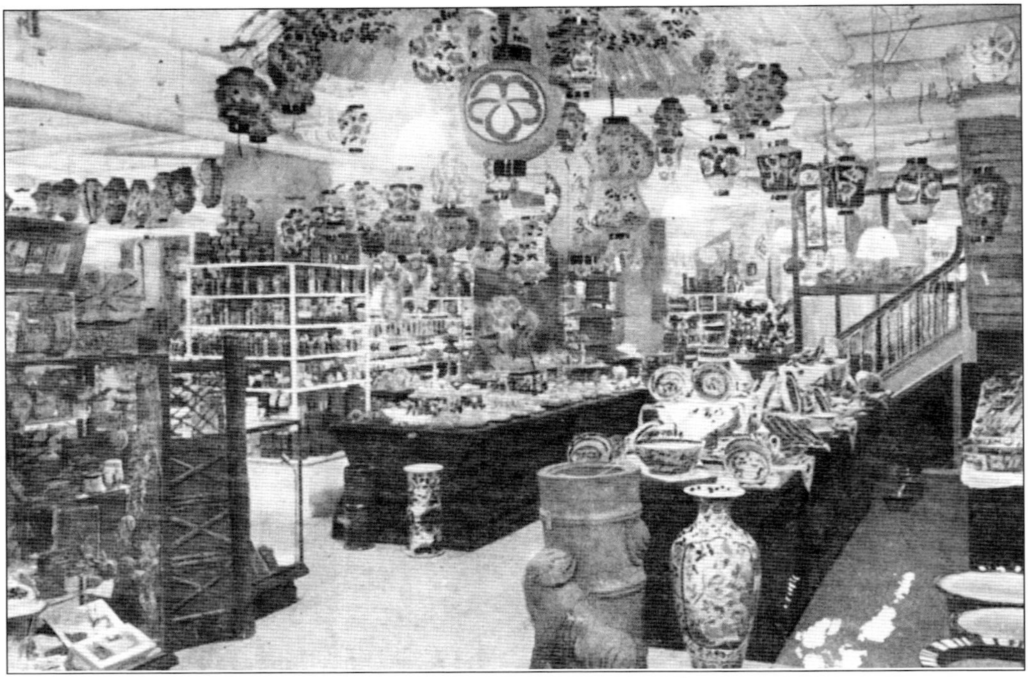

The interiors of Vantine's Department Store on the Ladies' Mile.

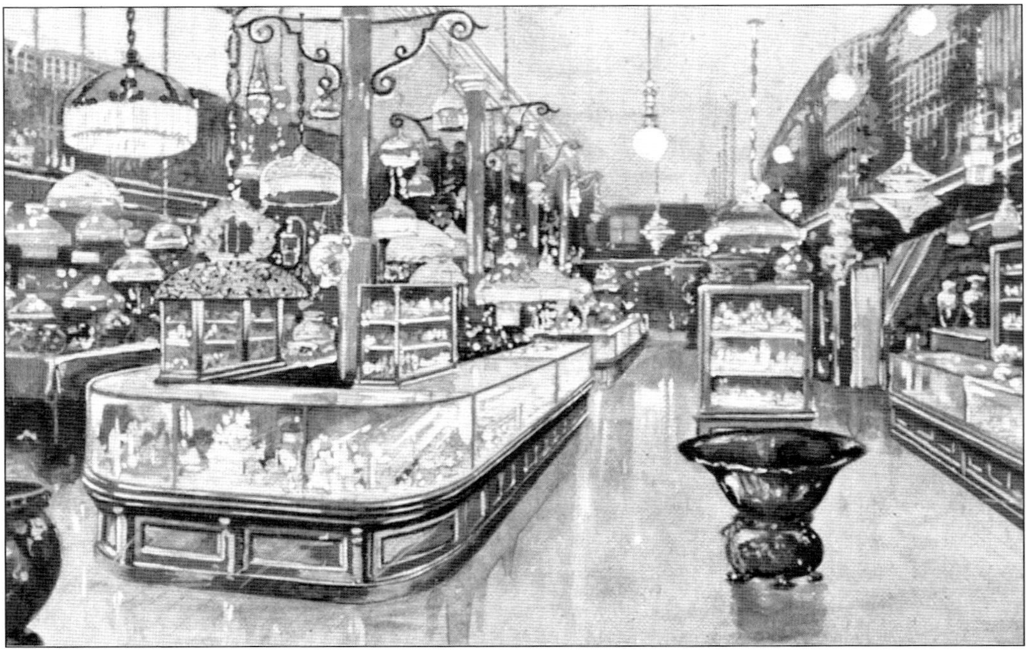

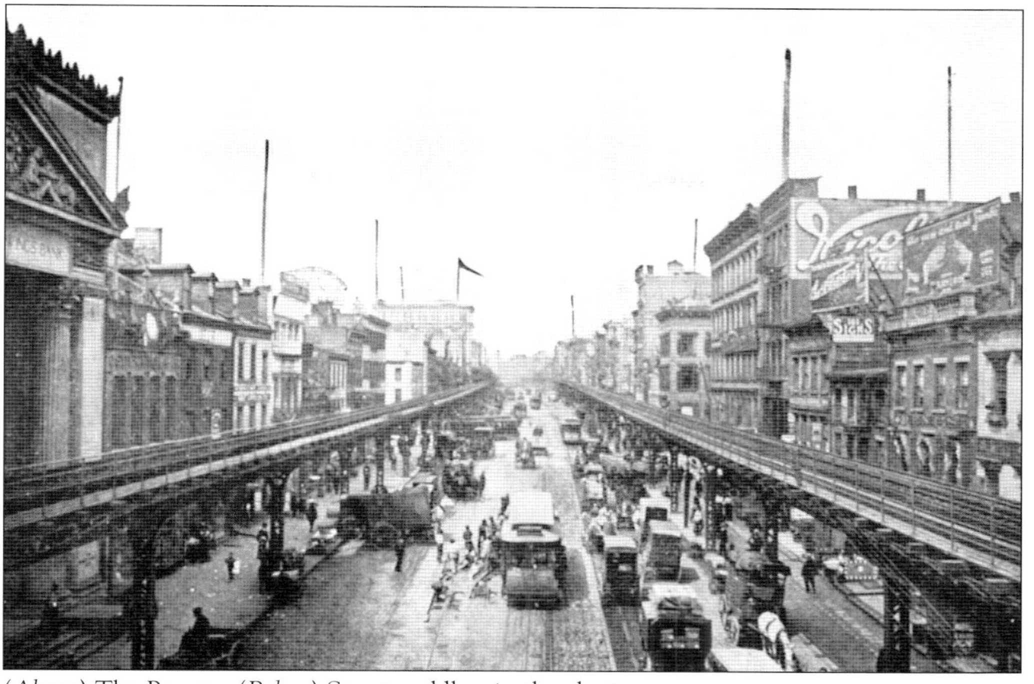

(*Above*) The Bowery. (*Below*) Street peddlers in the ghetto.

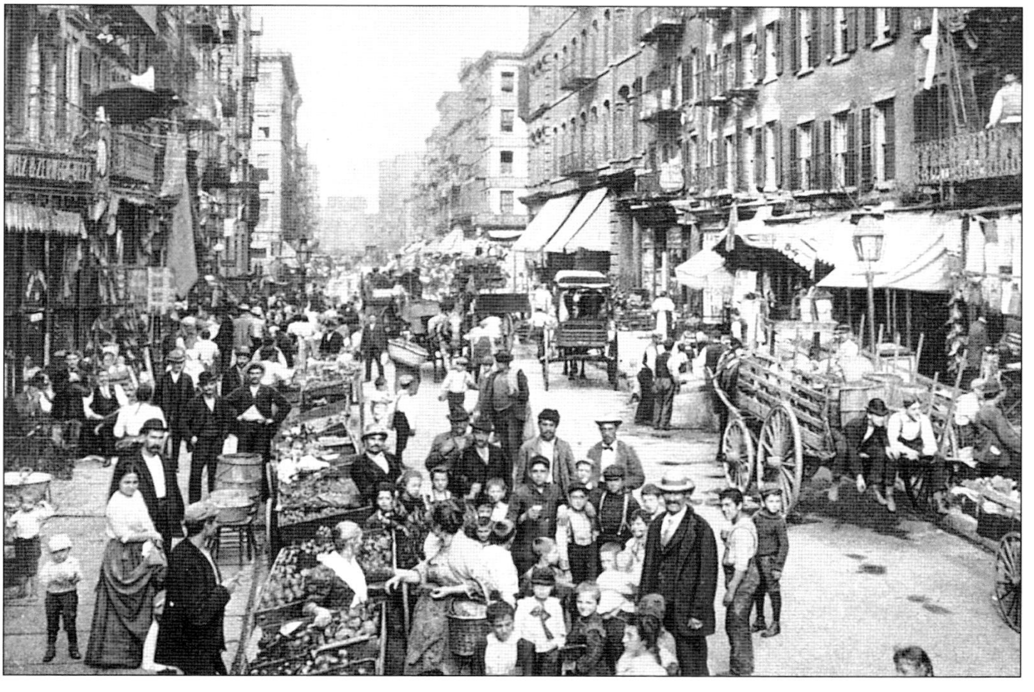

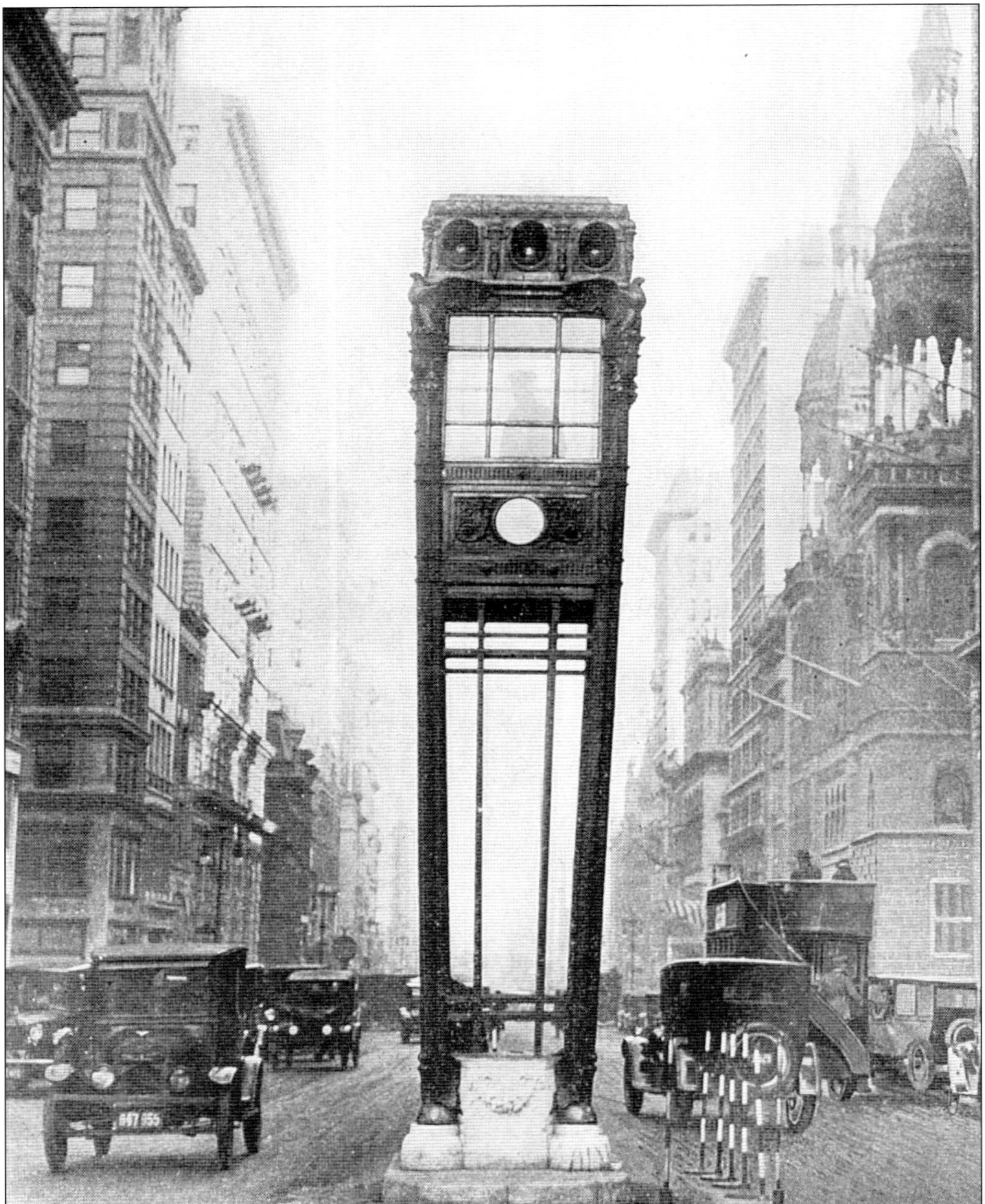

Bronze traffic signal, Fifth Avenue and Forty-Second Street, installed in 1922.

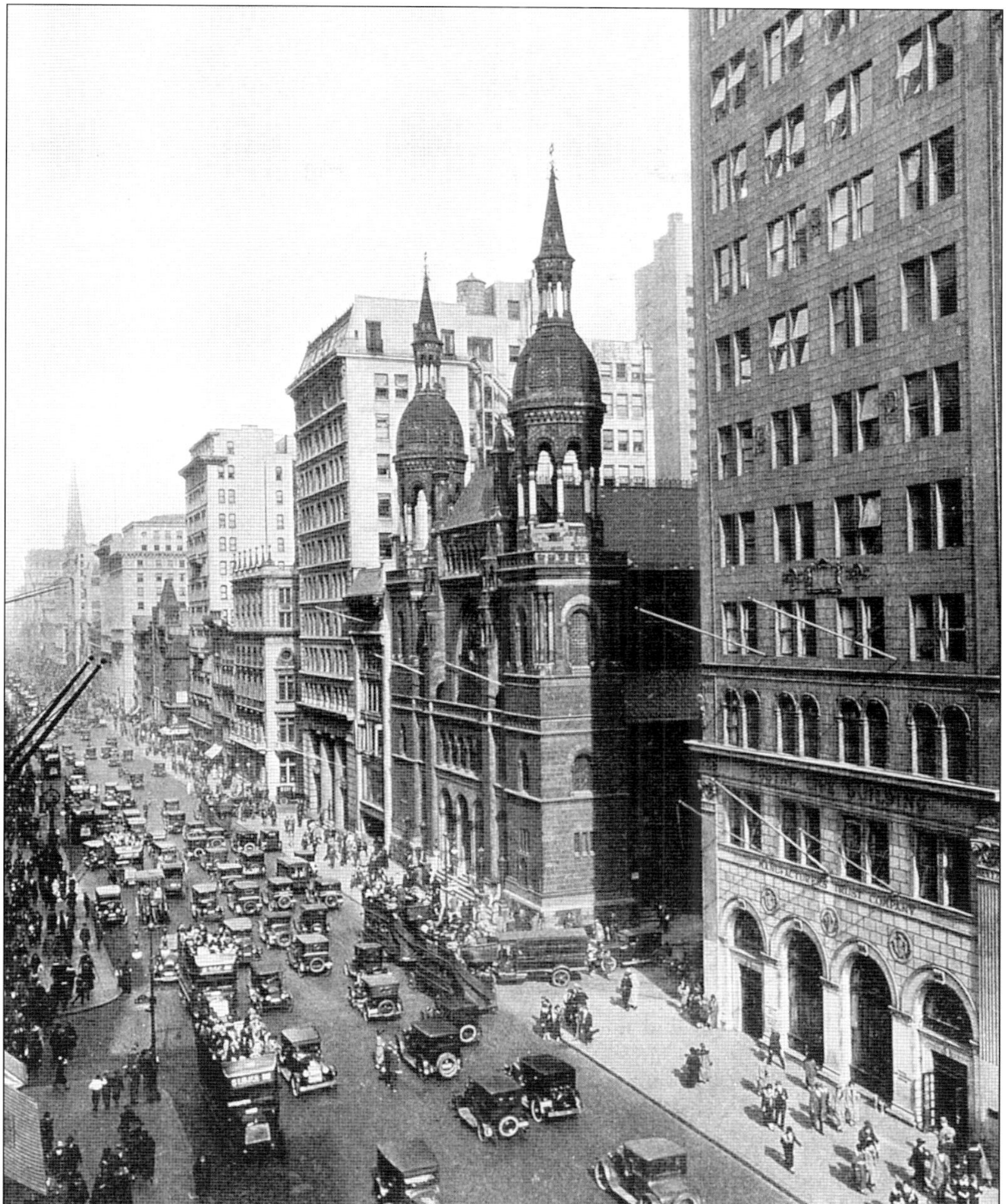

Fifth Avenue looking north from Forty-Second Street.

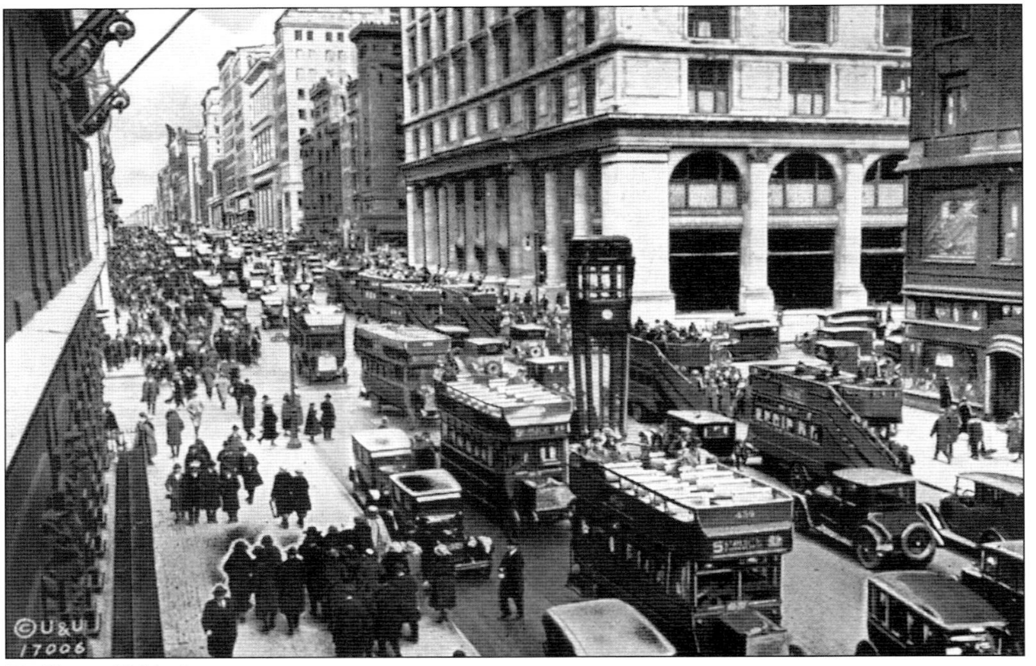

Traffic on Fifth Avenue.

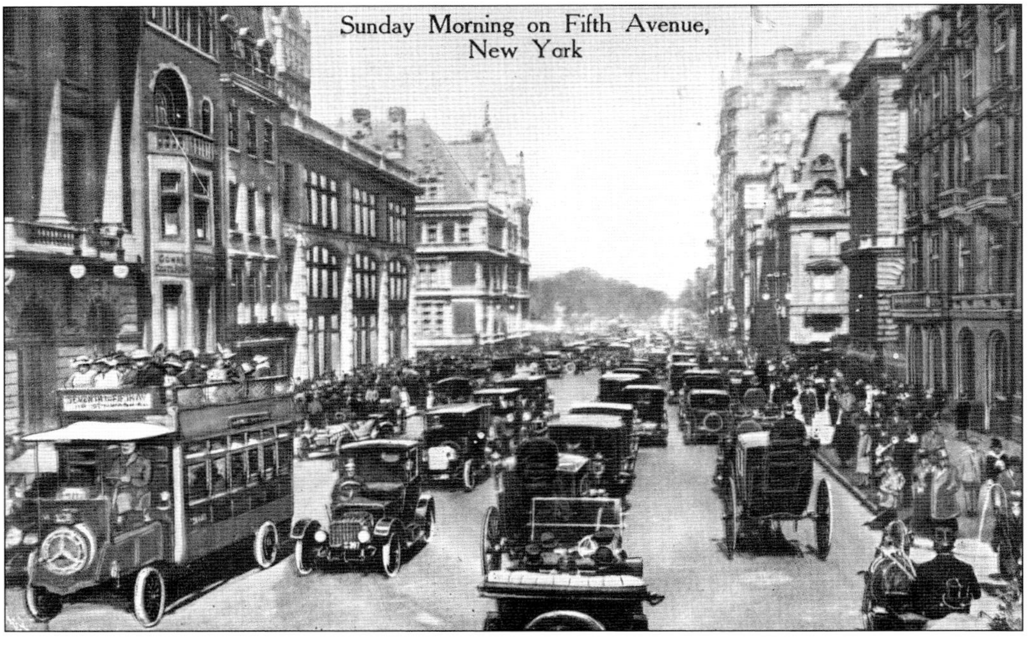

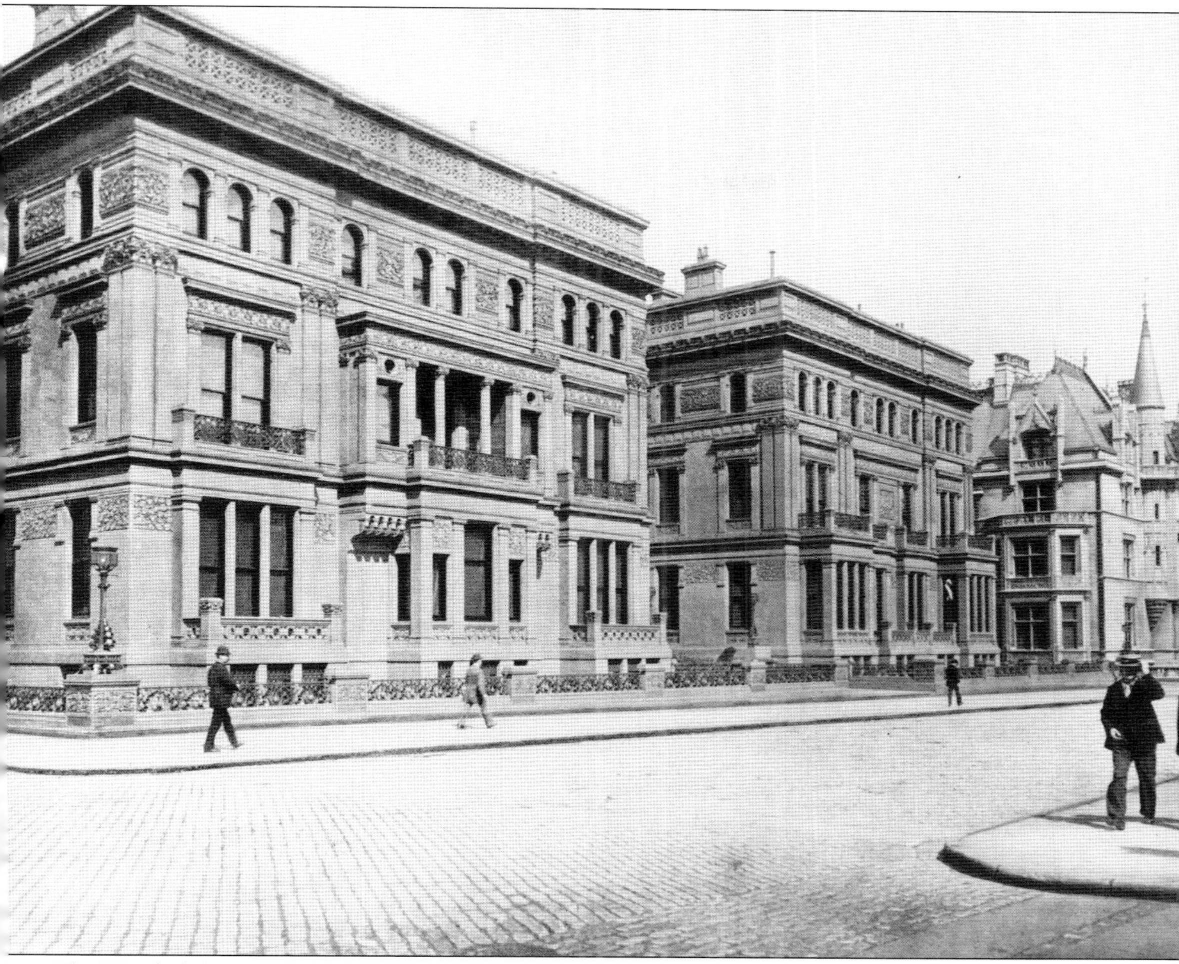

The Vanderbilt mansions on Fifth Avenue.

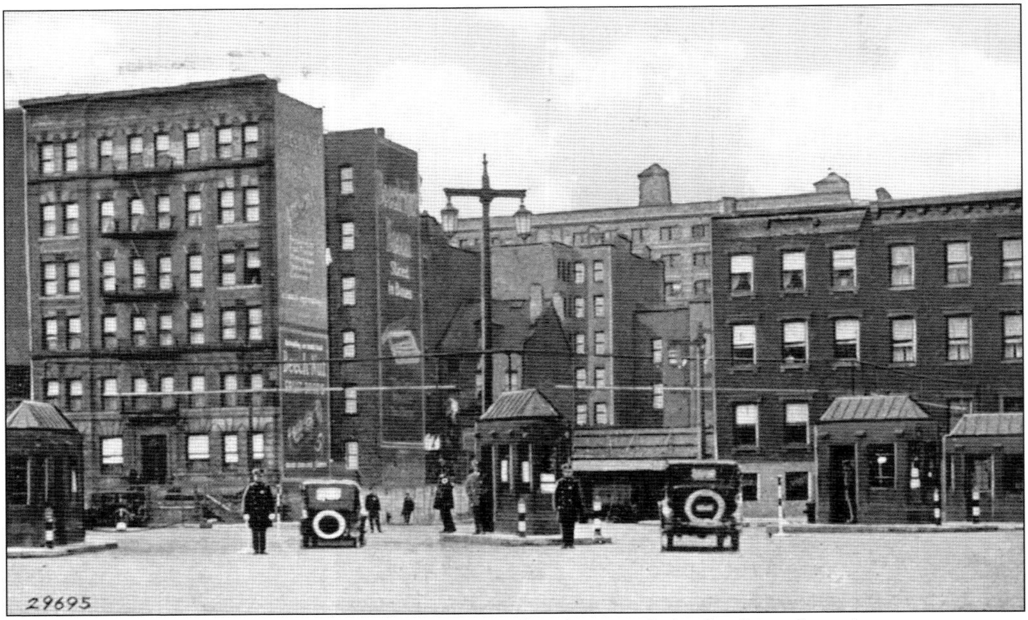

Leaving town. (*Above*) The entrance to the Holland Tunnel. (*Below*) In the tube.

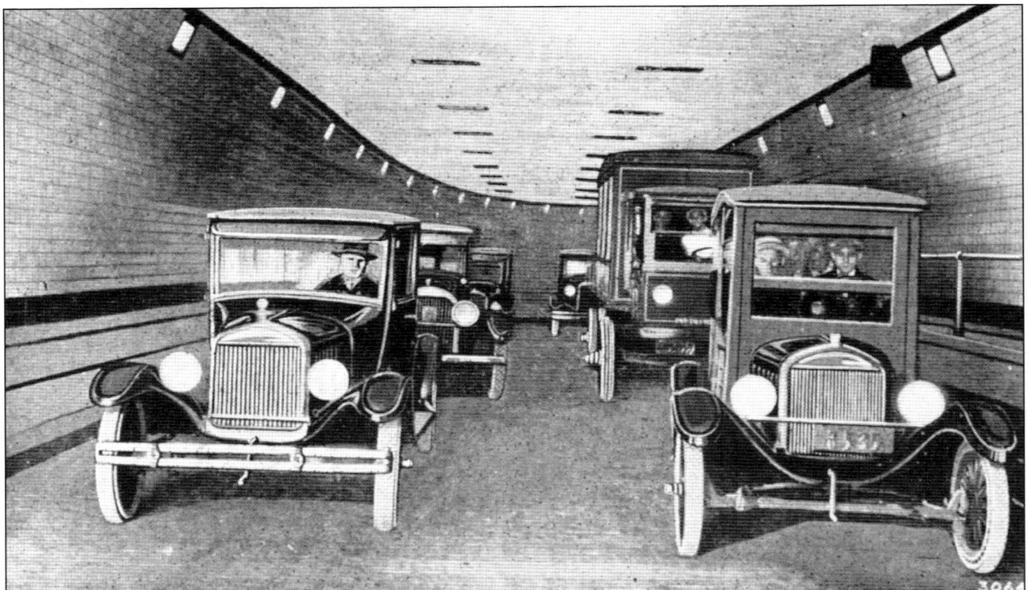

Three

NIGHT LIFE

Restaurants offering fine dining as opposed to tavern or coffeehouse fare had their start in America in 1831, when Delmonico's on William Street was taken over by Lorenzo Delmonico from his uncles. The concept was to provide leisurely dining for businessmen and other members of the city's elite.

Eventually Delmonico's expanded to a number of locations. The one at Fourteenth Street and Fifth Avenue was the scene of Samuel Morse's demonstration of the Atlantic cable. Delmonico's was followed along Broadway by such establishments as Churchills, Murray's Roman Gardens, Maxim's, and others.

By the 1880s restaurants had proliferated throughout Manhattan. Early waves of immigrants, such as the Germans, opened ethnic restaurants by mid-century. Later waves, such as Jews and Italians, began opening establishments before the turn of the century.

The theater district moved north in stages to Times Square, and fine dining establishments moved with it.

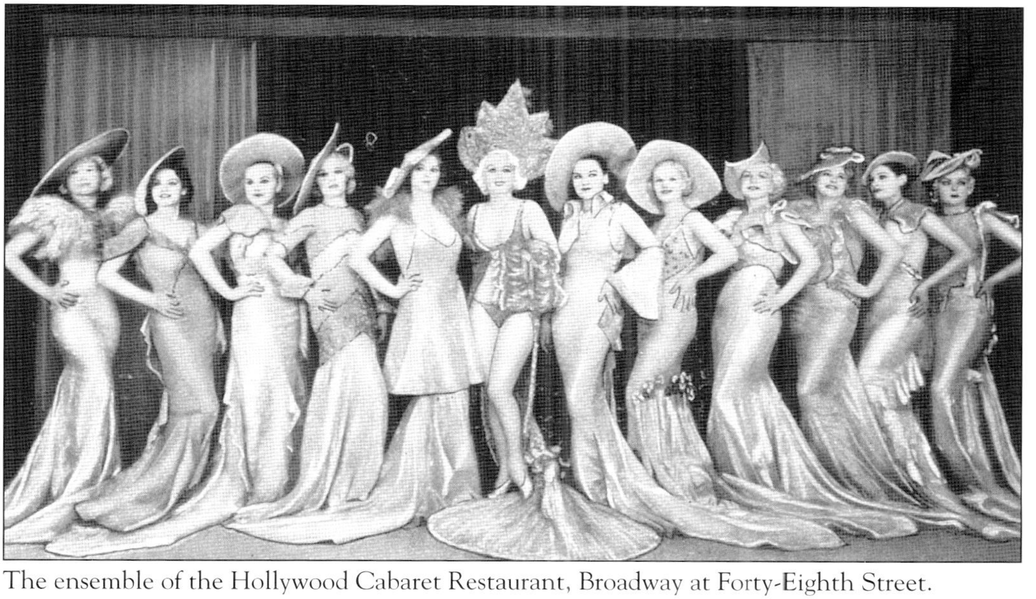

The ensemble of the Hollywood Cabaret Restaurant, Broadway at Forty-Eighth Street.

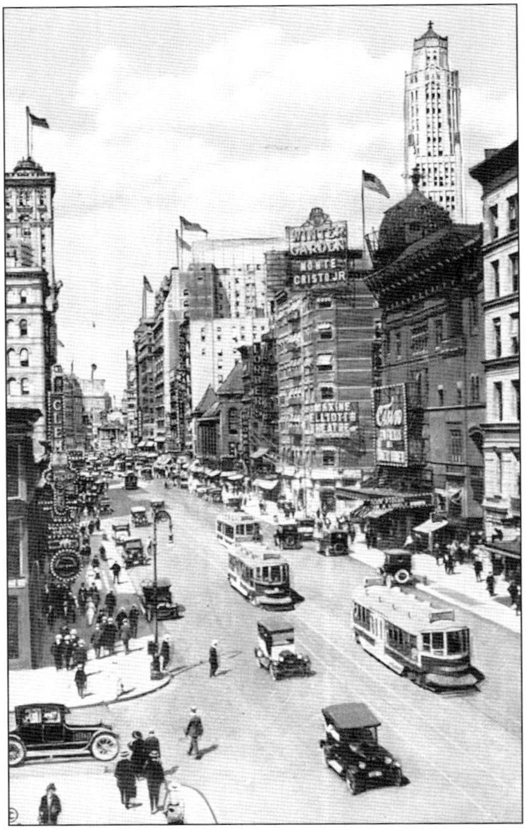

Hobble Skirt trolleys, introduced in 1914. They had center doors built just inches from the ground to accommodate women in long skirts. Broadway from Thirty-Third Street to Times Square, "The Great White Way," was the center for theater, hotels, and fine dining.

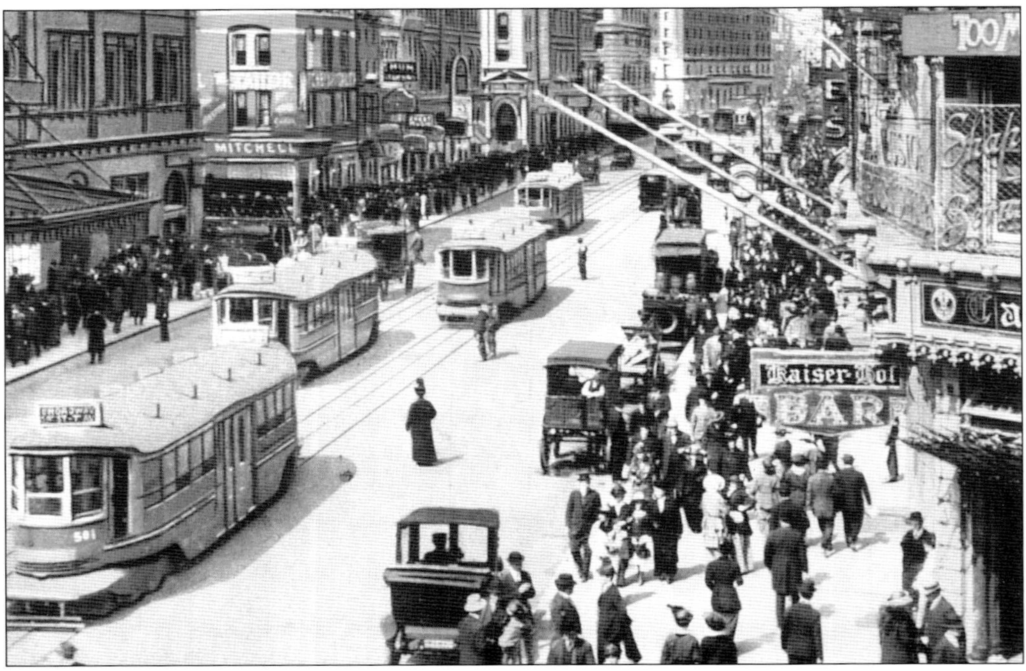

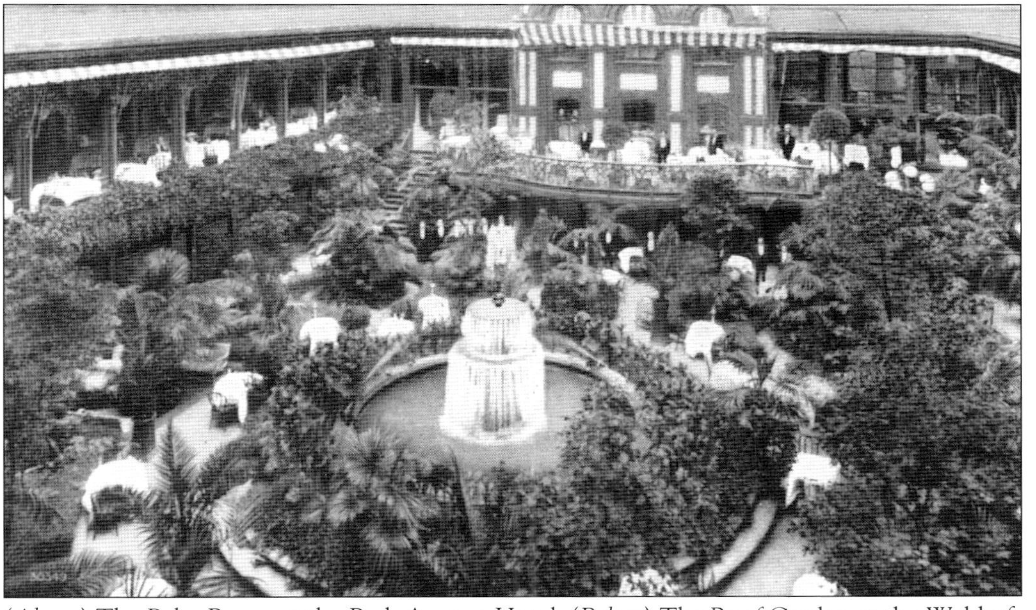

(*Above*) The Palm Room at the Park Avenue Hotel. (*Below*) The Roof Garden at the Waldorf-Astoria.

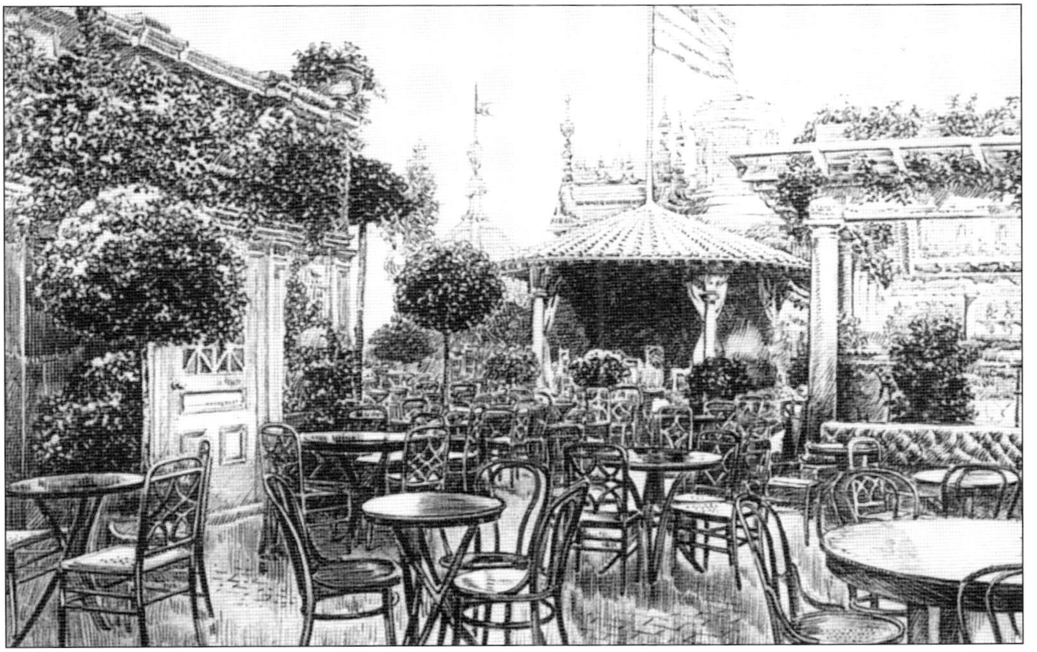

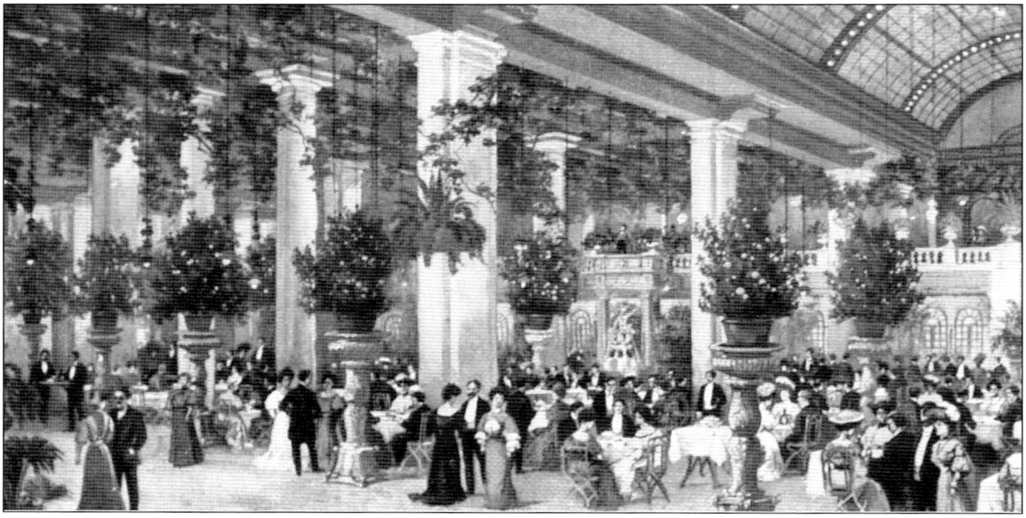

(*Above*) The Orangerie at the Hotel Astor. (*Below*) The Belvedere, Hotel Astor.

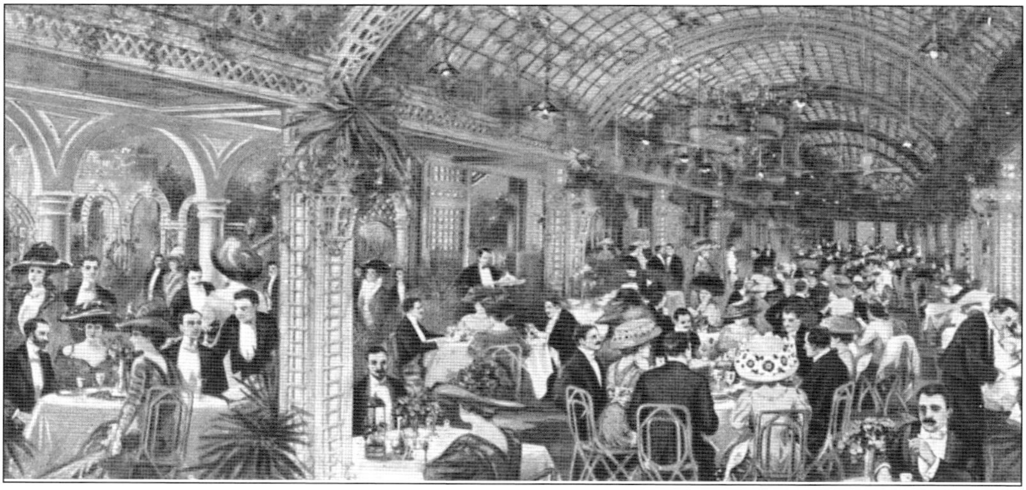

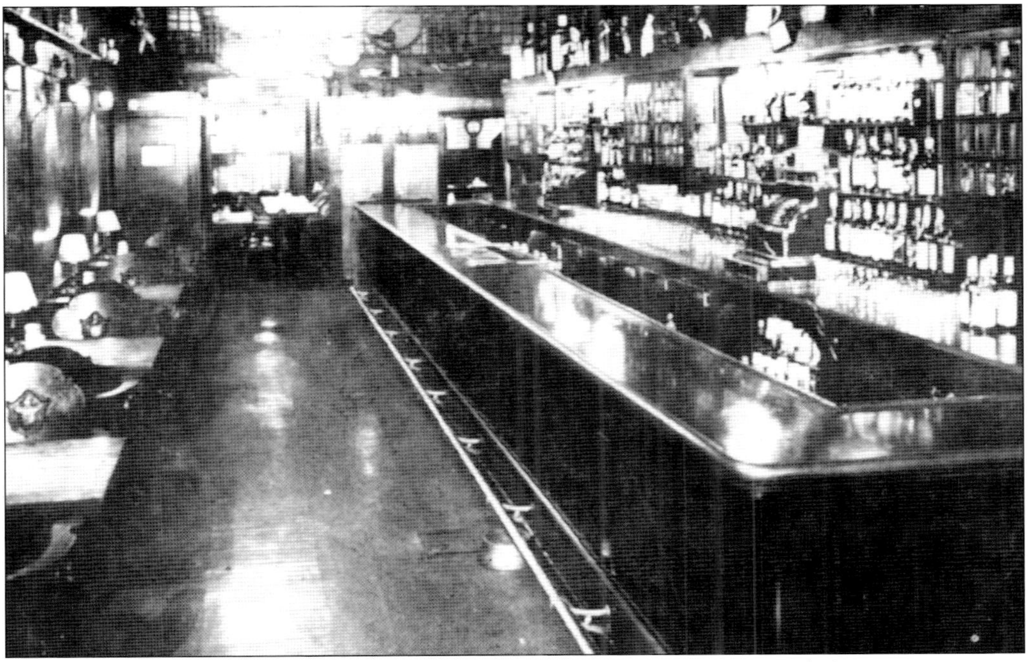

The bar and dining room of the Artist's and Writer's Restaurant on Fortieth Street.

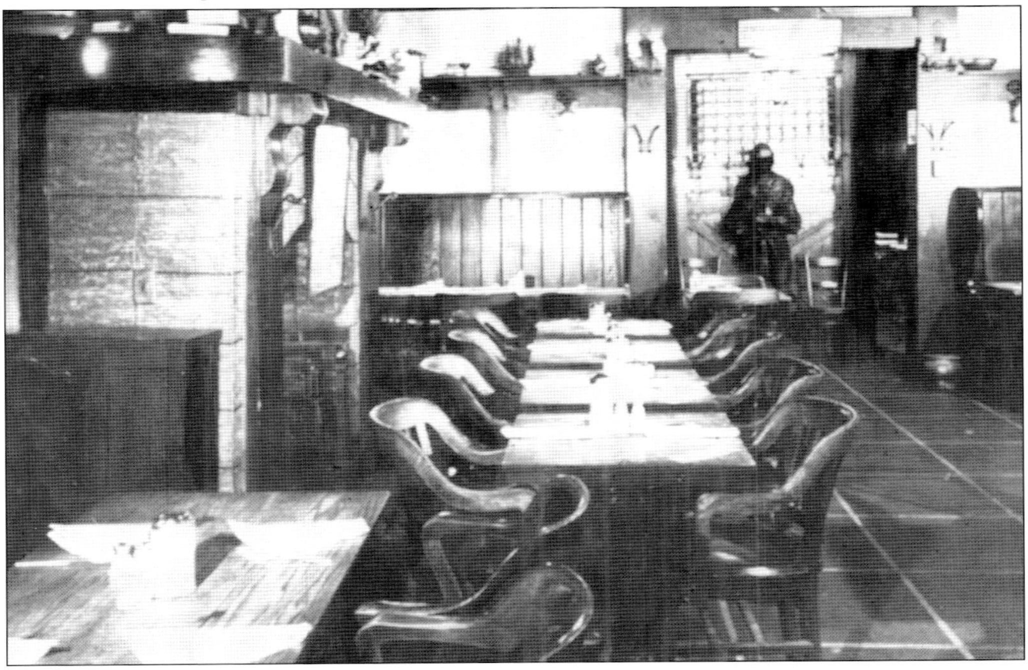

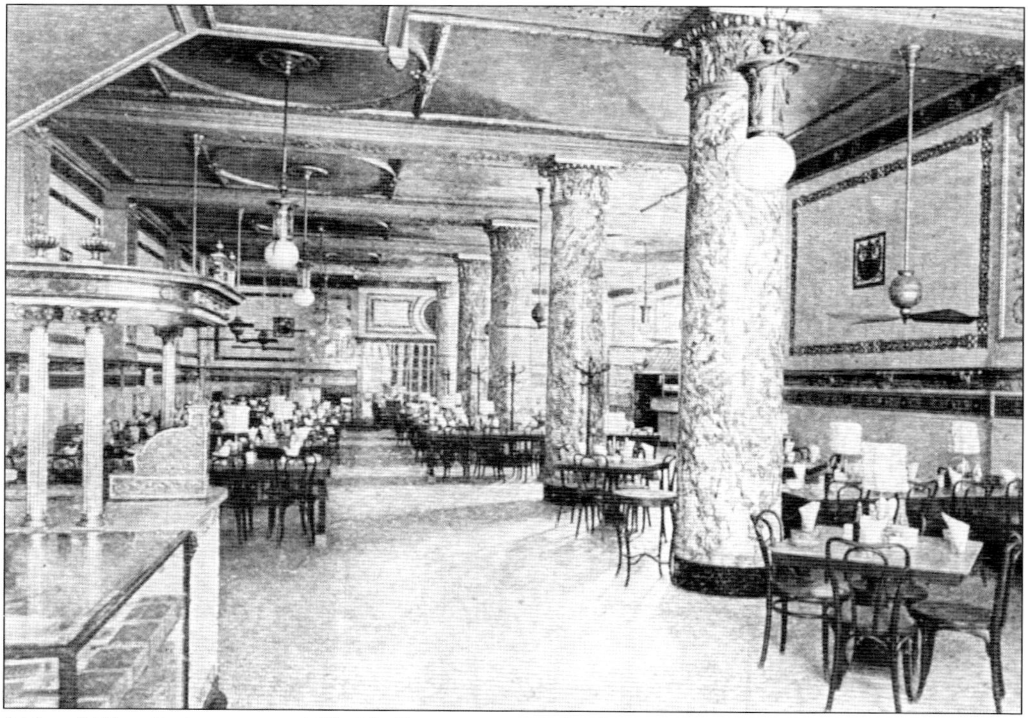

(*Above*) The dining room of Child's Restaurant. (*Below*) Horn & Hardart's Automat.

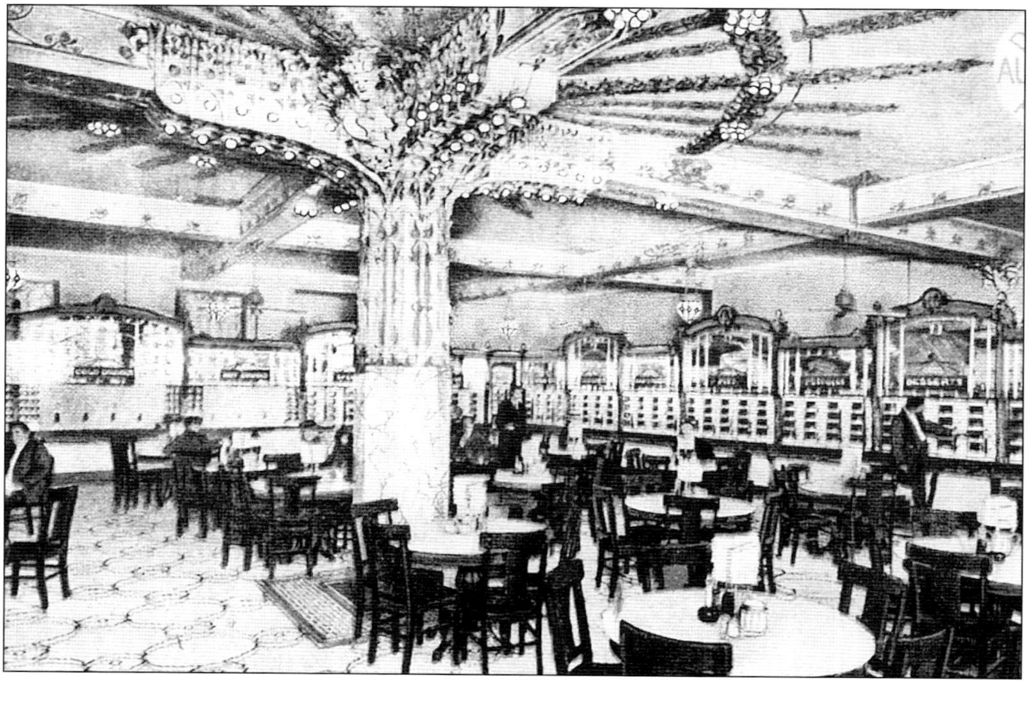

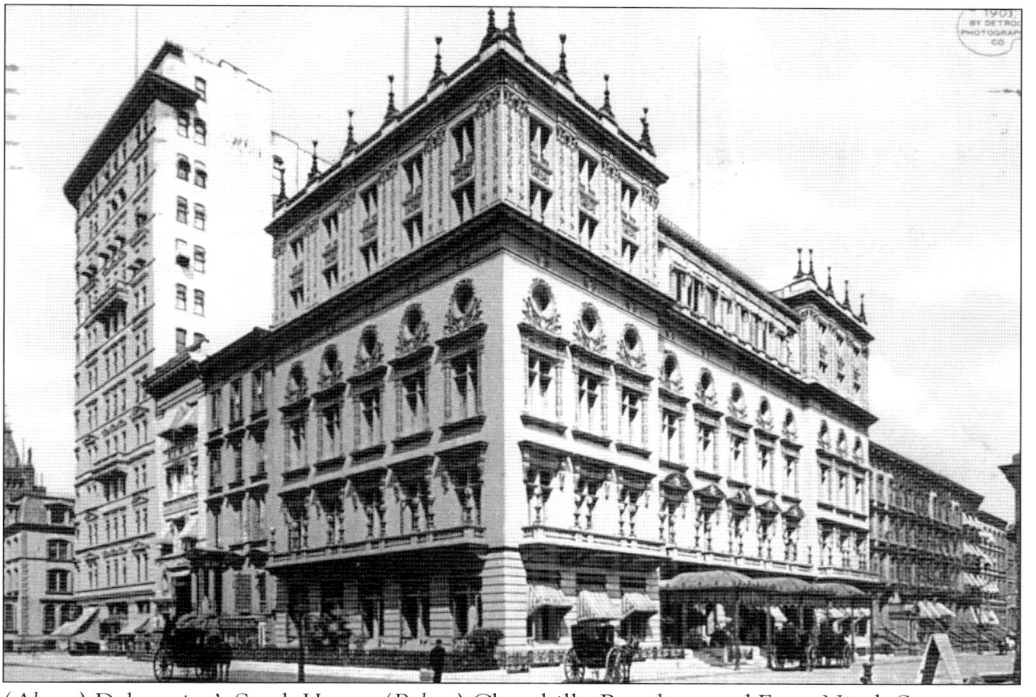

(*Above*) Delmonico's Steak House. (*Below*) Churchills, Broadway and Forty-Ninth Street.

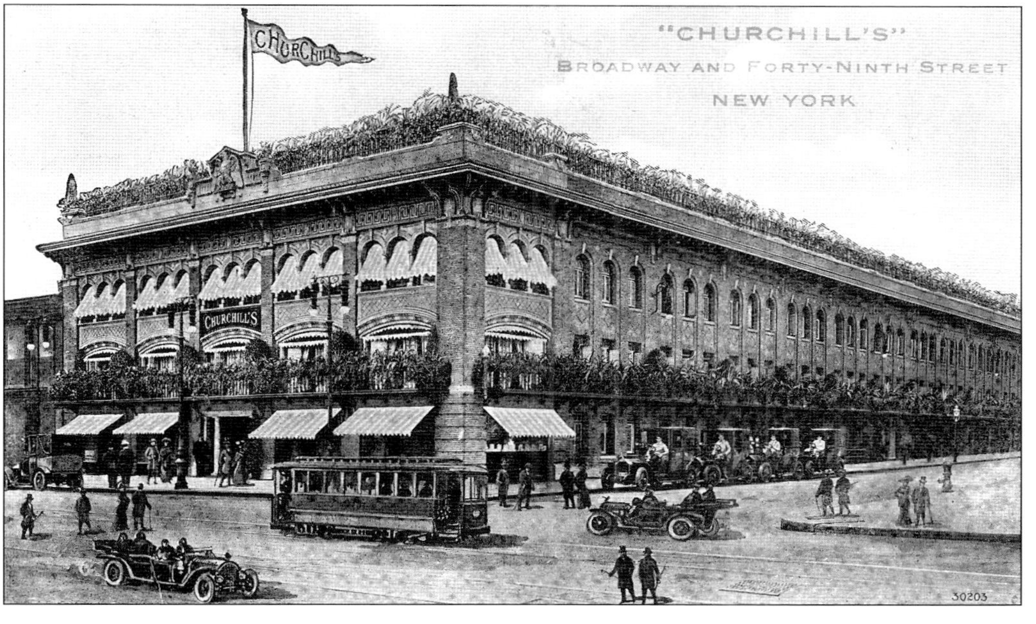

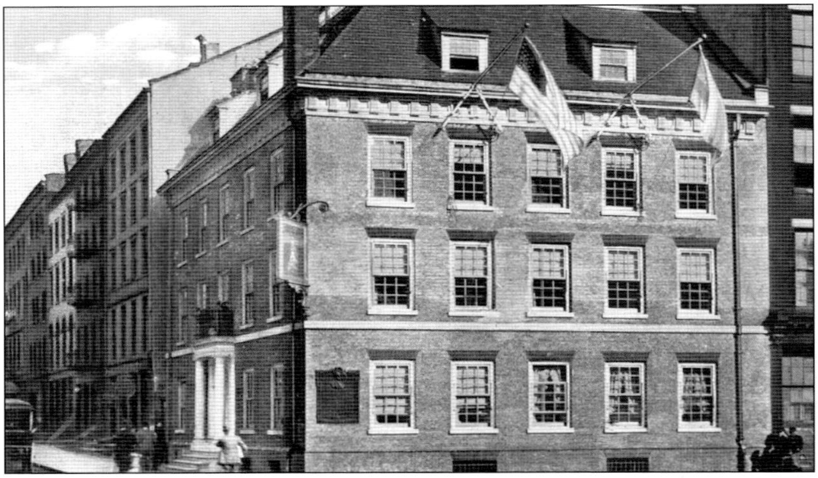

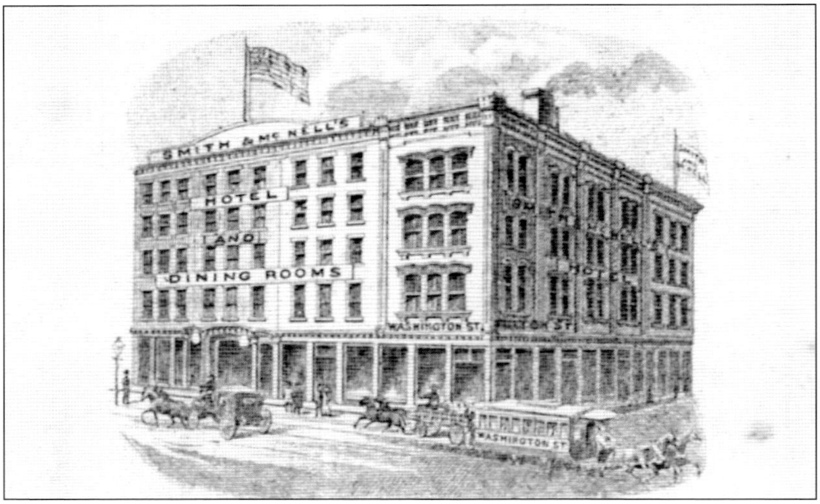

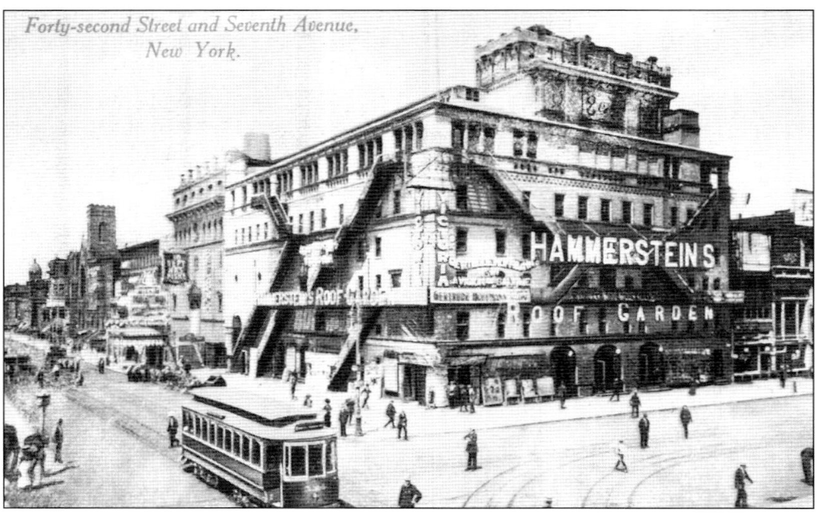

(*Top*) One of the city's more luxurious taverns, Faunce's, at Broad and Pearl Streets. (*Center*) Smith & McNell's, an early restaurant at Greenwich & Washington Streets. It catered mainly to businessmen. (*Bottom*) Hammerstein's, Seventh Avenue and Forty-Second Street.

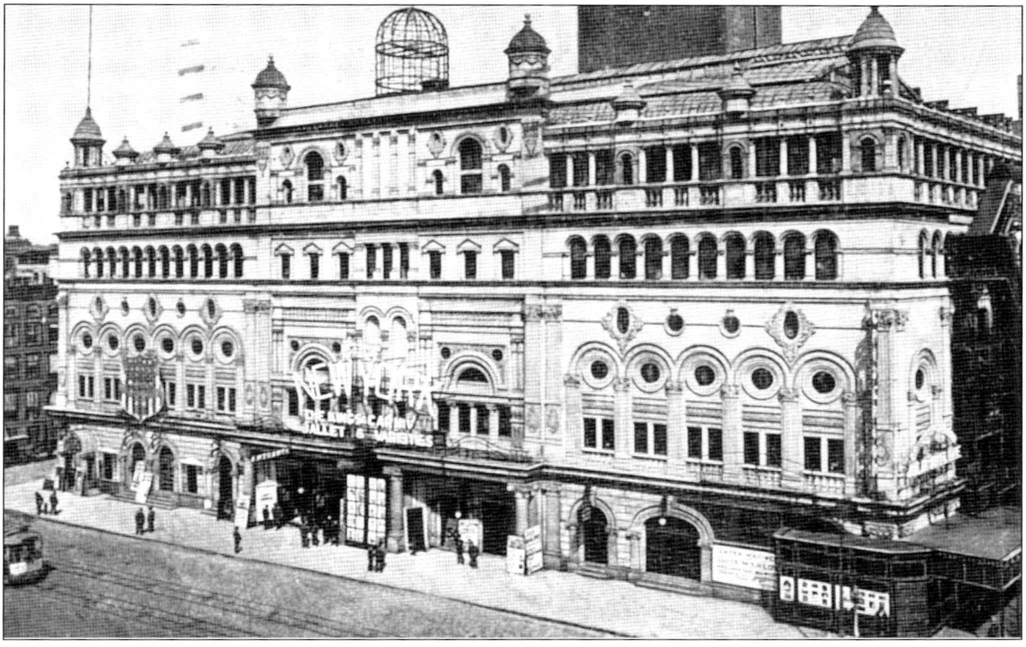

(*Above*) The New York and Criterion Theaters. (*Below*) The New Theater.

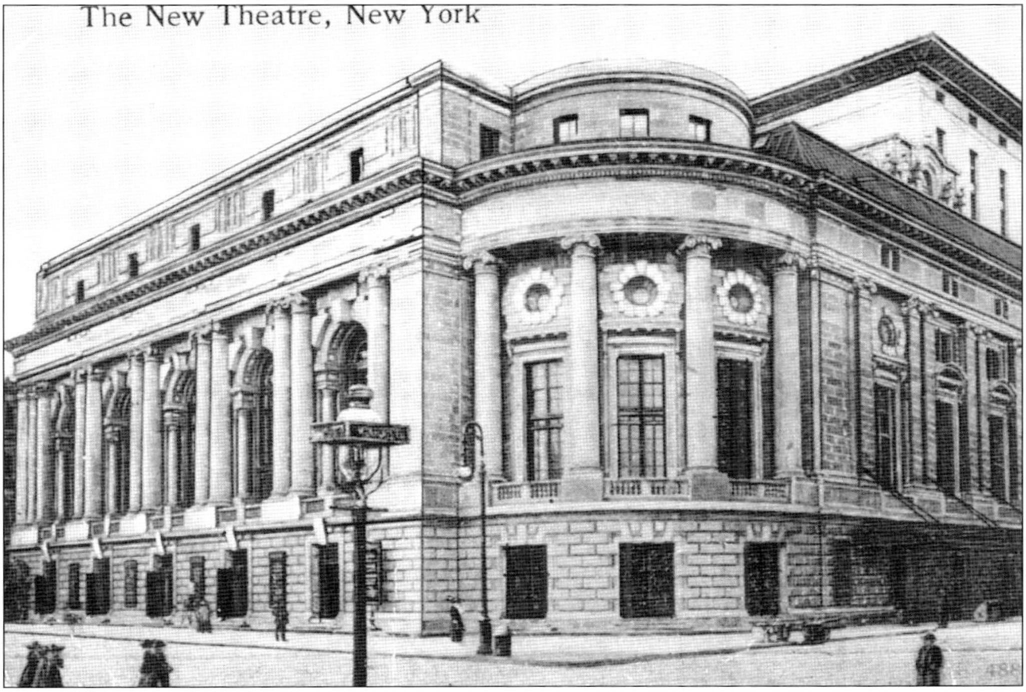

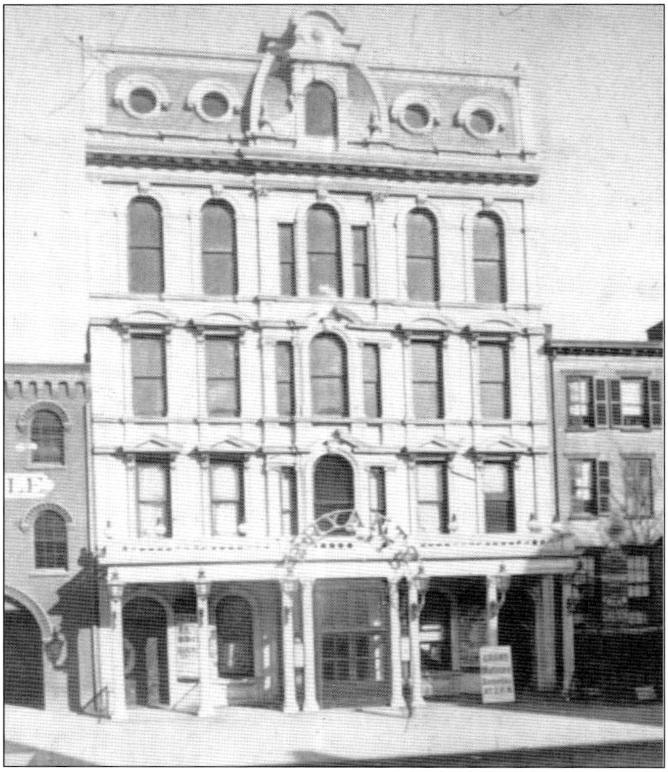

(*Left*) Bryant's Opera House. (*Below*) Manhattan Opera House on Thirty-Fourth Street, founded by Oscar Hammerstein.

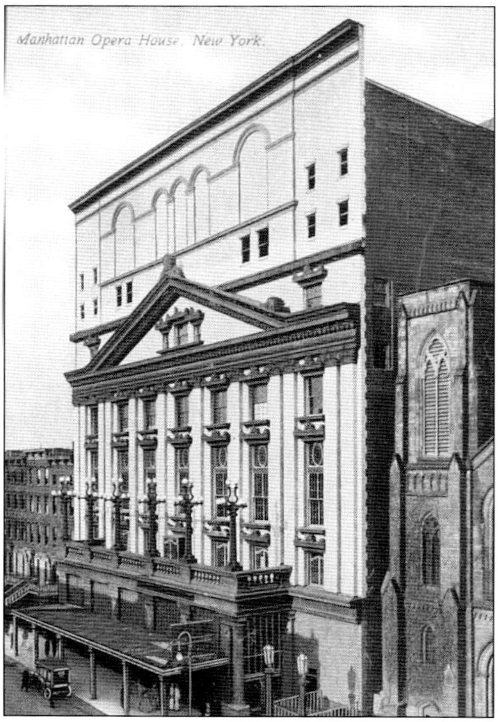

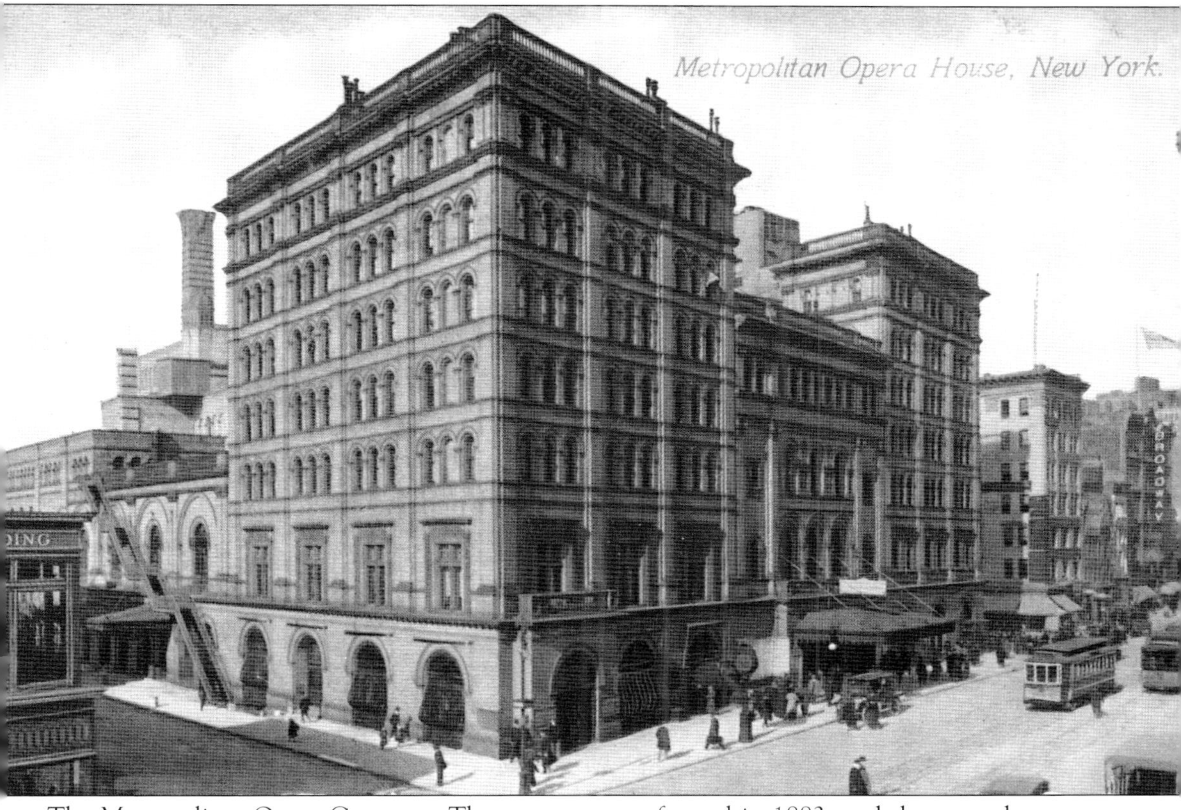

The Metropolitan Opera Company. The company was formed in 1883, and the opera house at Thirty-Ninth Street and Broadway opened for its first season in that year. The Italian Renaissance structure was designed by J.C. Caddy. Its conservative facade inspired critics to call it the yellow brick brewery.

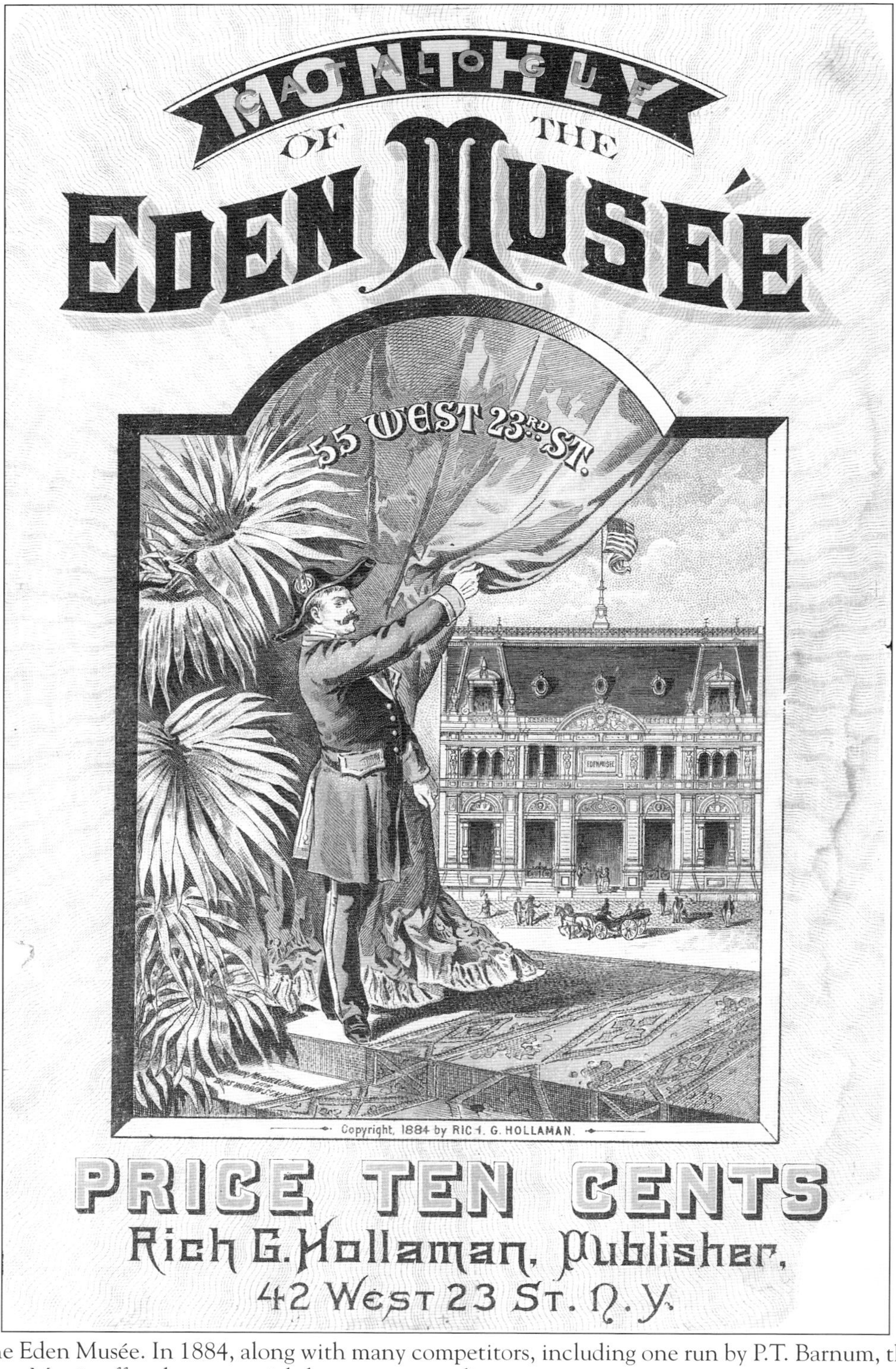

The Eden Musée. In 1884, along with many competitors, including one run by P.T. Barnum, the Eden Musée offered commercial shows masquerading as museums.

Four

COMMERCE

The last two decades of the 19th century were exciting years for Wall Street. On December 15, 1886, for the first time in the history of the New York Stock Exchange, share volume exceeded one million. It was not until the end of the century that industrial securities were traded on the exchange. In 1901, U.S. Steel became the first corporation in history capitalized at more than $1 billion.

The current headquarters of the New York Stock Exchange, designed by George B. Post, was opened in 1903. Behind the magnificent Renaissance facade is a trading floor that is 100 feet wide and 183 feet deep, with a ceiling that is 79 feet high.

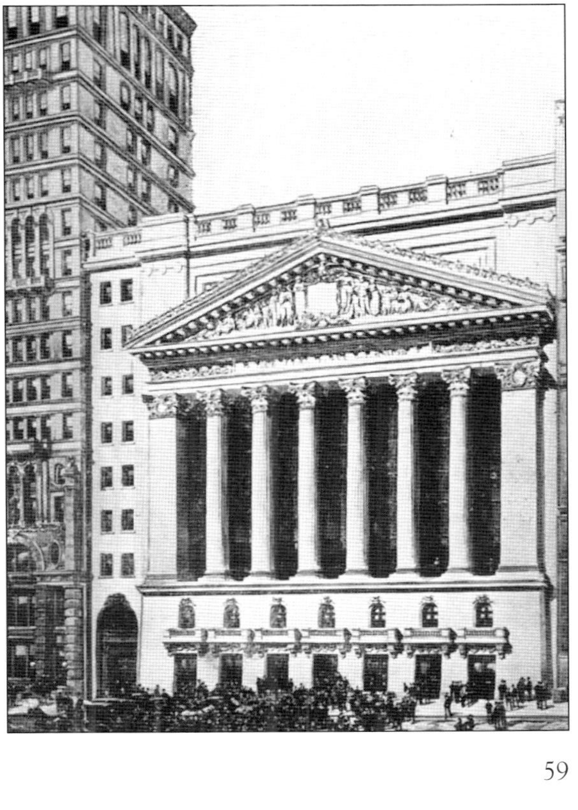

The New York Stock Exchange.

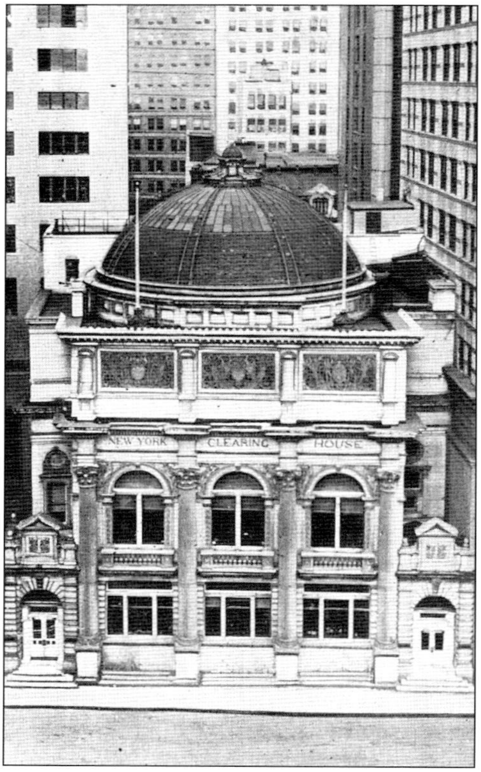

(*Left*) The New York Clearing House, 77 Cedar Street. In 1913 it handled transactions averaging nearly $324 million a day. (*Below*) Curb brokers who dealt in the street. These were the predecessors of what would in 1953 become the American Stock Exchange. In 1921 the exchange moved indoors at 113 Greenwich Street.

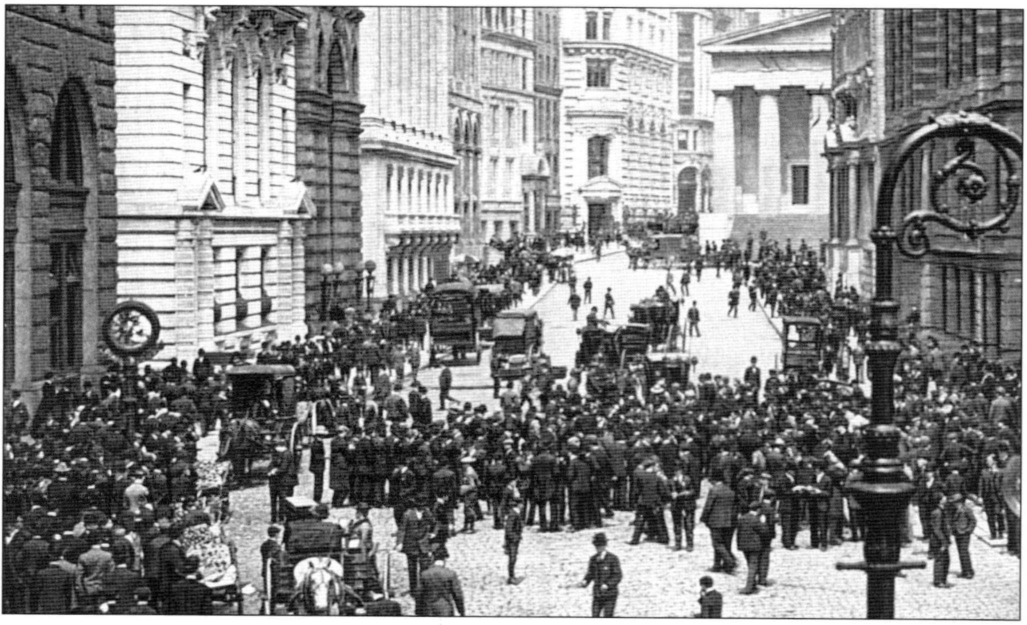

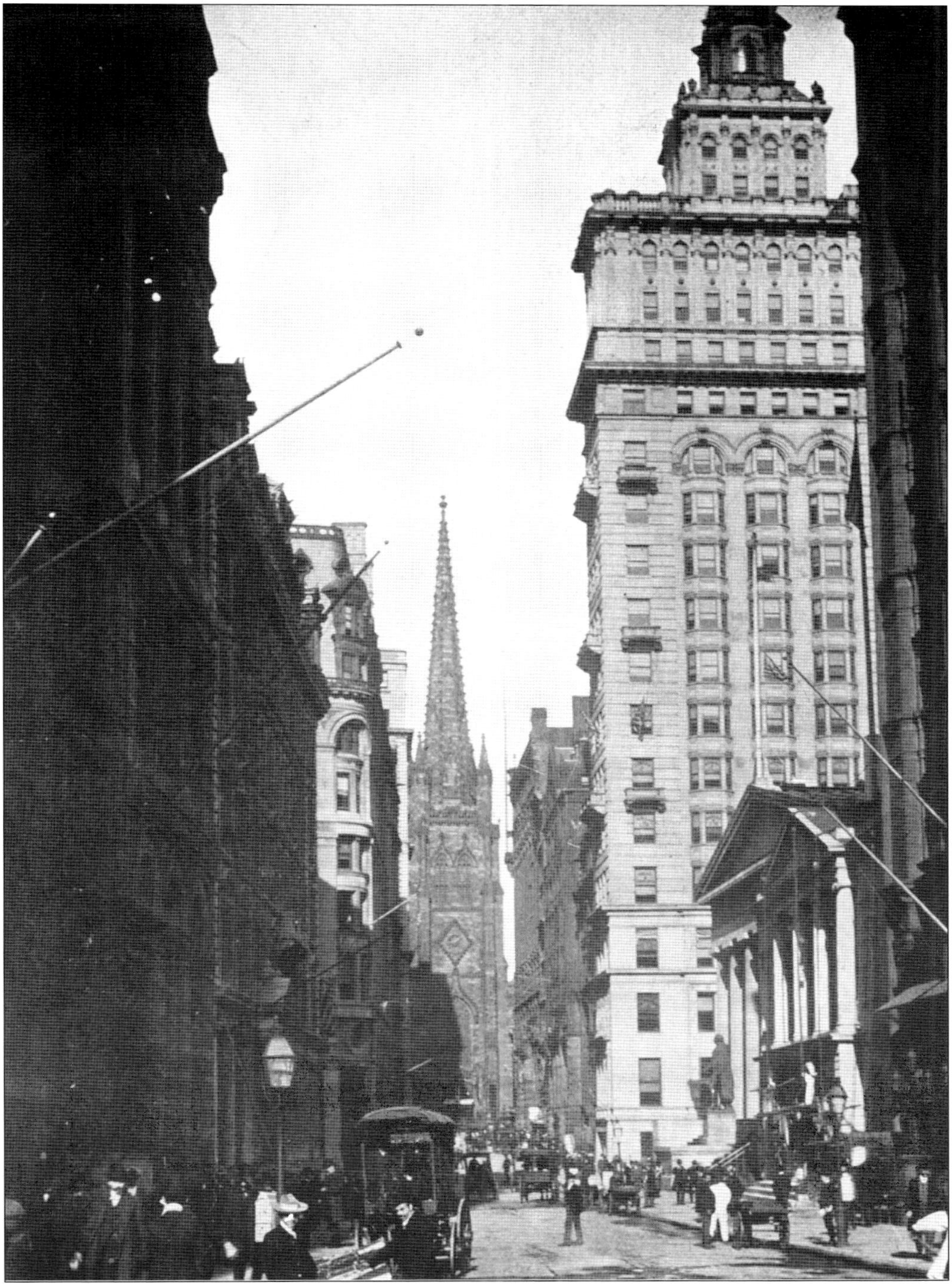

Trinity Church at the end of Wall Street. The low building on the right is the United States Treasury. The skyscraper next to it is the Gillender Building.

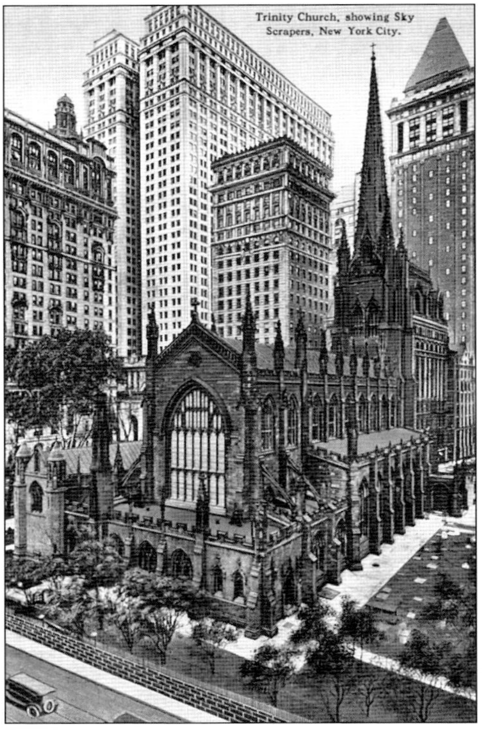

(*Left*) Trinity Church dwarfed by early-20th-century skyscrapers. (*Below*) City hall and City Hall Park. In the background are several of the buildings on Newspaper Row.

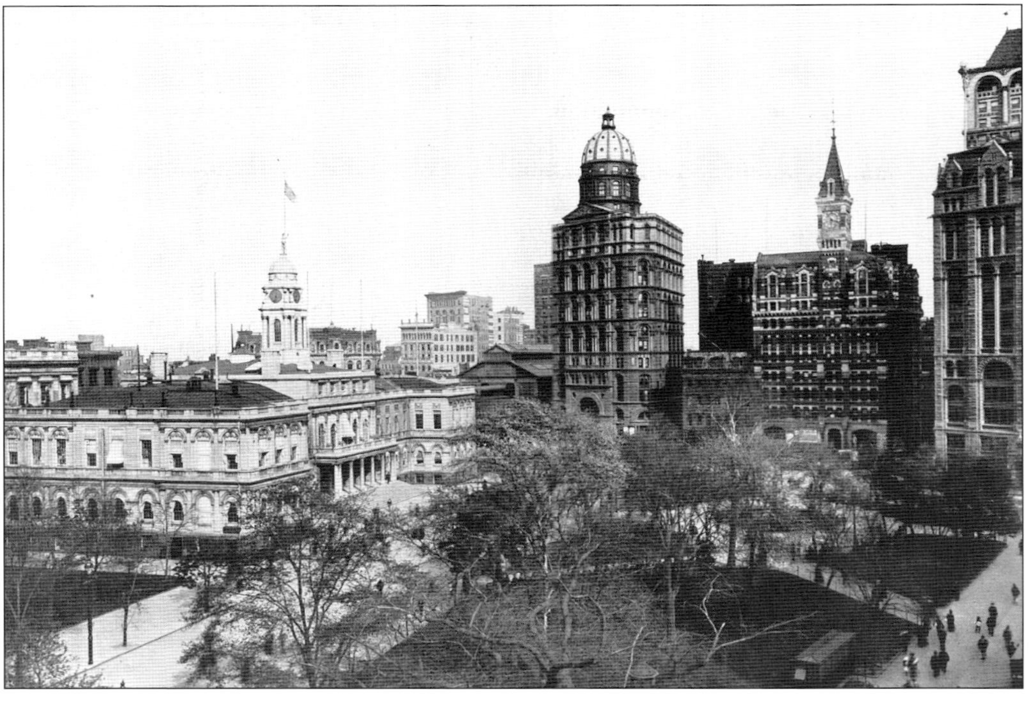

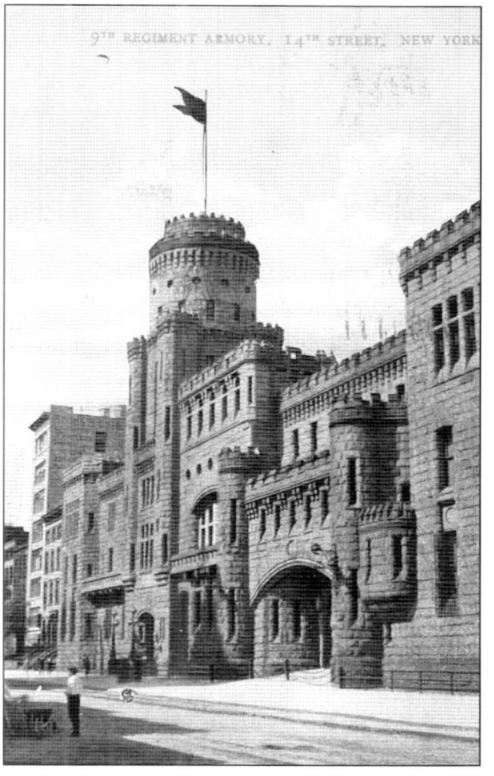

(*Right*) The 9th Regiment Armory on Fourteenth Street. (*Below*) The city prison, a Neo-Egyptian-style building known as "The Tombs." The "Bridge of Sighs" in the center leads to the Criminal Court Building.

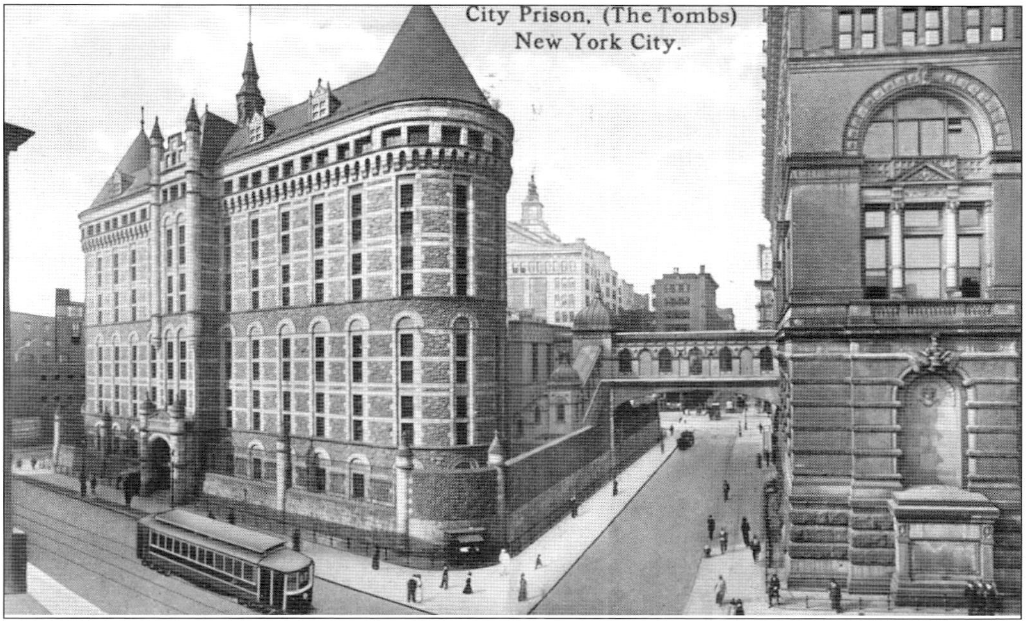

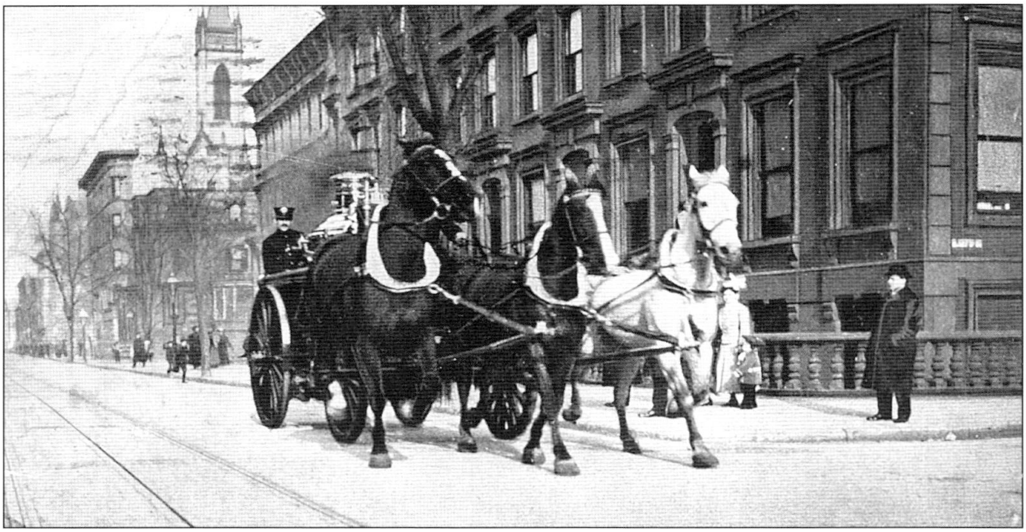

(*Above*) A horse-drawn pumper. This pumper was captured on film as it sped to a fire. (*Below*) Battling a fire. Achieving sufficient water pressure became an increasing problem in the early 20th century as ever higher buildings were built.

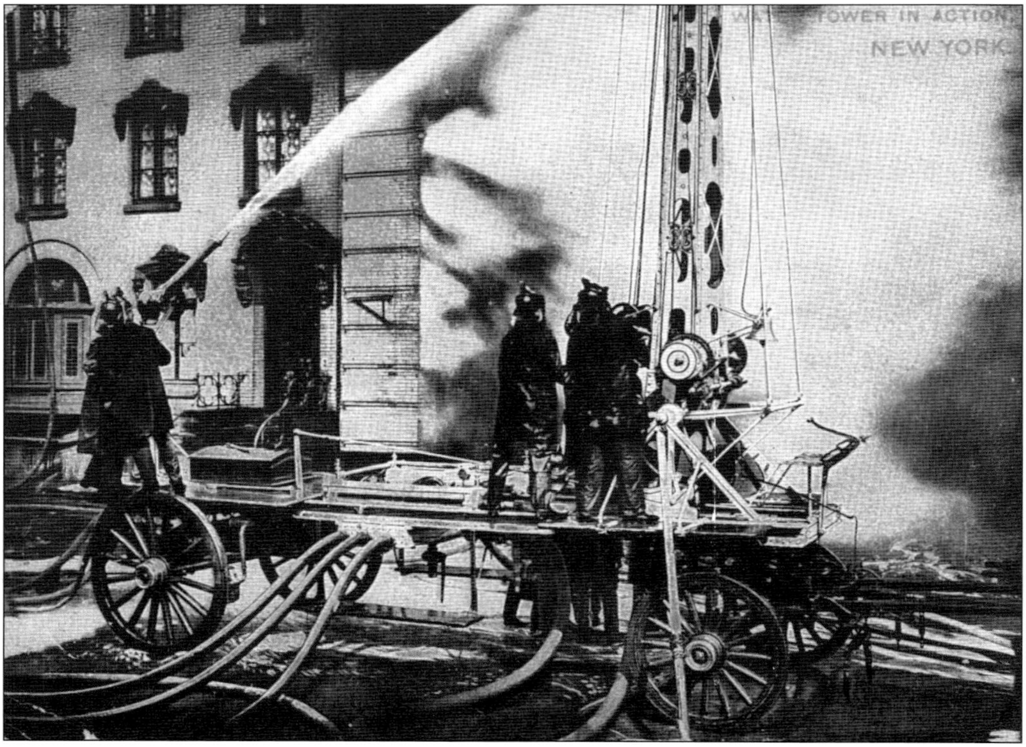

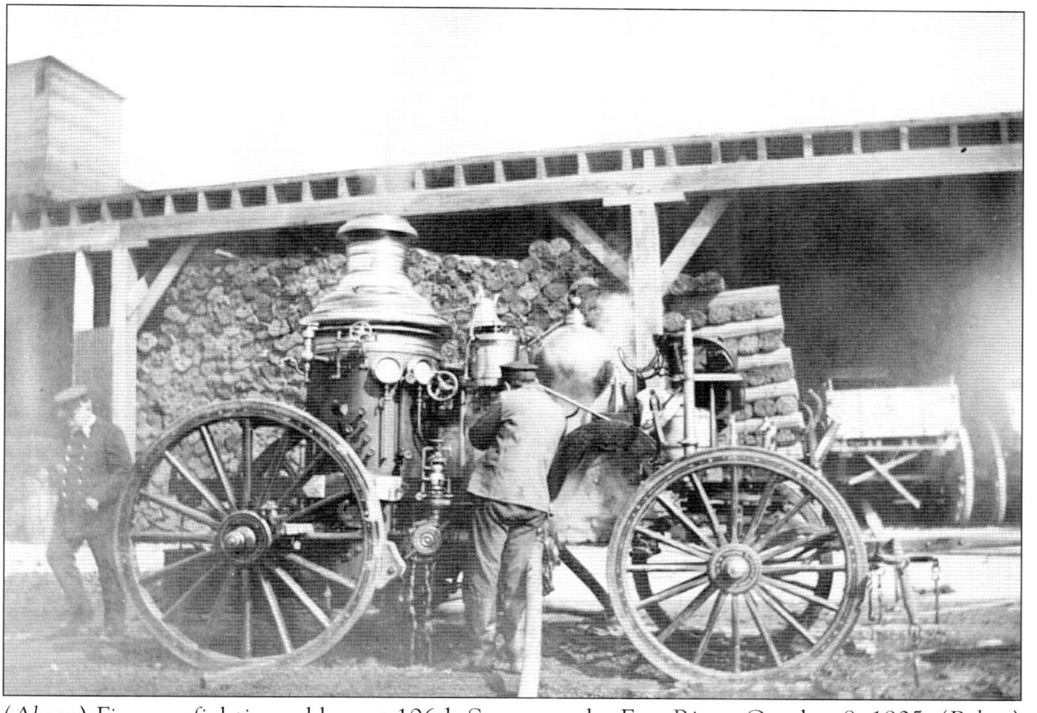

(*Above*) Firemen fighting a blaze at 106th Street on the East River, October 8, 1905. (*Below*) Motor-propelled engines, introduced in 1907. By 1922 all horse-drawn vehicles were replaced.

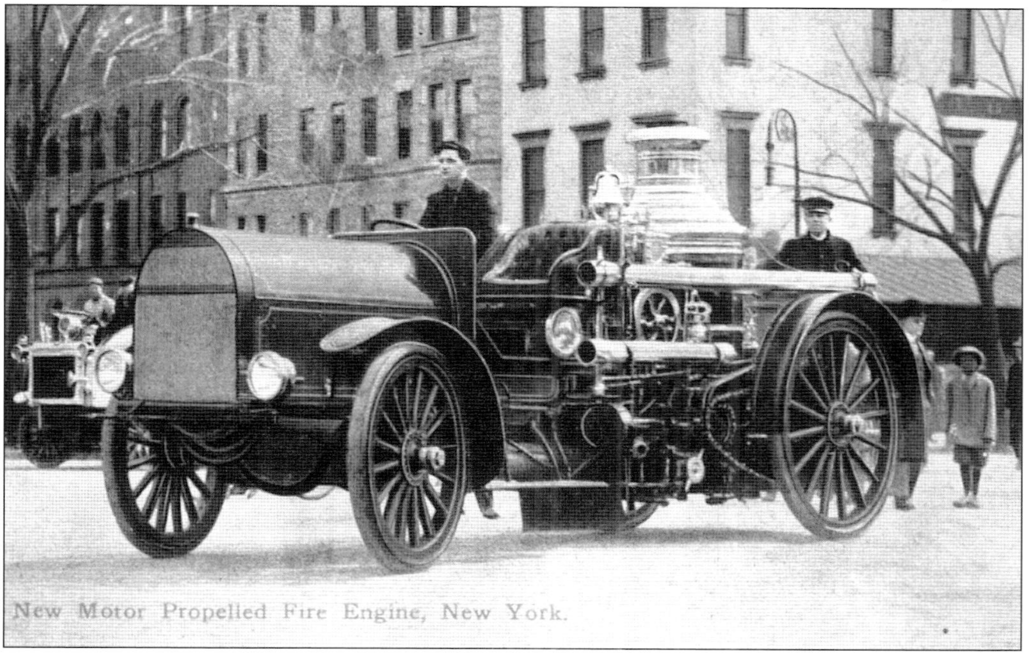

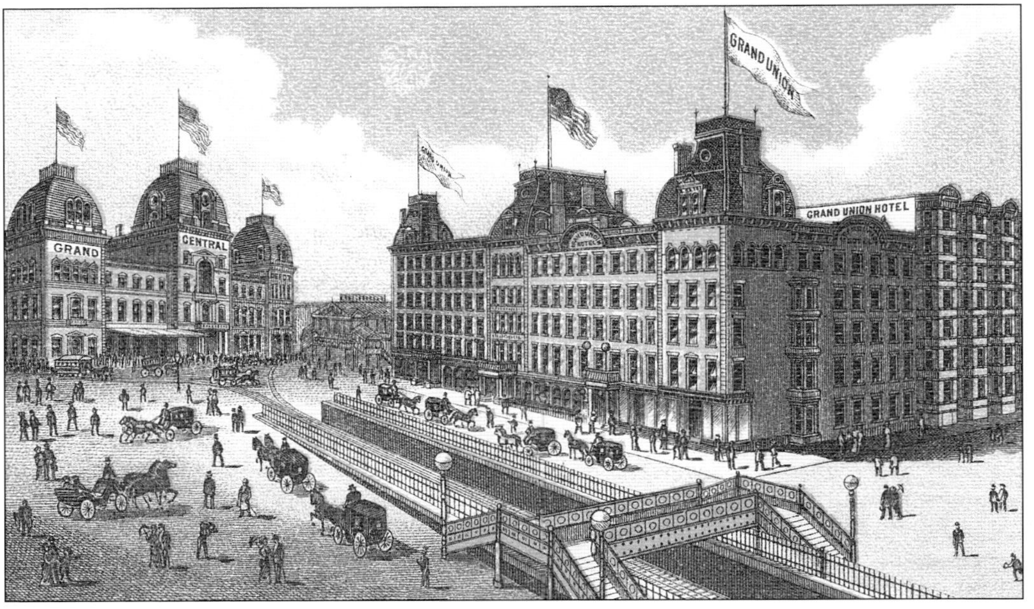

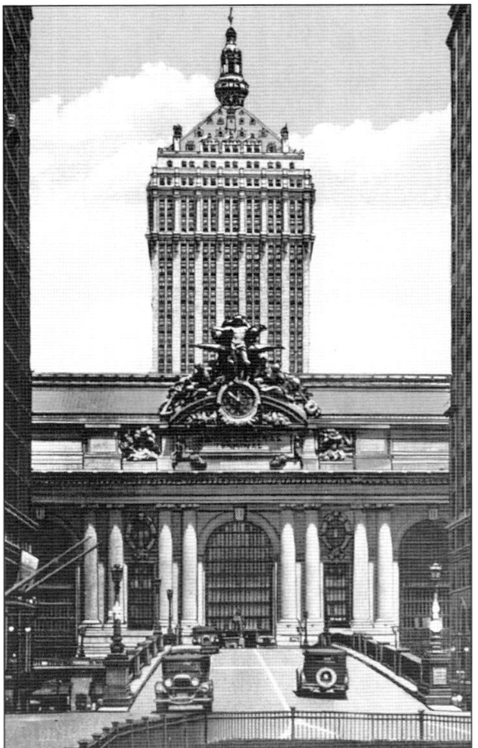

(*Above*) Grand Central Depot and the Grand Union Hotel as they appeared around 1890. (*Left*) Grand Central and the New York Central Building from Park Avenue.

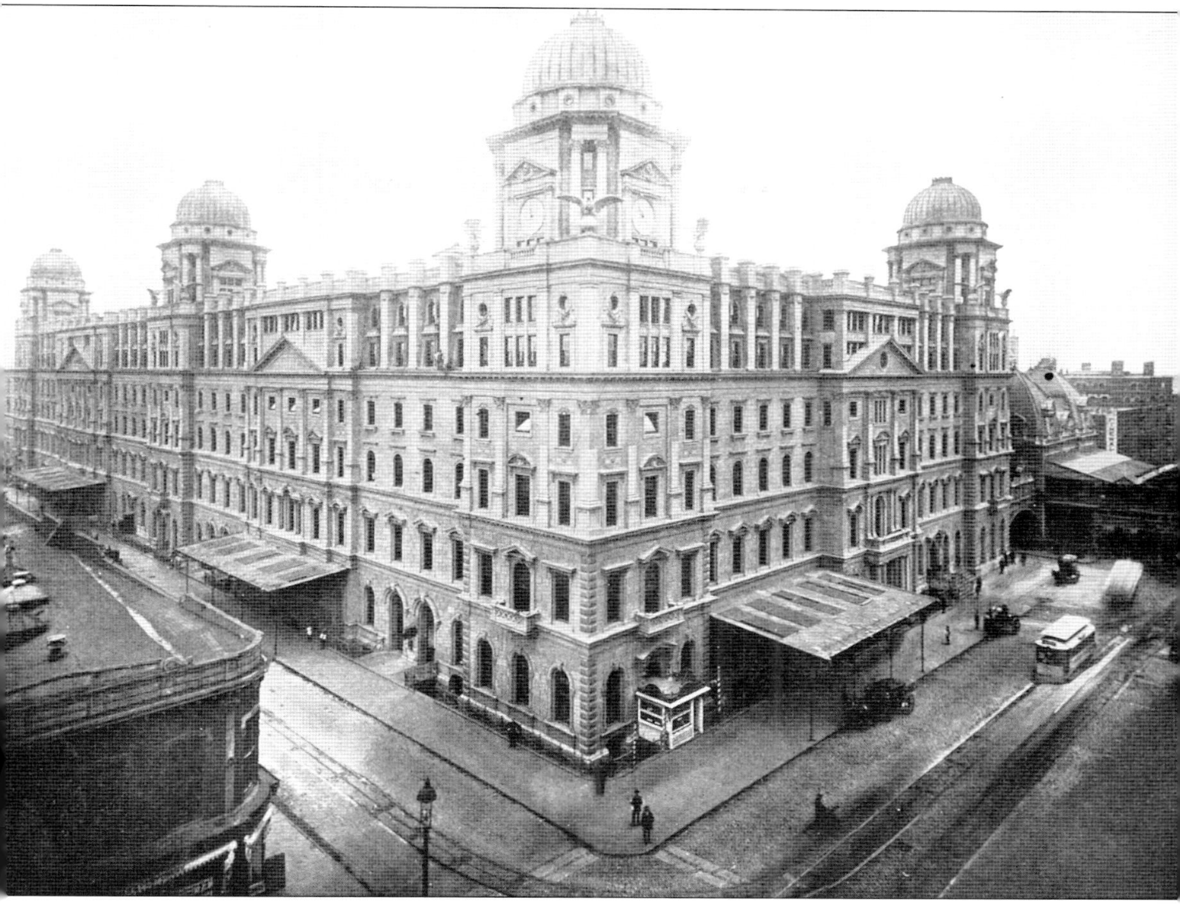

The new Grand Central as it appeared in 1904.

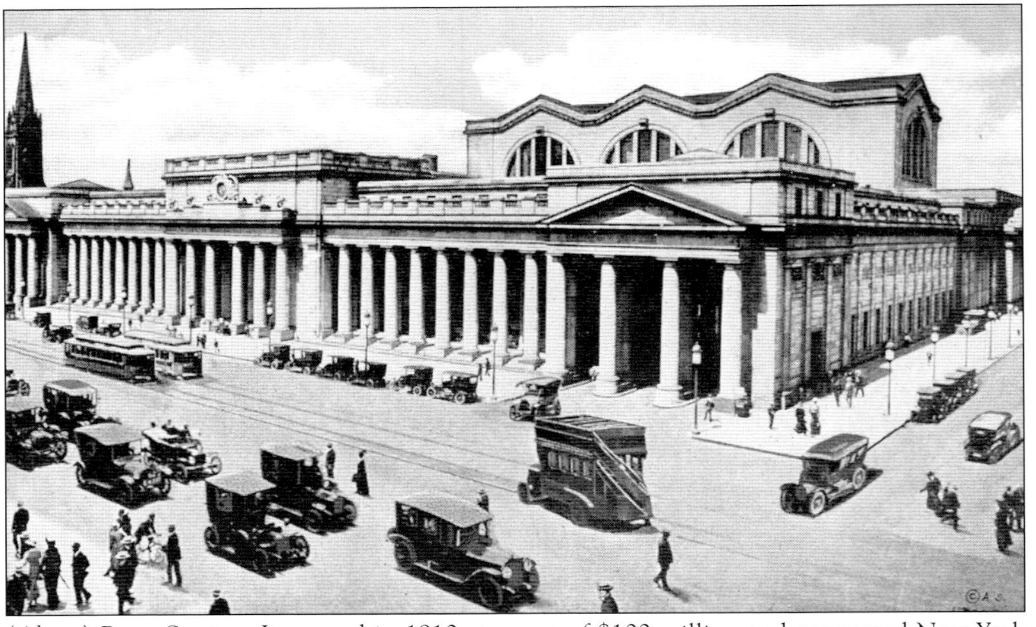

(*Above*) Penn Station. It opened in 1910 at a cost of $100 million and connected New York and New Jersey via twin tunnels under the Hudson River. (*Below*) The main concourse at Penn Station. The concourse is over 200 feet wide and runs the full length of the station. It was roofed by a spectacular dome of iron and glass.

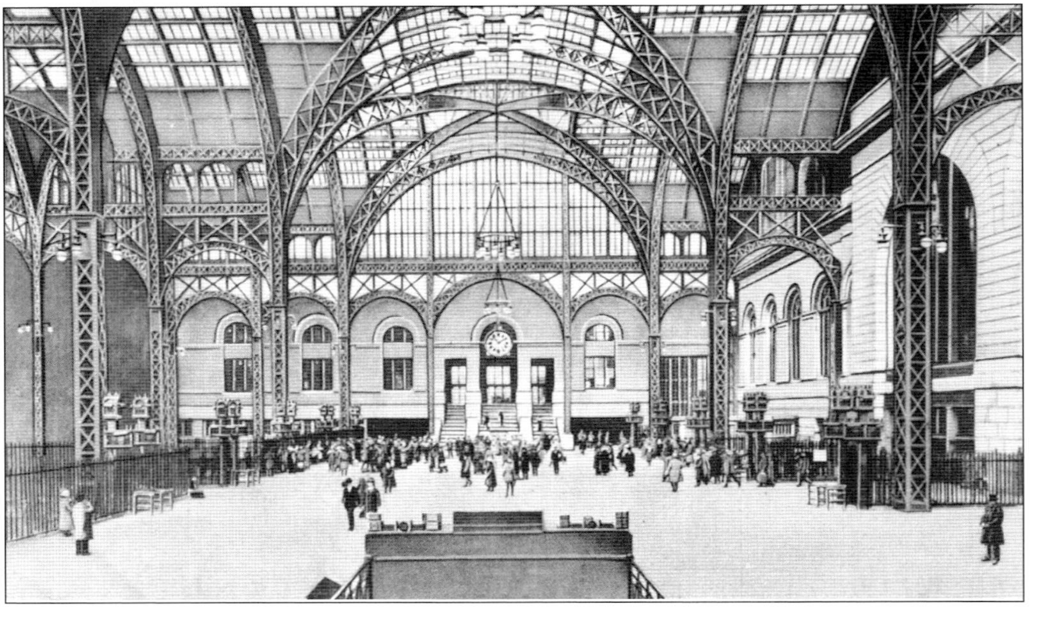

Five

SKYSCRAPERS: THE BEGINNING

Around the end of the Civil War, as the commercial district grew ever more congested, the need for tall office buildings began to be recognized. All large buildings at the time, whether masonry or cast iron, had load bearing walls. This limited their height to less than ten stories.

Another limiting factor was the human heart. Stairs were still far more common than the rudimentary elevators.

By the end of the 1880s, skeletal steel construction was starting to evolve. This made possible much higher buildings as load bearing walls were eliminated. The elevator, too, had developed far beyond the primitive "vertical steam-engines" of the 1860s. The stage was set for the emergence of the skyscraper.

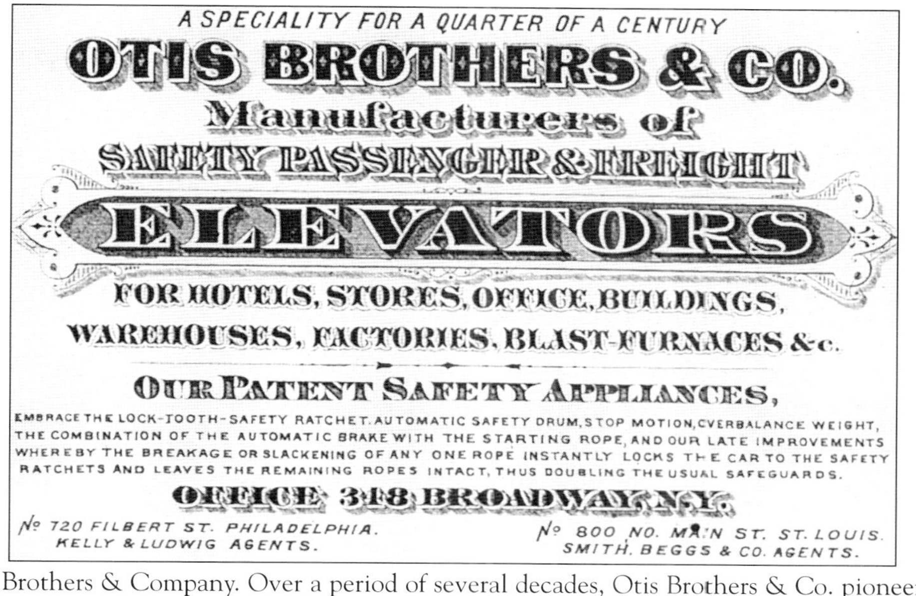

Otis Brothers & Company. Over a period of several decades, Otis Brothers & Co. pioneered a succession of safety devices and improvements that made the elevator suitable for handling the demands of service in a skyscraper.

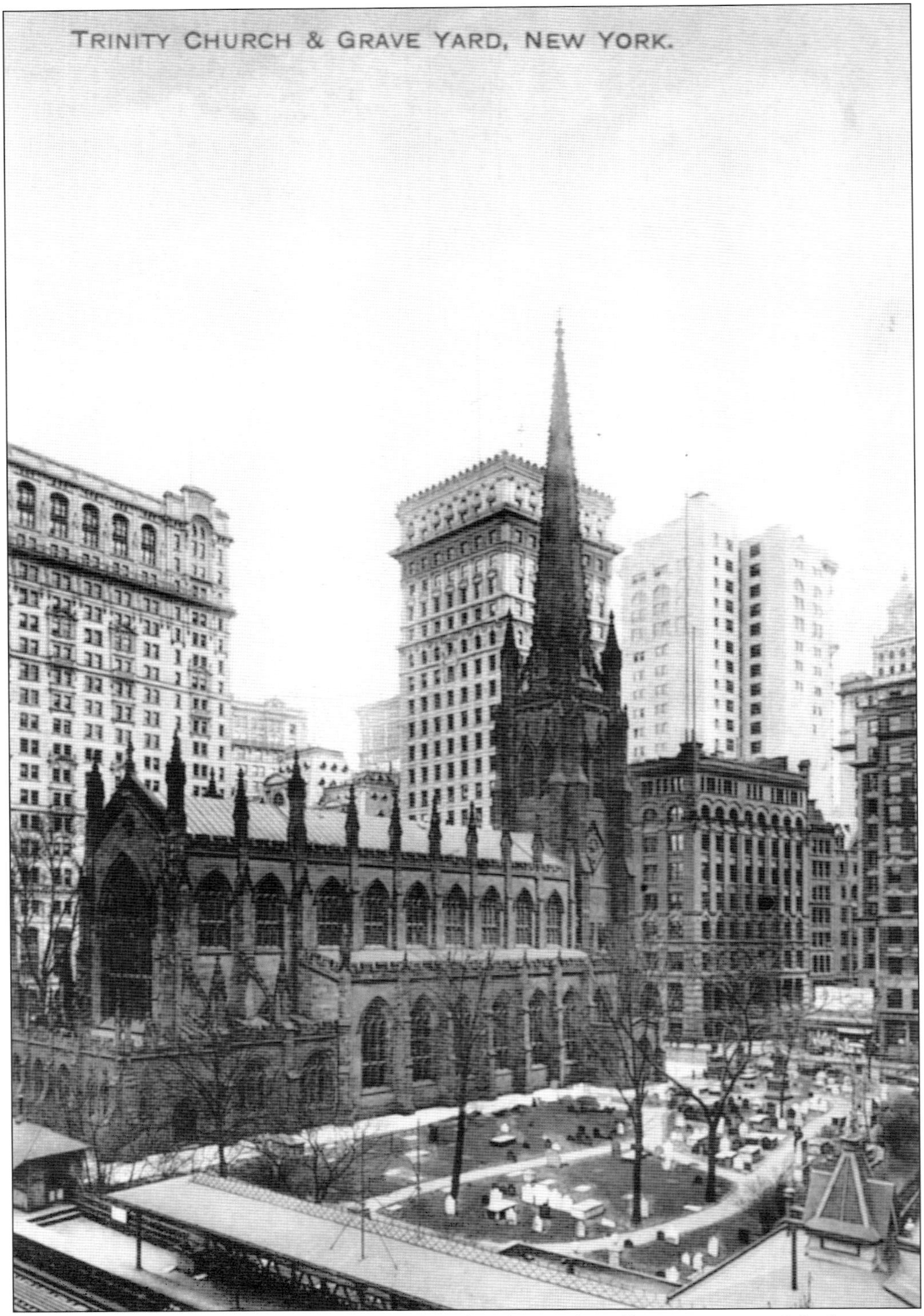

Trinity Church. Until early in the 1890s, this church was the tallest structure in Manhattan.

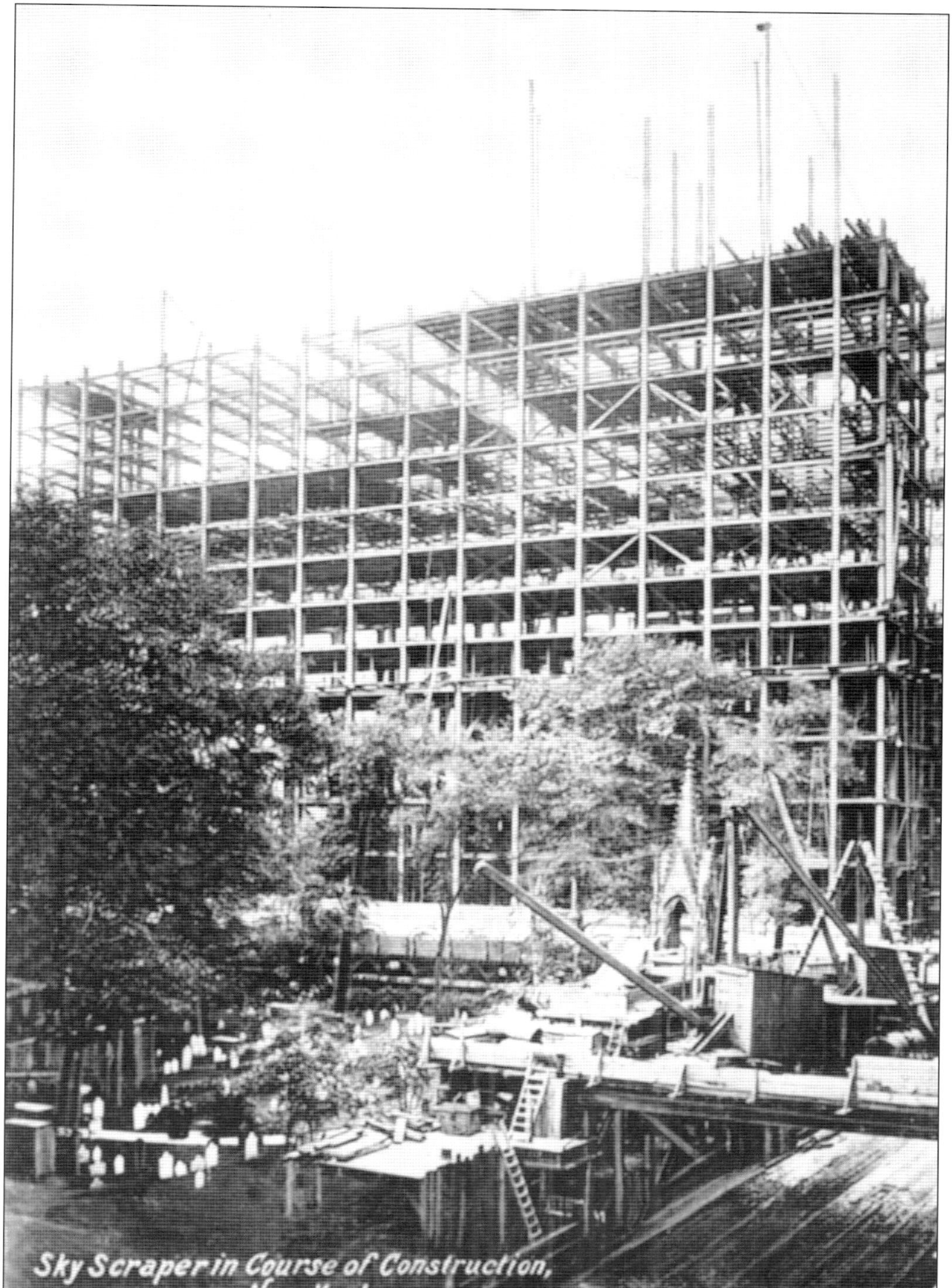

Steel cage construction, the technology that made the skyscraper feasible, shown here at a turn-of-the-century construction site.

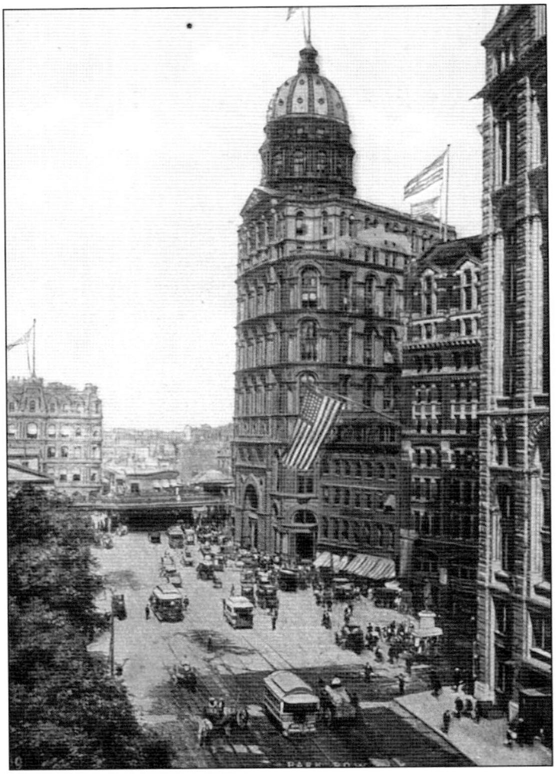

(*Left*) George B. Post's 309-foot Pulitzer (World) Building, with its famed golden dome. It was the first building in New York City to rise above the steeple of Trinity Church. Its construction (1889–90) marked the beginning of the wave of skyscraper construction that created what is now the Manhattan skyline. (*Below*) The elegant 21-story American Surety Building at 100 Broadway (1894–96). Designed by Bruce Price, it was one of the earliest skyscrapers erected on pneumatic caisson foundations.

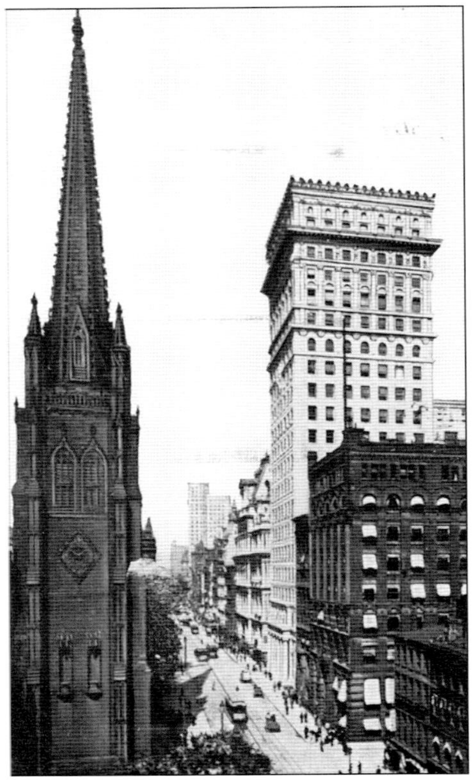

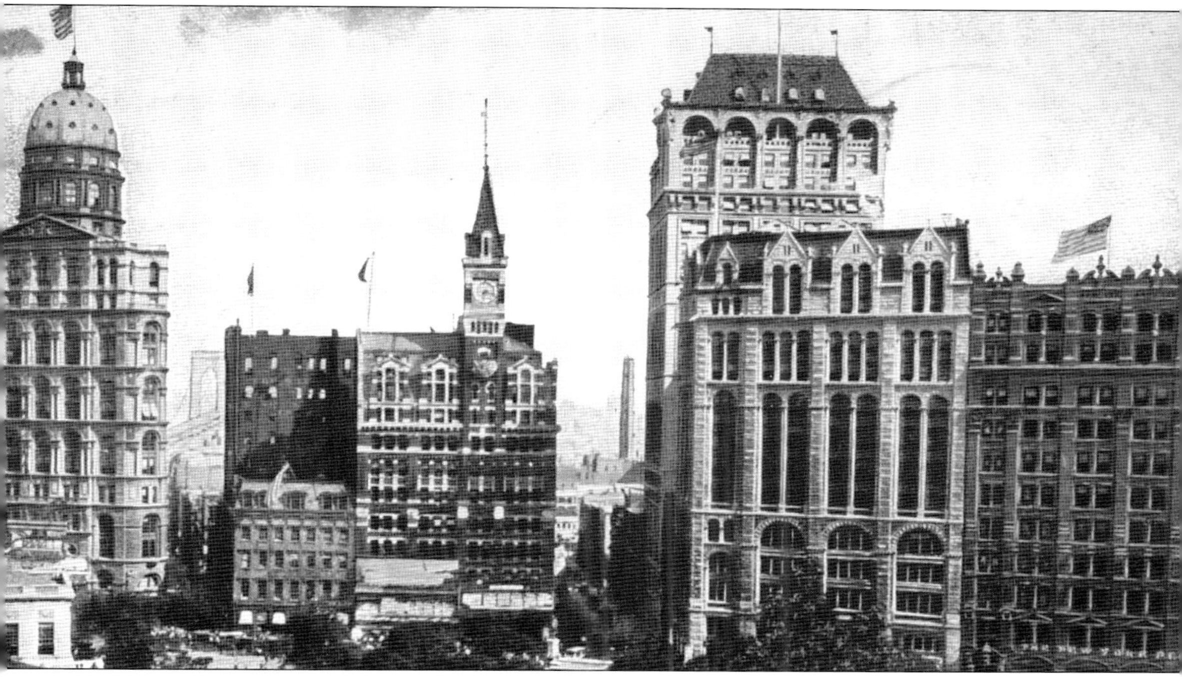

Newspaper Row: the World Building, New York Sun, and the Tribune Building (1873–75), designed by Richard Morris Hunt.

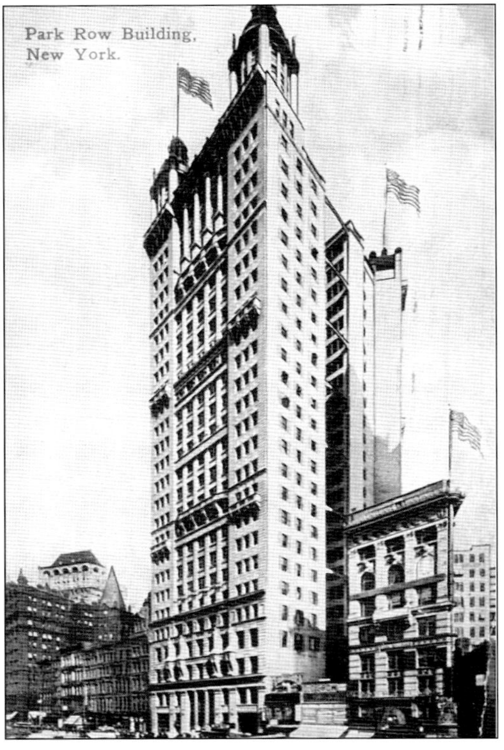

(*Left*) The Syndicate Building. R.H. Robertson set a new height record (381 feet counting the tower) with his 30-story Park Row Building (1896–99), also known as the Syndicate Building. The reported cost of the structure was $3.5 million. (*Below*) The Equitable Building (1868–70). Designed by Gilman and Kendall with George B. Post, it was just seven-and-a-half-stories tall (shown here after it was destroyed by fire). It was the first Manhattan office building to include elevators in its design and was a precursor of the modern skyscraper.

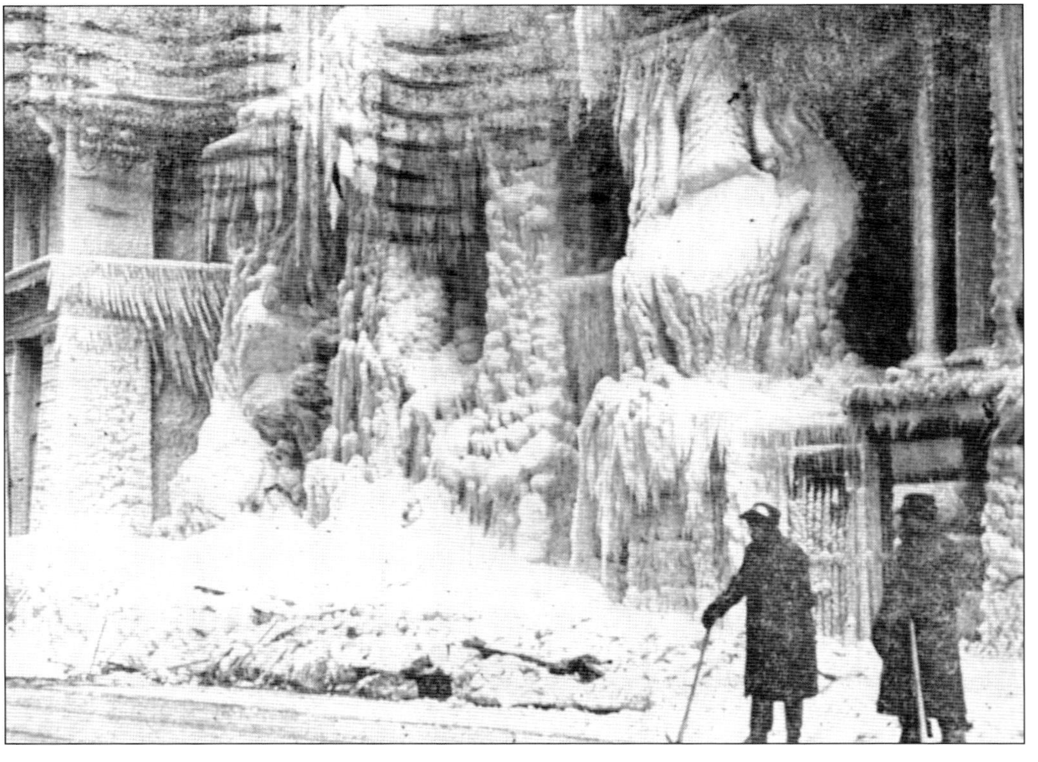

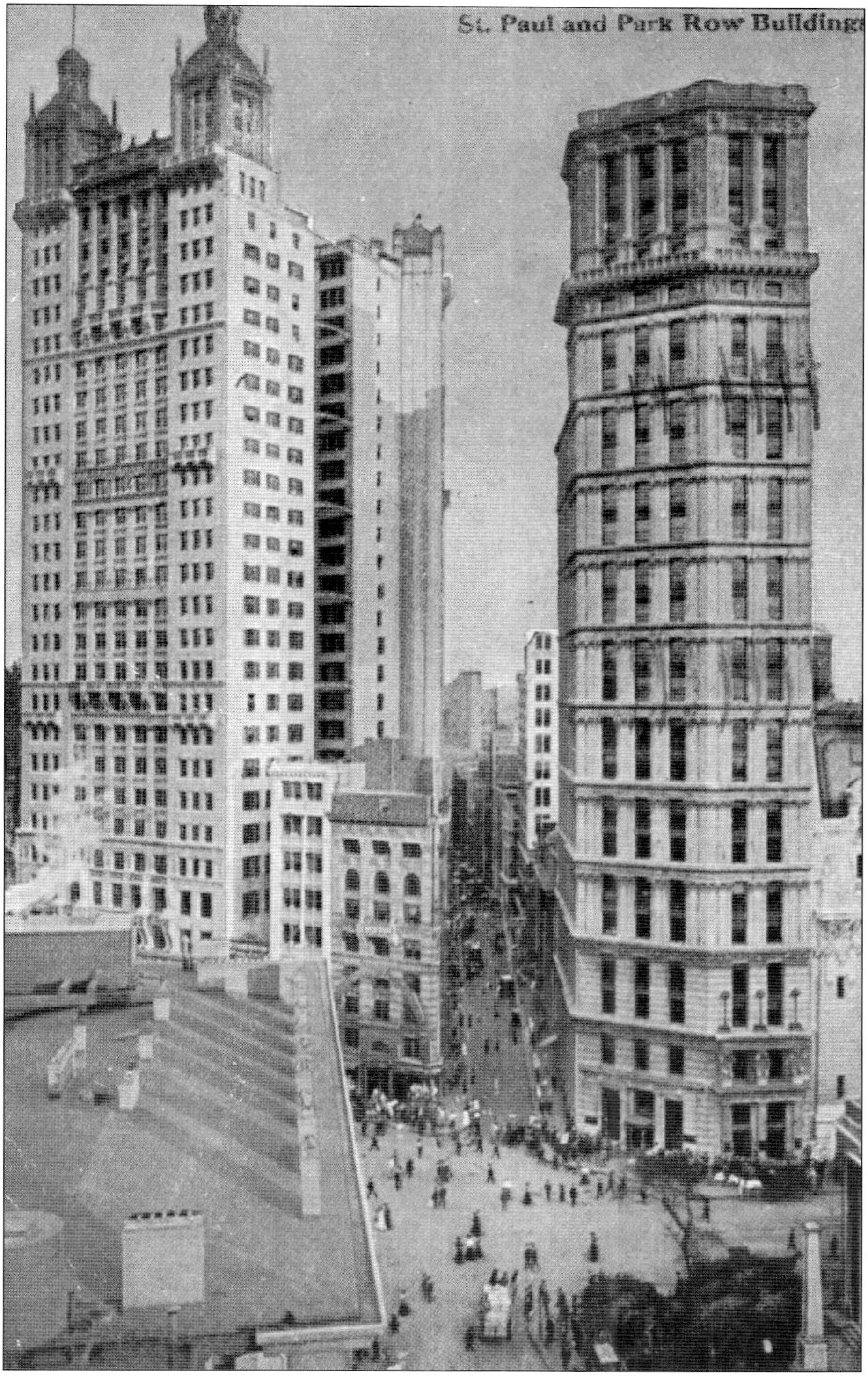

The St. Paul Building, down the block and across the street from the Park Row Building.

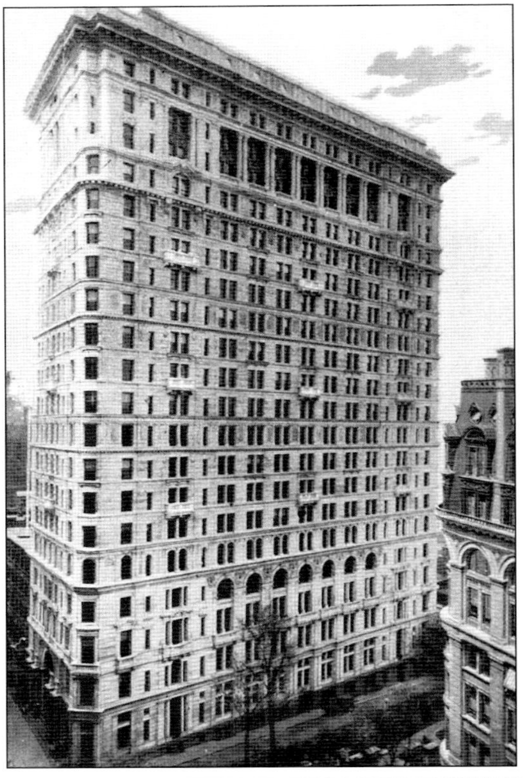

New structures. Toward the end of the 1890s, the three part facade came into vogue. One such building (left) was the Empire Building (1897–98) designed by Kimball and Thompson. Another in the same style (below) is the Bowling Green Building (1895–98) by W. and G. Audsley.

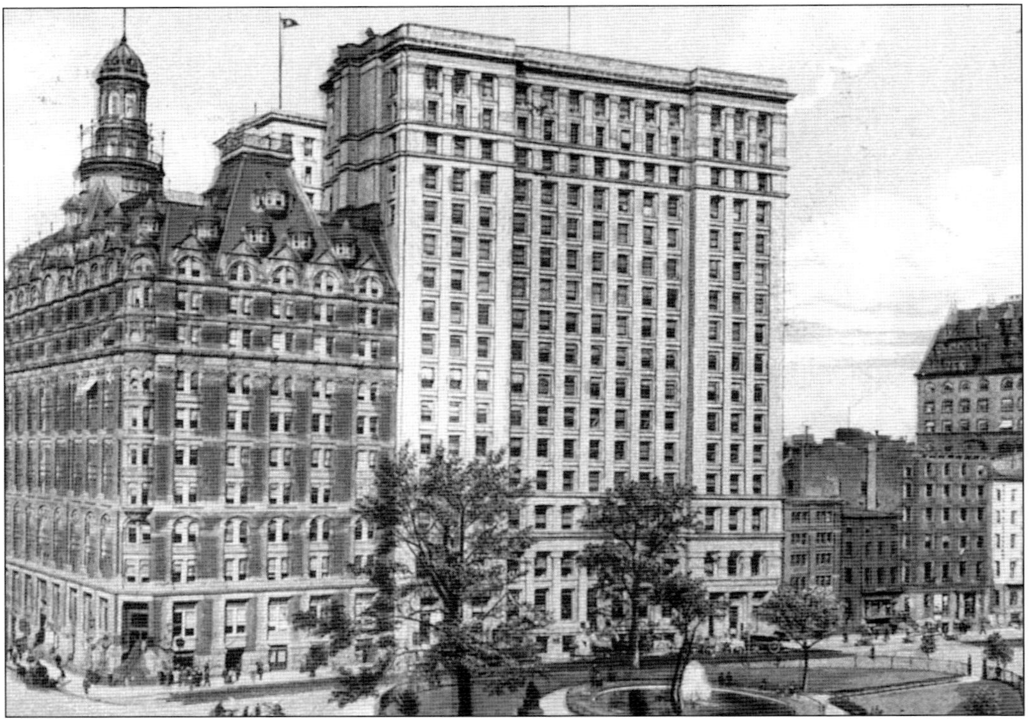

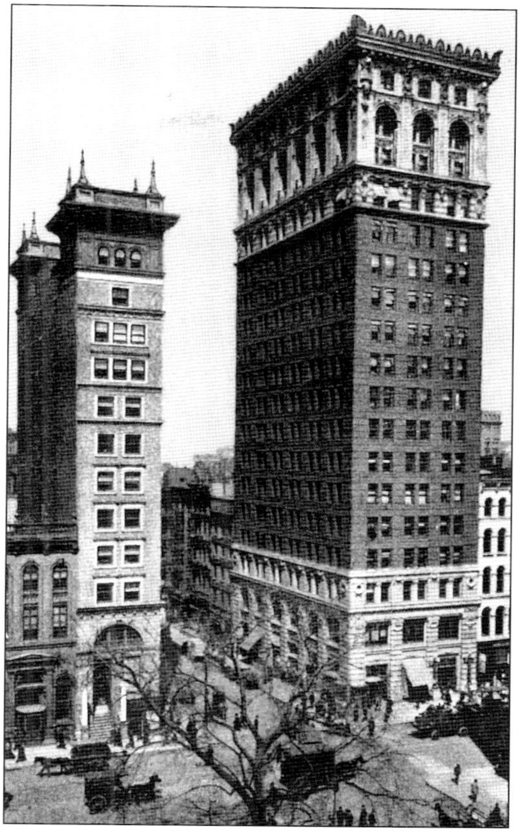

(*Right*) The first of many exceptional Manhattan skyscrapers designed by Cass Gilbert. The Broadway and Chambers Building (1899–1900) is located across from City Hall Park. The tower is noted for its colorful brick and terra-cotta-clad facade. The smaller building to the left was the Shoe & Leather Bank. (*Below*) The Washington Life Building, 141 Broadway.

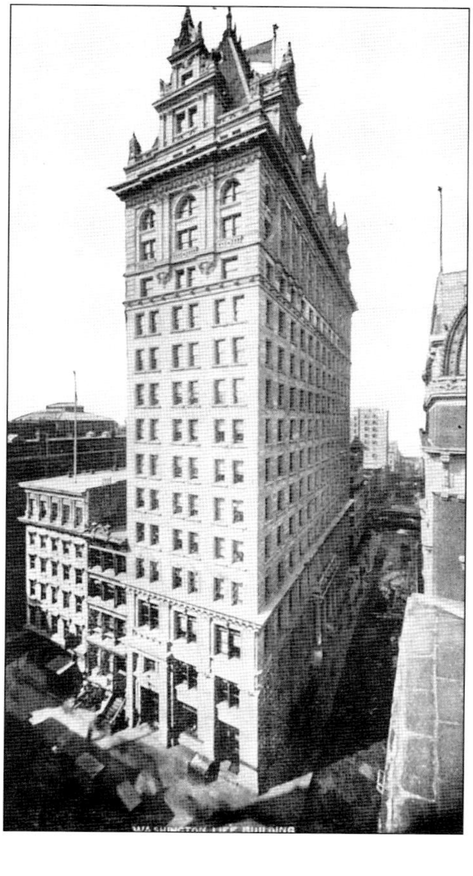

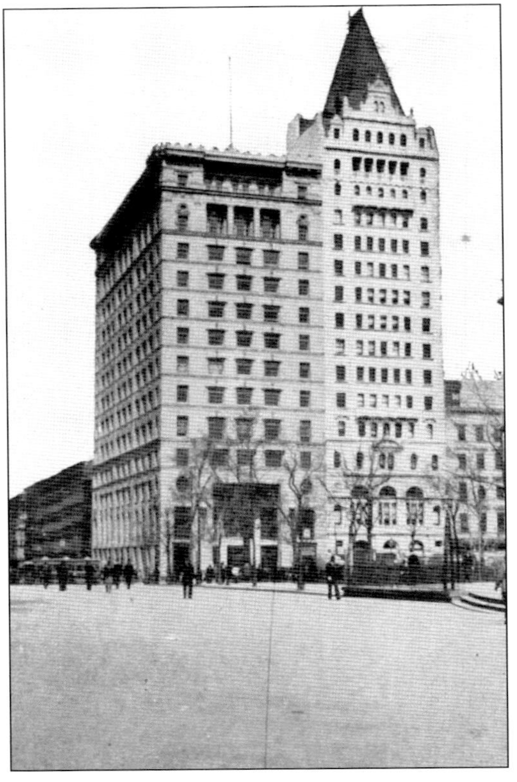

(*Left*) The Western Union Building, another early skyscraper precursor by George B. Post. It was built between 1873 and 1875. Next to it is the Home Life Building. (*Below*) The Washington Building.

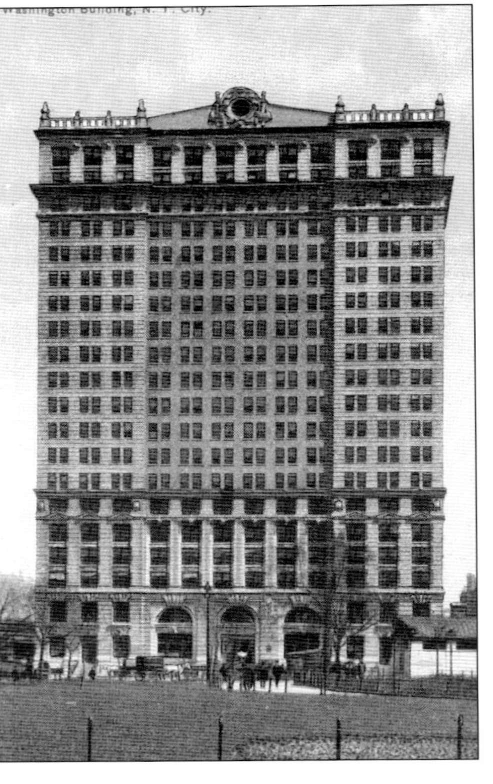

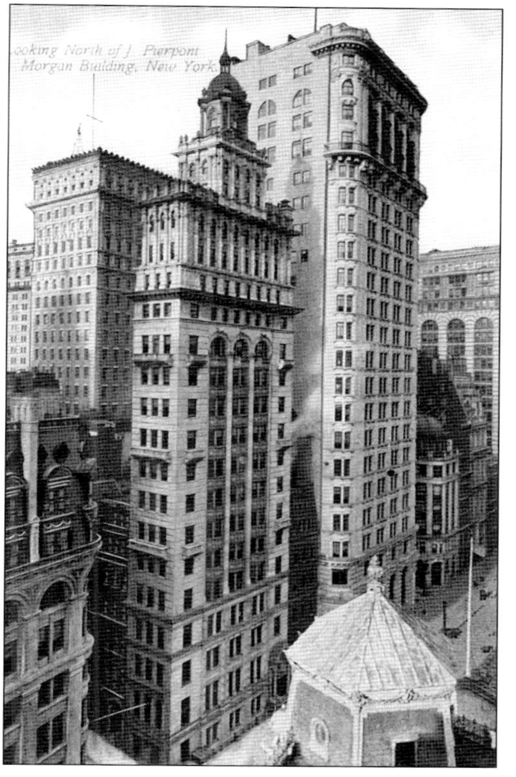

(*Right*) The Gillender Building, corner Broad and Wall Streets. (*Below*) Bankers Trust Company Building. This building replaced the Gillender in 1897 with a 39-story, 540-foot-high structure.

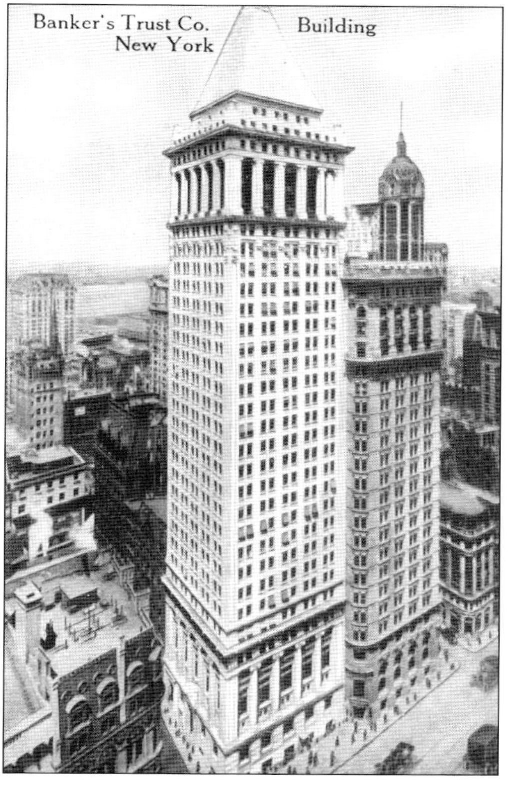

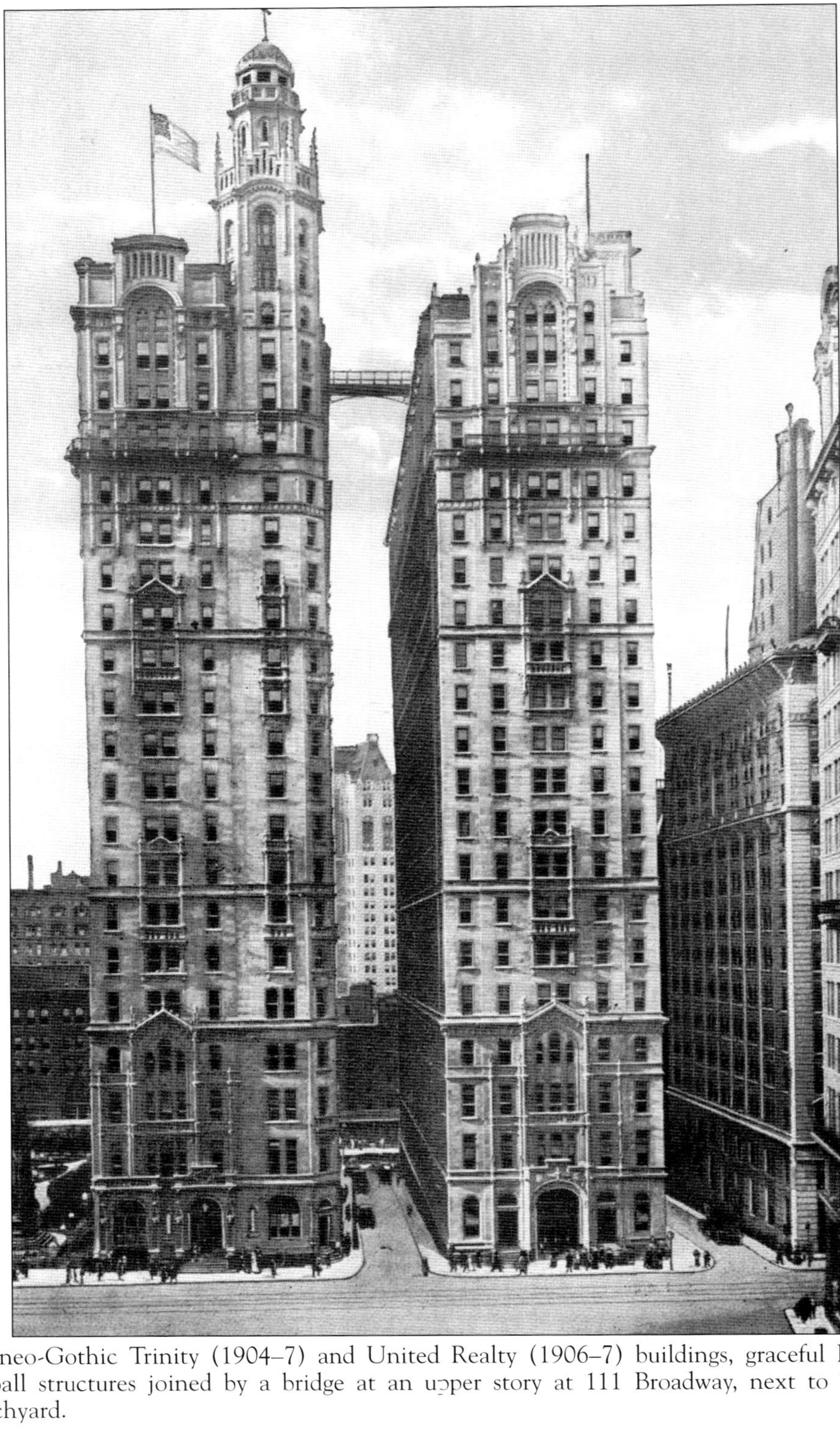

The neo-Gothic Trinity (1904–7) and United Realty (1906–7) buildings, graceful Francis Kimball structures joined by a bridge at an upper story at 111 Broadway, next to Trinity churchyard.

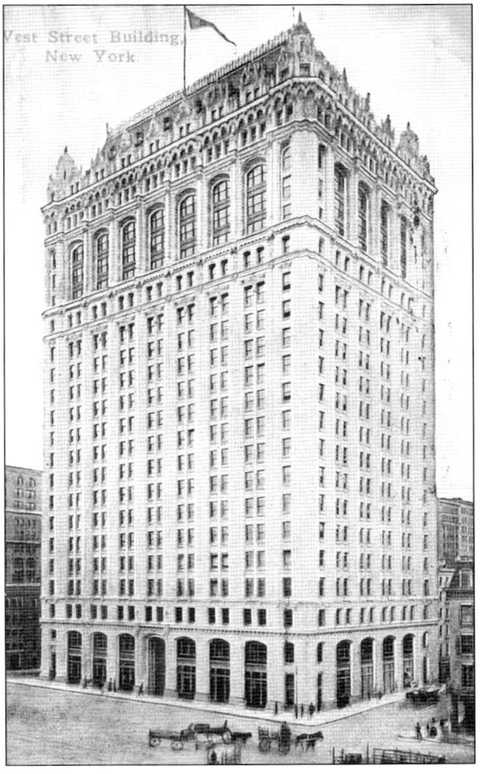

(*Right*) The neo-Gothic West Street Building (1906–7). Designed by Cass Gilbert, it was known for its elegant appointments. In 1907, the building housed the sales department of the American Woodworking Machinery Company. (*Below*) Two-Broadway Building, designed by Henry Ives.

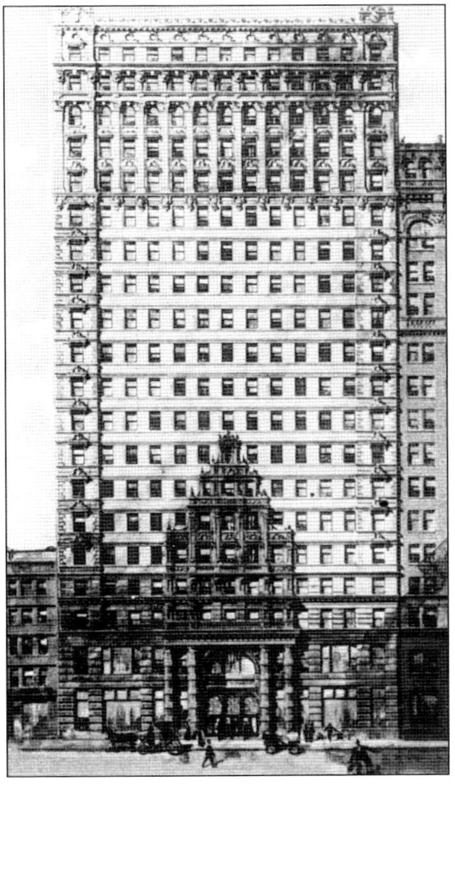

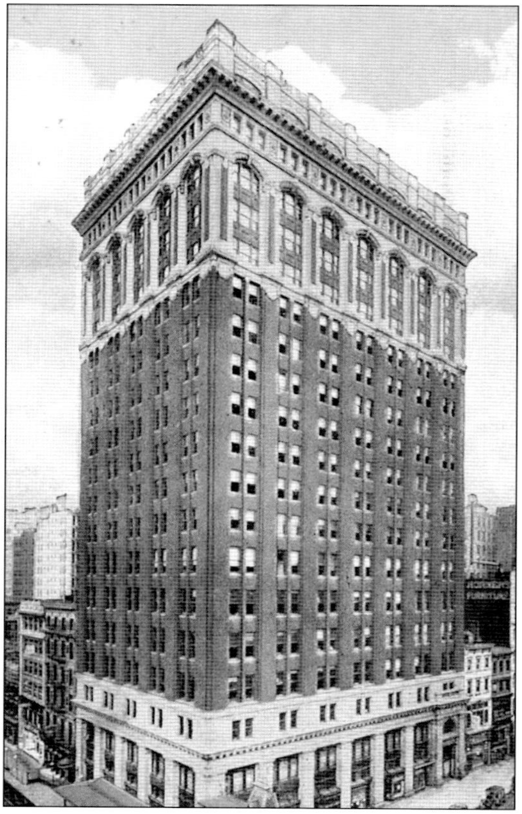

(*Left*) The Masonic Building, Sixth Avenue and Twenty-Third Street. (*Below*) River and street-side views of the Hudson Terminals of the Hudson and Manhattan Railroad Company.

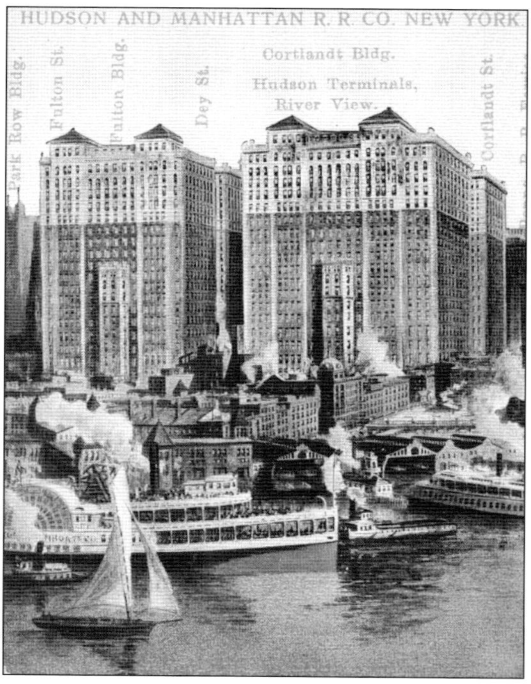

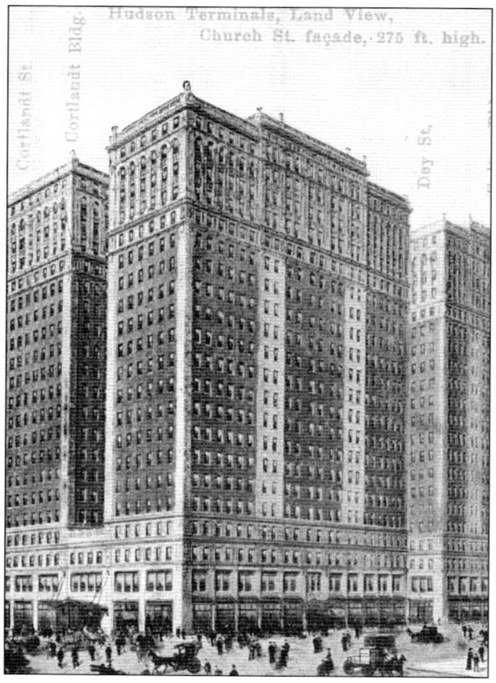

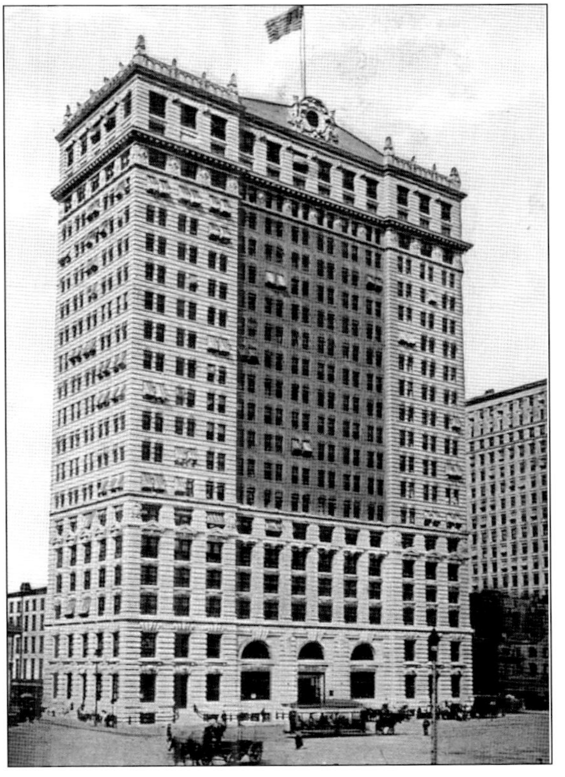

(*Right*) Henry Hardenbergh's neoclassical Whitehall Building (1902–3), located at Battery Place and West Street. Hardenbergh was also responsible for the Waldorf Astoria and the new Plaza Hotel. (*Below*) The Telephone and Telegraph Building.

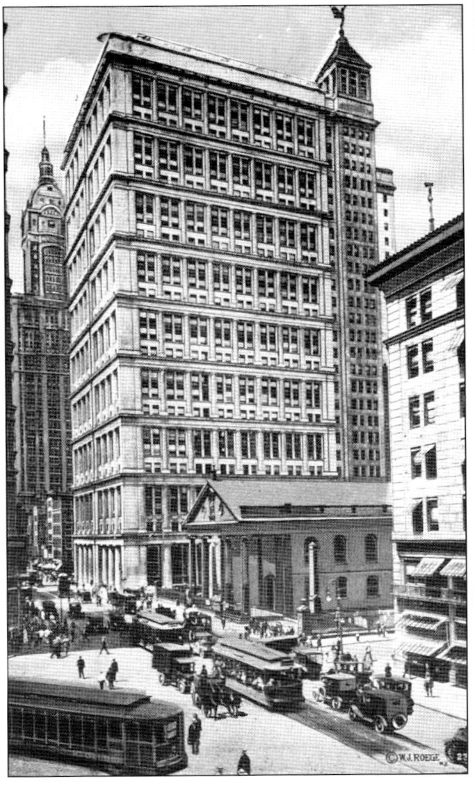

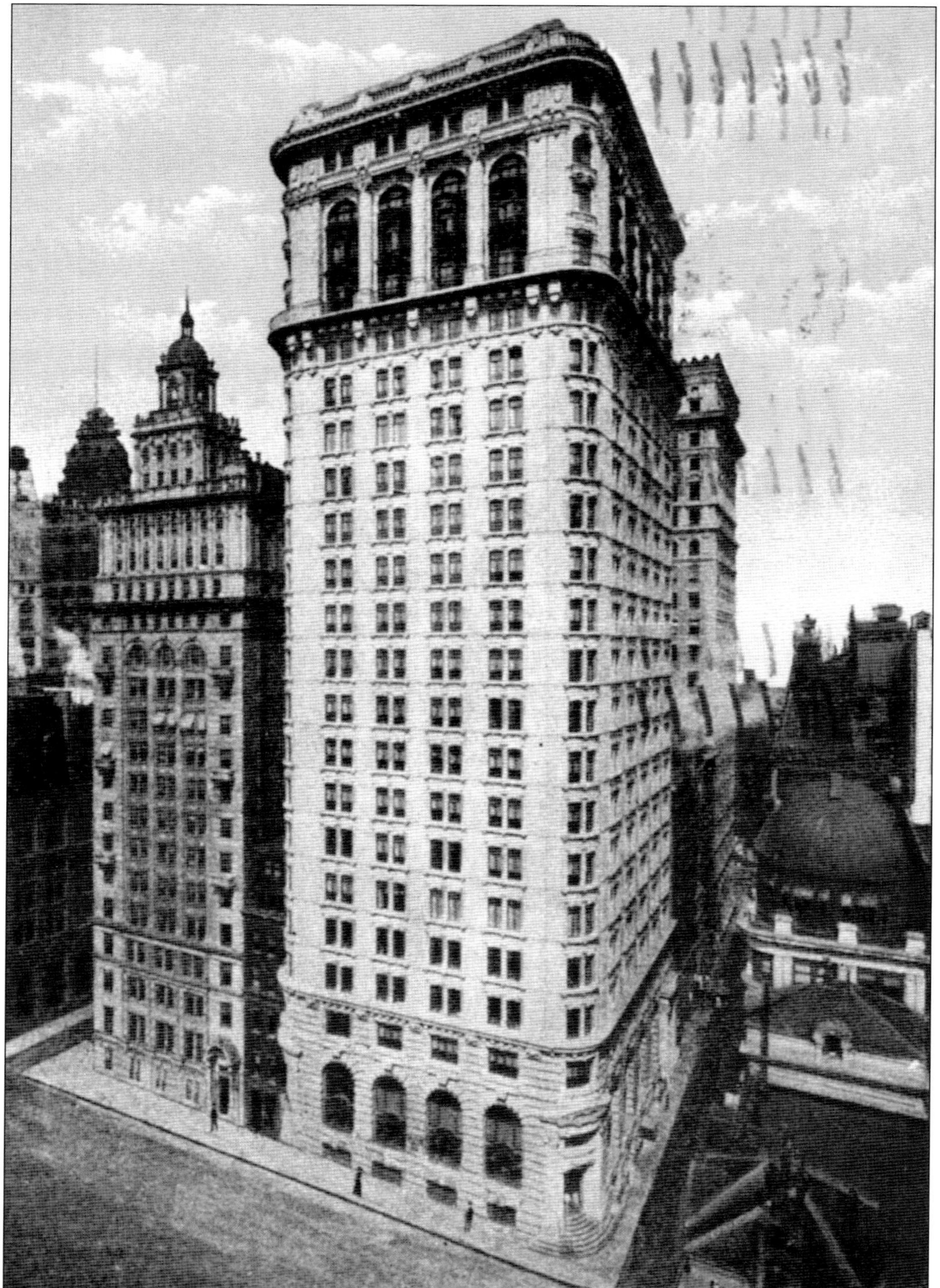

The Hanover National Bank Building.

Six

SKYSCRAPERS: THE EVOLUTION

If you were to pick a spot for the museum of skyscrapers, it would have to be in Manhattan. Much of the best work on the development of the skyscraper was done by architects of the Chicago school. For example, the aesthetic concept of "soaring verticality" was the work of great Chicago architect Louis Sullivan, a mentor of Frank Lloyd Wright.

Even so, like many other ideas that came to town, the skyscraper was done to the max in Manhattan. In short order the skyscraper came to be viewed as a "New York thing." In less than a decade, Manhattan had more skyscrapers than any other city on the planet.

As big egos came face to face with big buildings, the scramble was on to build the world's tallest building. From the last decade of the 19th century until the Great Depression, a succession of massive edifices turned Manhattan into a city of canyons.

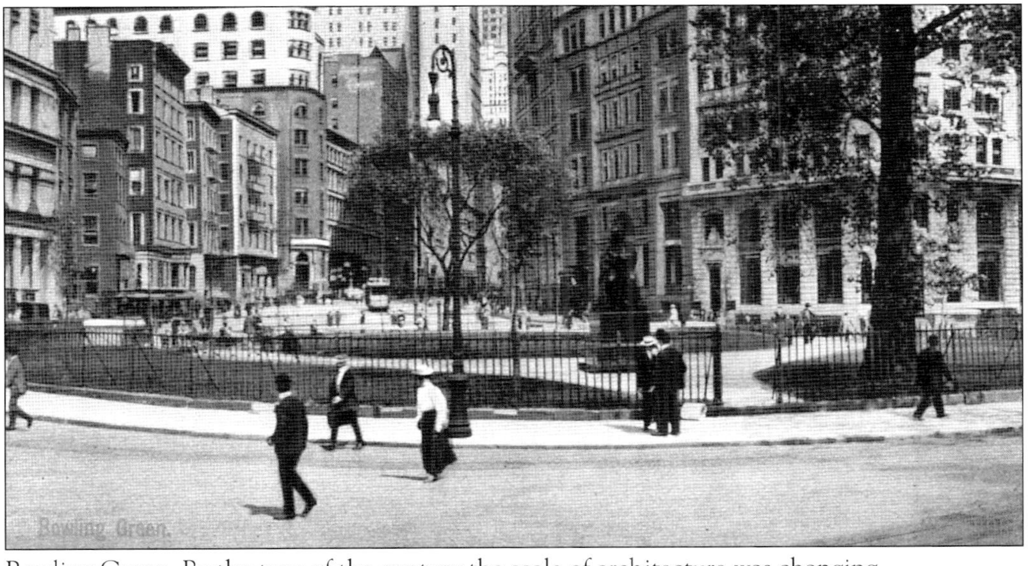

Bowling Green. By the turn of the century the scale of architecture was changing.

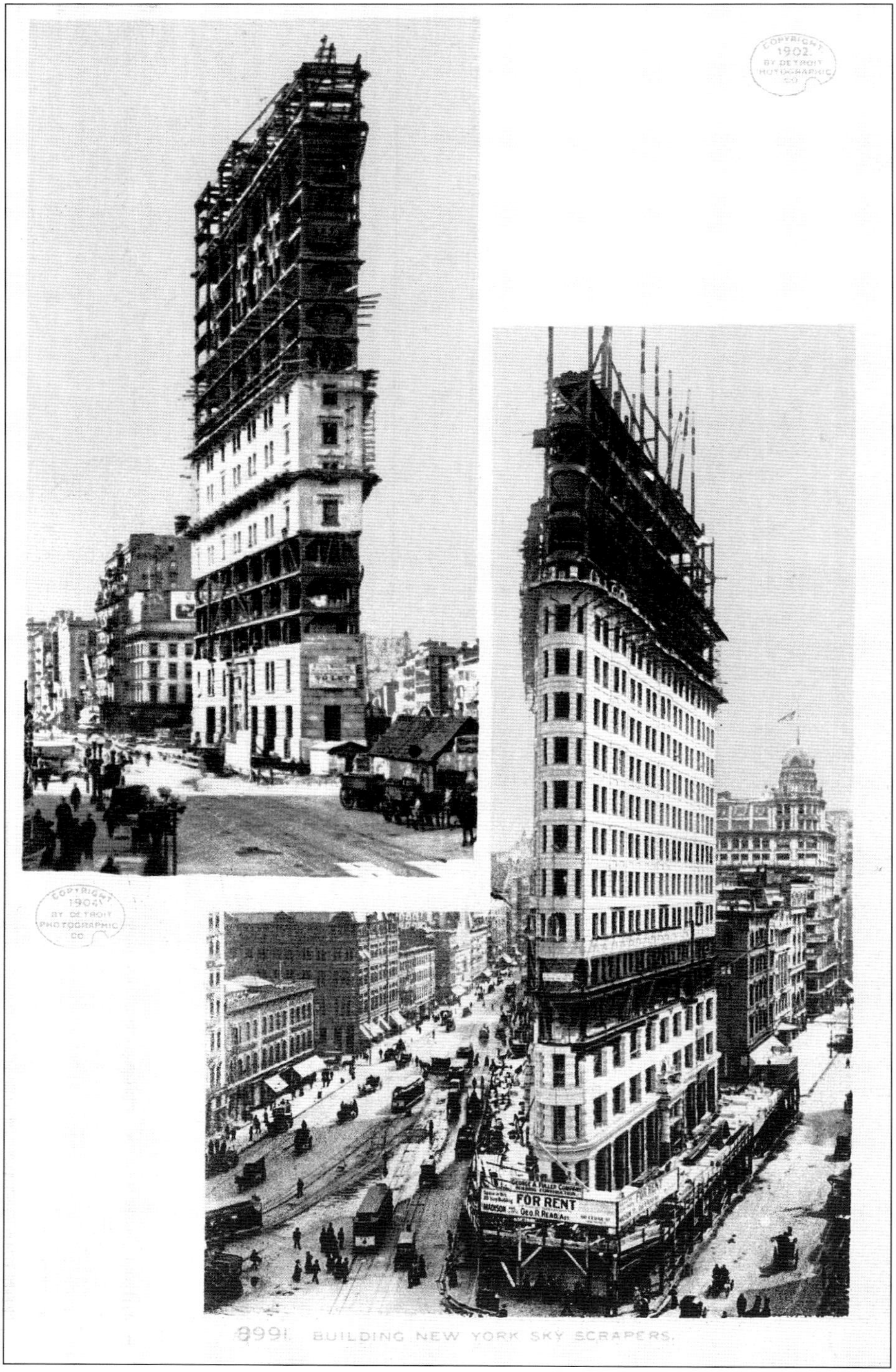

The New York Times and Flat Iron buildings under construction. Skeletal steel construction used in these two buildings was still something of a novelty in the first years of the 20th century. Many people were convinced that the Flat Iron Building would blow over in high winds.

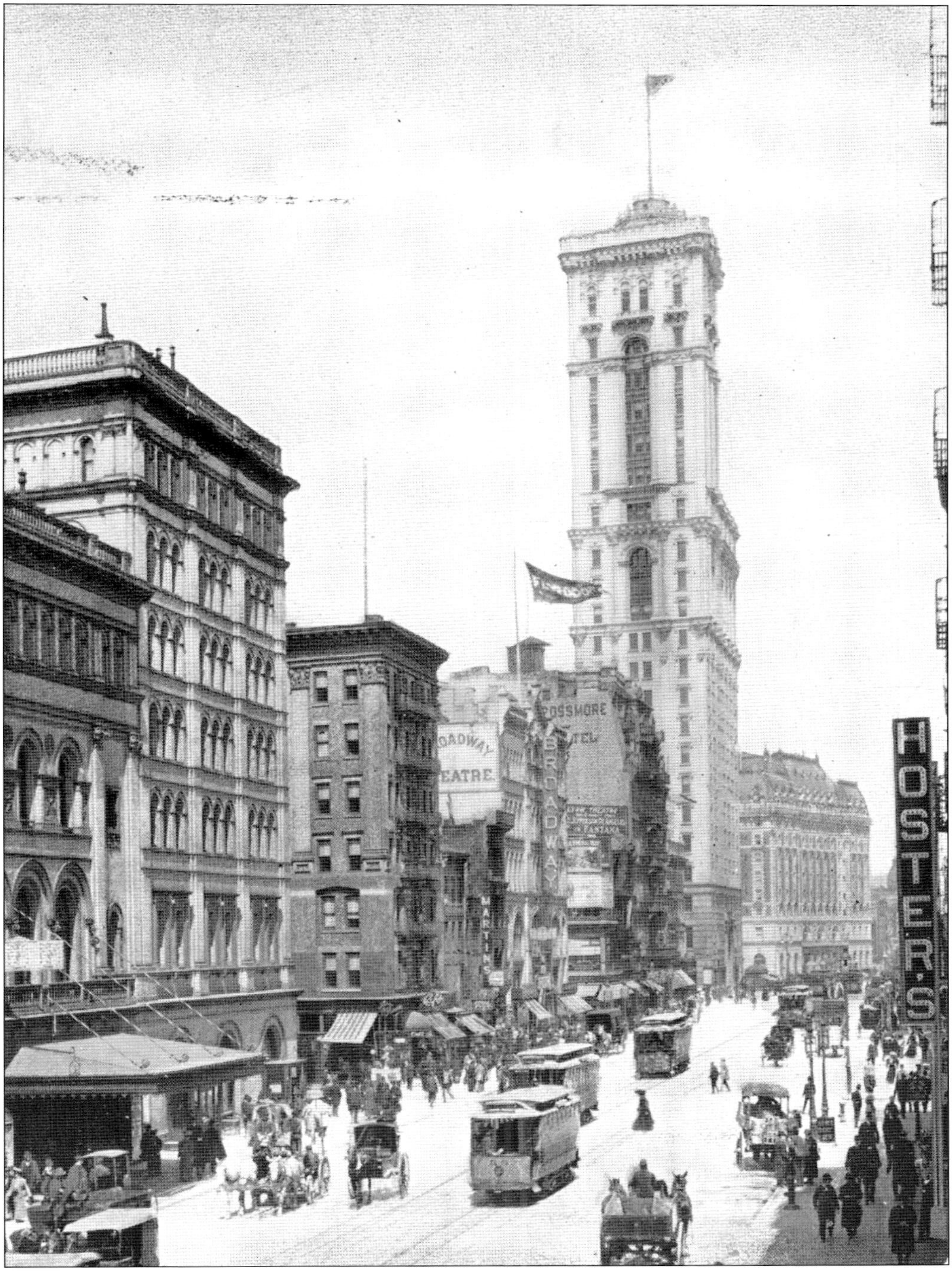

Broadway looking toward the Times Building. In the distance is the Astor Hotel.

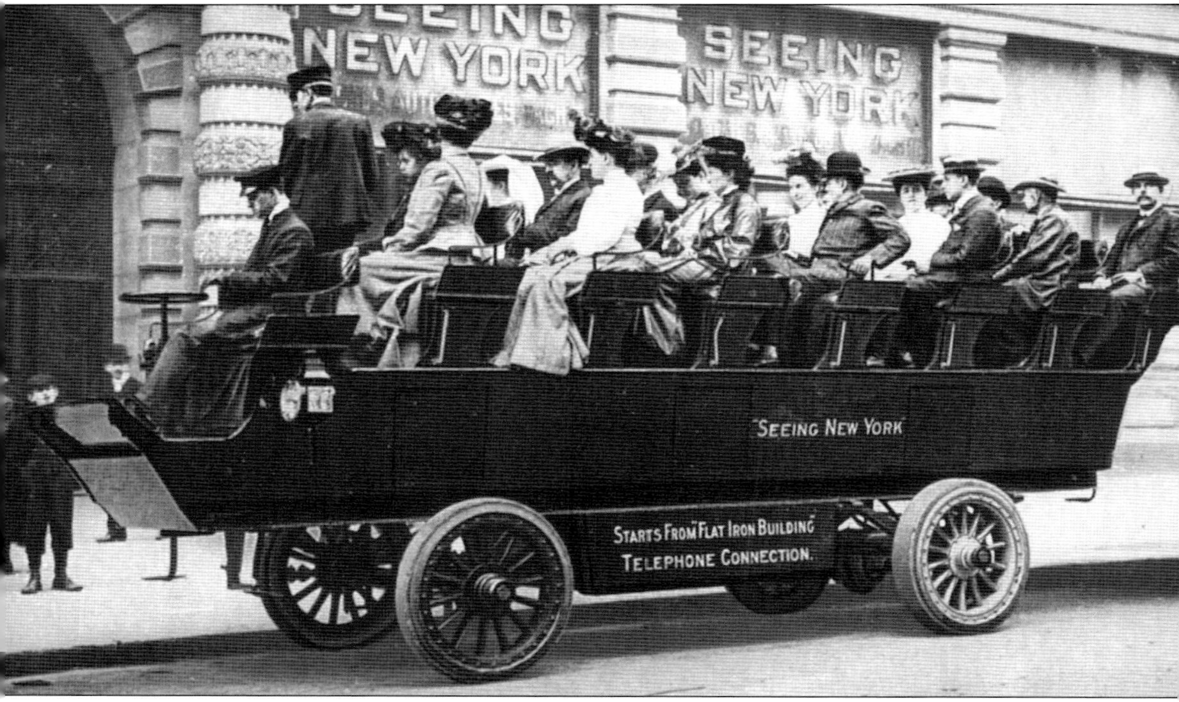

The Flat Iron Building (1902), an instant tourist attraction. It was the departure point for this early bus tour of the city.

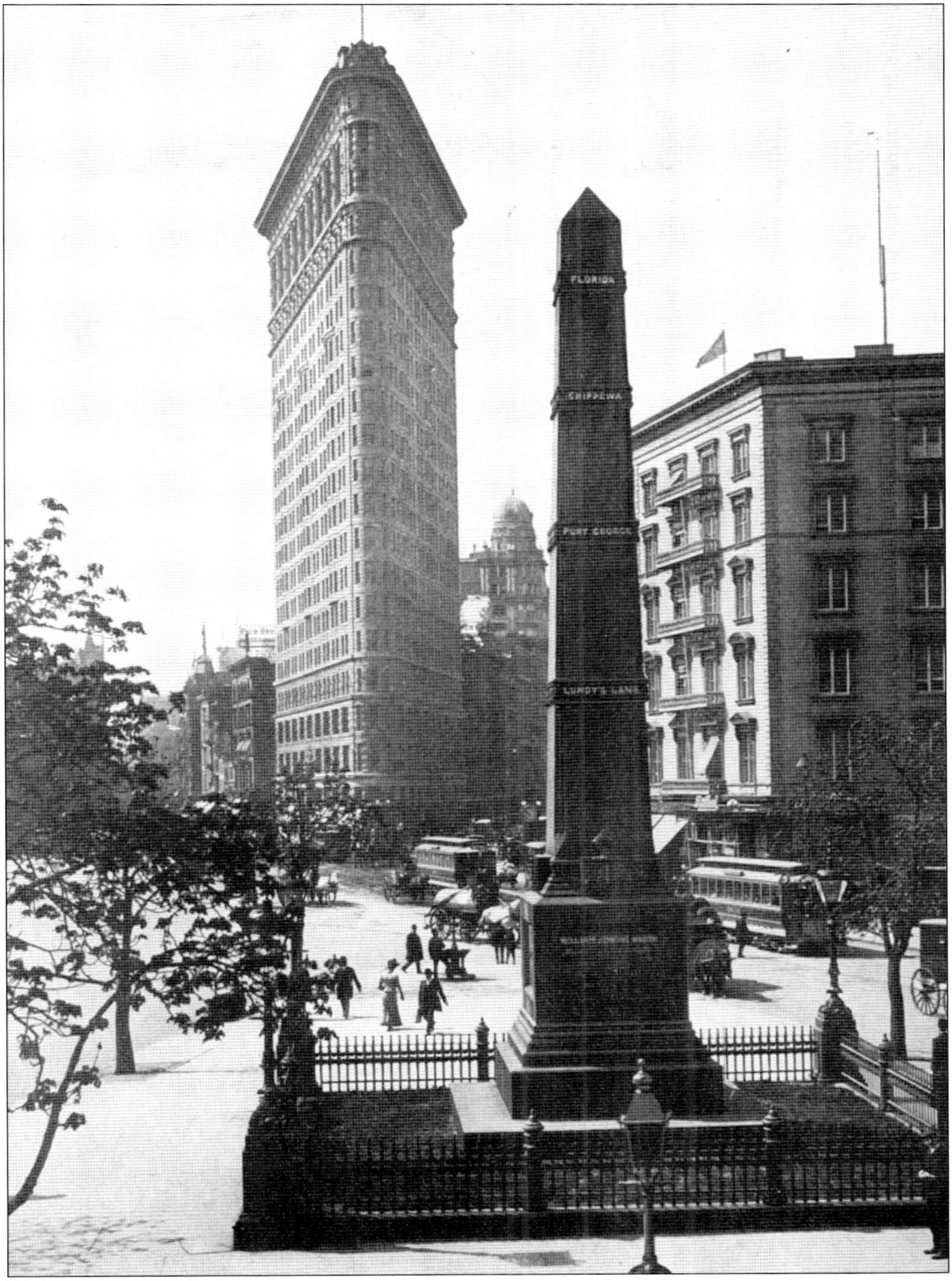

The 22-story Fuller Building. Better known as the Flat Iron Building (1902), it was the work of Chicago architect Daniel Burnham. He called it the structural steel-frame "inhabited tower standing forever free." Monumental and religious in its ambitions, the Flat Iron Building turned the skyscraper into a permanent symbol of corporate pride.

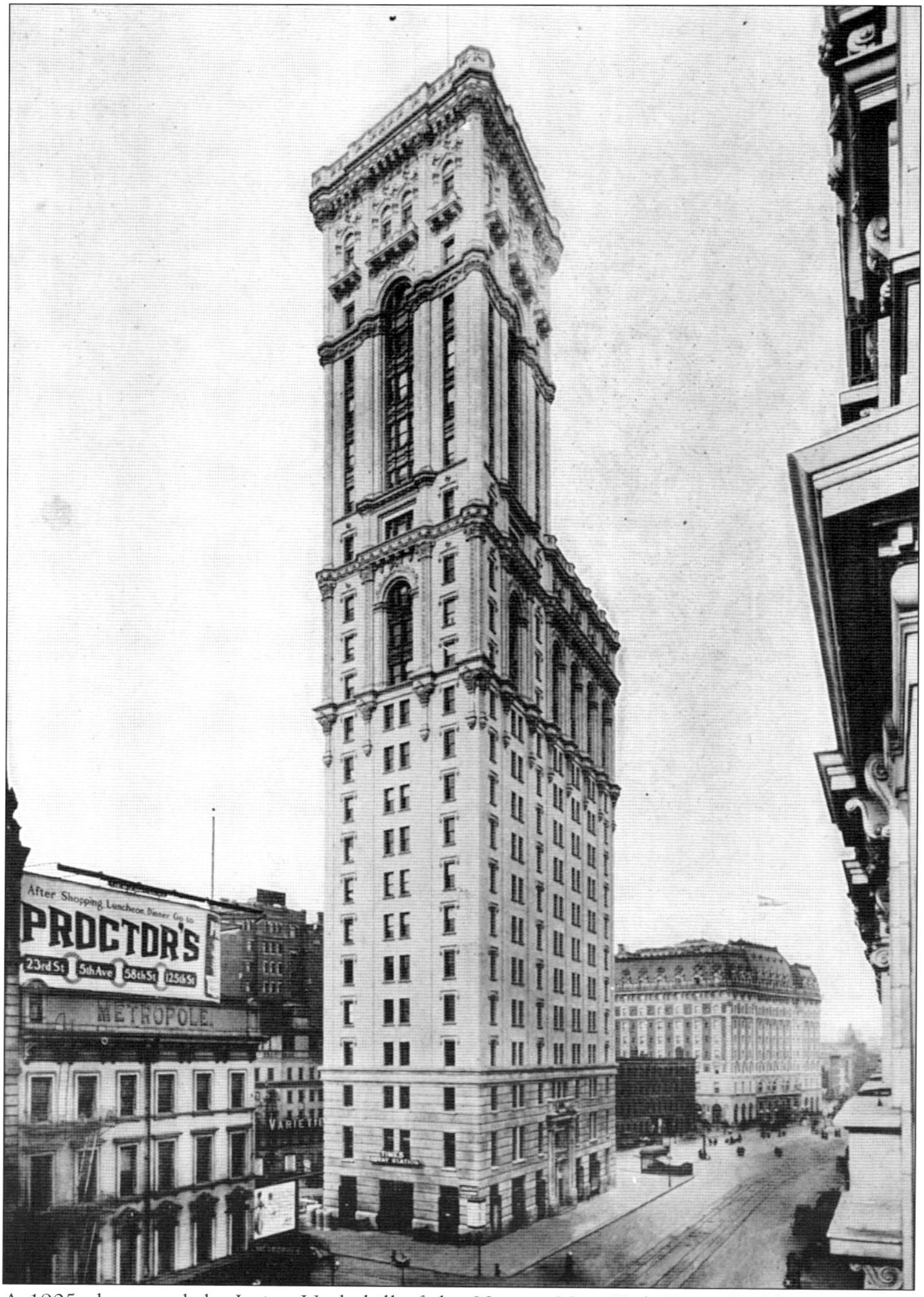

A 1905 photograph by Irving Underhill of the 22-story New York Times Building (1903–4), designed by Eidlitz and McKenzie.

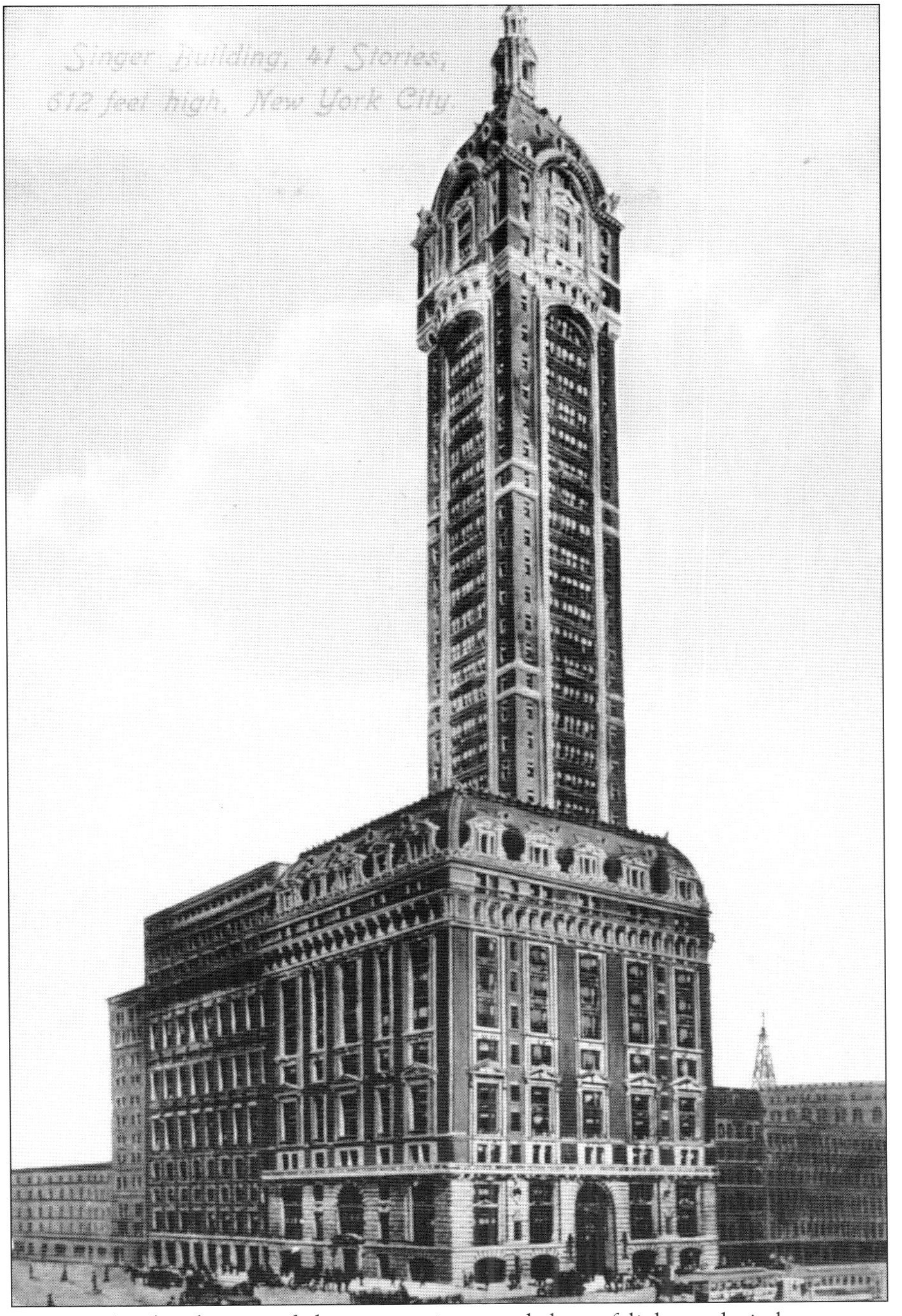

Rising issues. As the density of skyscrapers increased, loss of light and air became a widely recognized problem. Architect Ernest Flagg insisted that this would not be the case if a skyscraper occupied no more than 25 percent of its site, no matter what the building's height. To demonstrate this, he designed the Singer Tower (1906–8), at the time the world's tallest building. Flagg's ideas ran into stiff opposition, but they were eventually incorporated into the city's revolutionary building code of 1916.

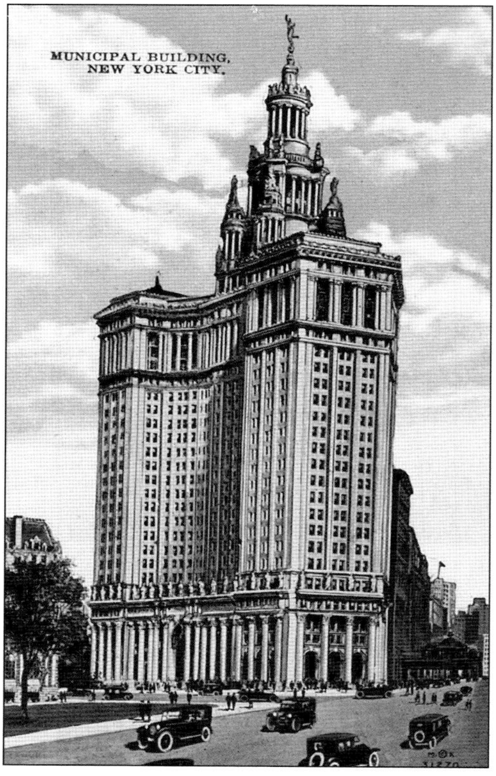

(*Left*) The massive Municipal Building (1909–14) by W.M. Kendall of McKim, Mead, and White, at Chambers and Centre Streets. (*Below*) The Equitable Building (1913–15) by E.R. Graham. Along with the Municipal Building, it is one of the last skyscrapers built just prior to the 1916 regulations regulating the height and bulk of these structures.

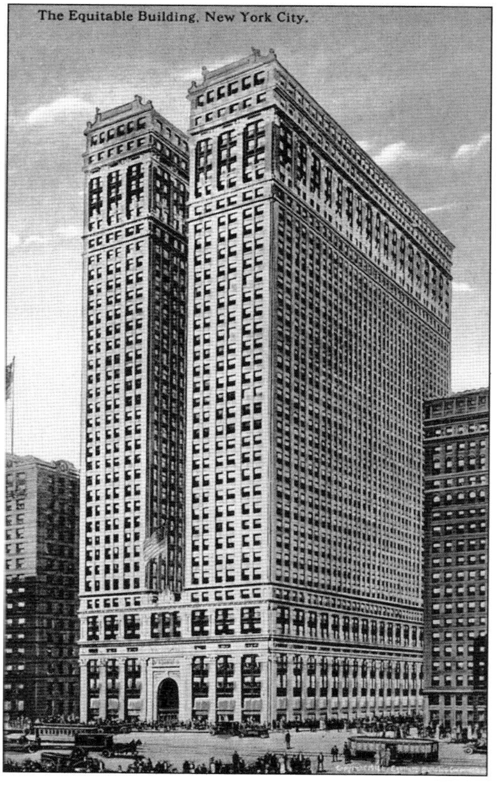

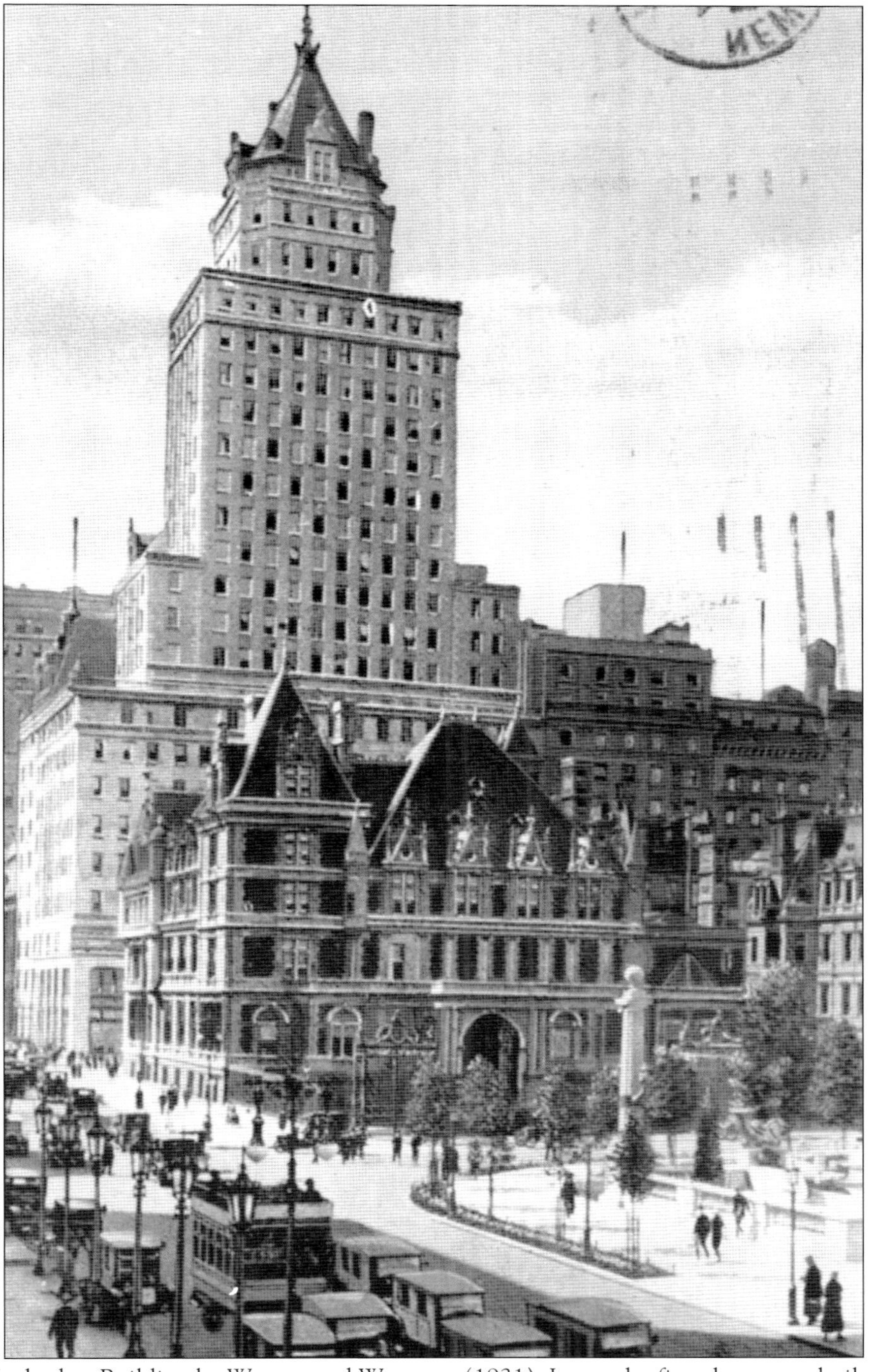

The Heckscher Building by Warren and Wetmore (1921). It was the first skyscraper built under New York's innovative 1916 zoning law. The regulations mandated setbacks of upper stories that led to the "wedding cake" look. The Museum of Modern Art opened in 1929 in rented space in the Heckscher Building, which is now known as the Crown Building.

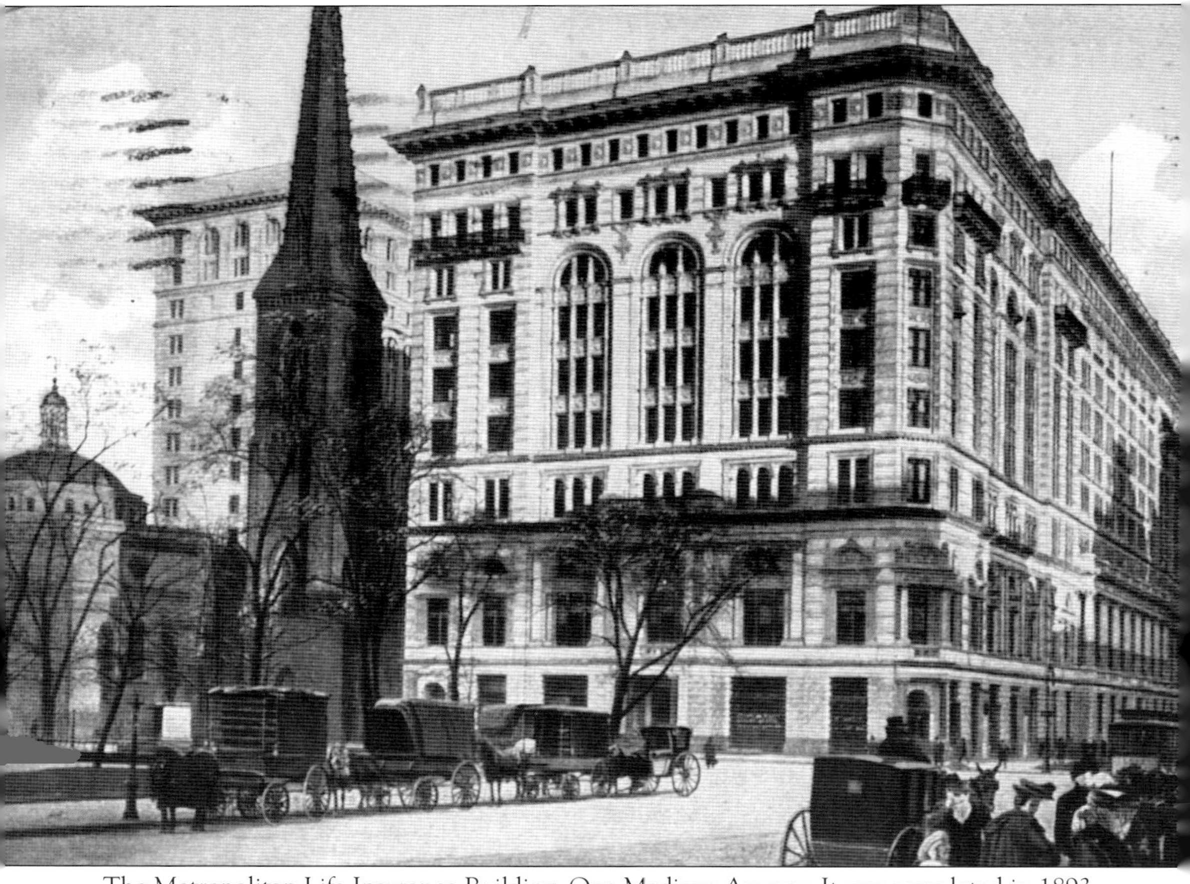

The Metropolitan Life Insurance Building, One Madison Avenue. It was completed in 1893.

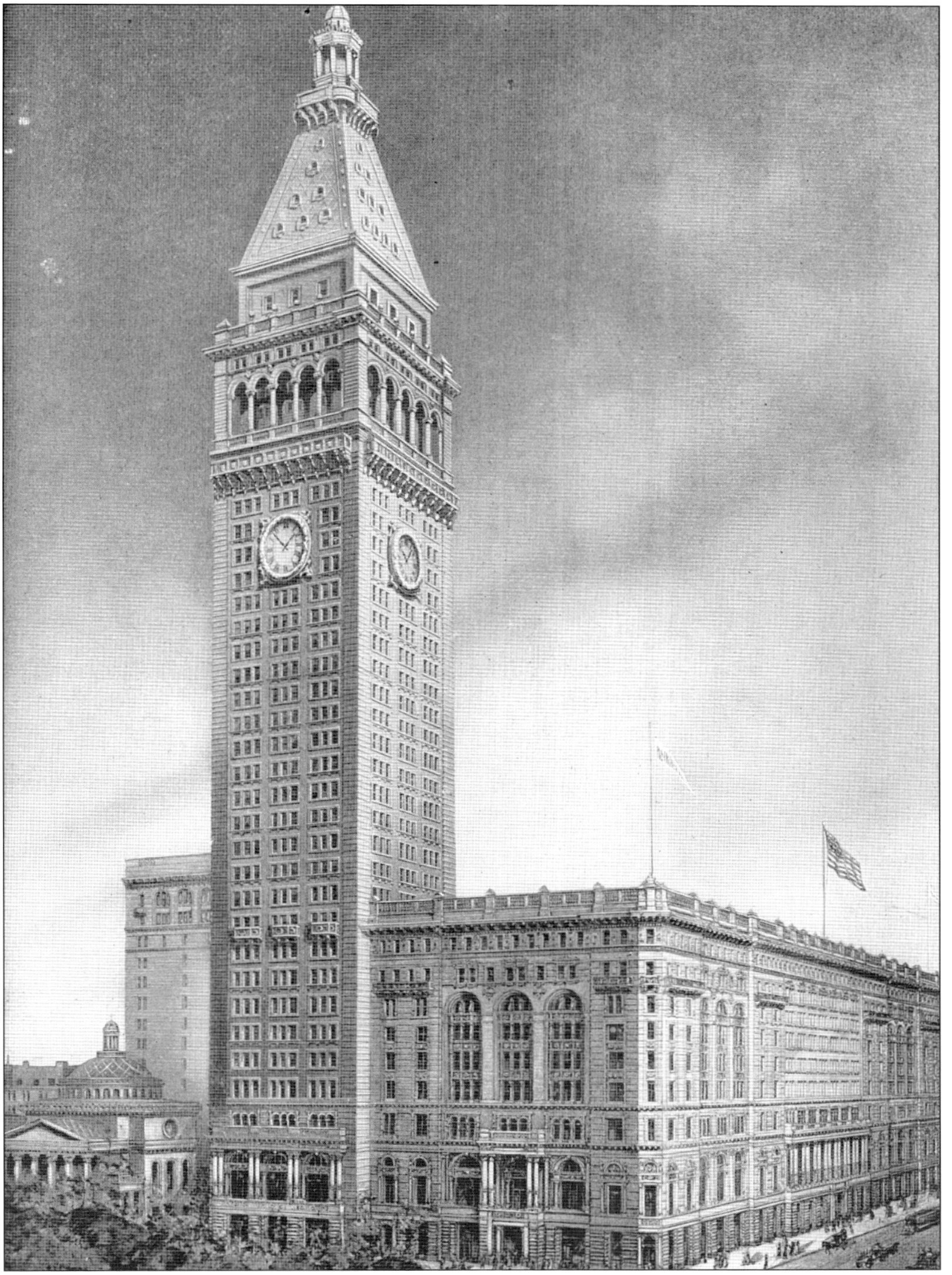

The 51-story Metropolitan Life Tower (1907–9) by Napoleon Le Brun and his sons. This structure surpassed the Singer Tower as the world's tallest. Modeled after the Campanile of San Marco in Venice, the tower was an effort by Le Brun to upstage Stanford White's nearby Giralda Tower at Madison Square Garden.

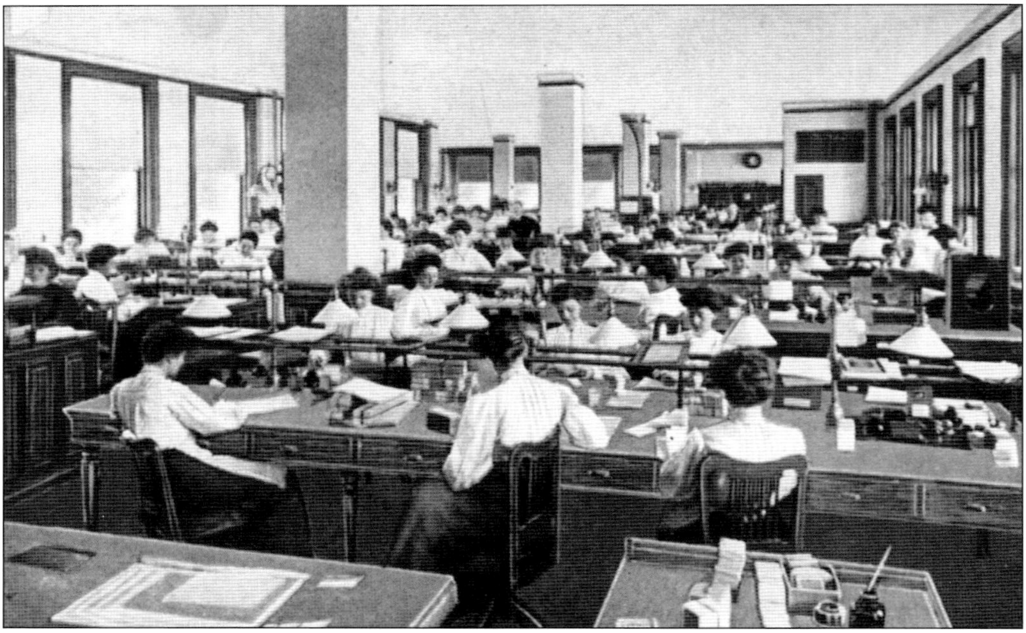

Women working in the Actuarial Division in the Metropolitan Life Insurance Building. Over ten million records were stored on cards in this room.

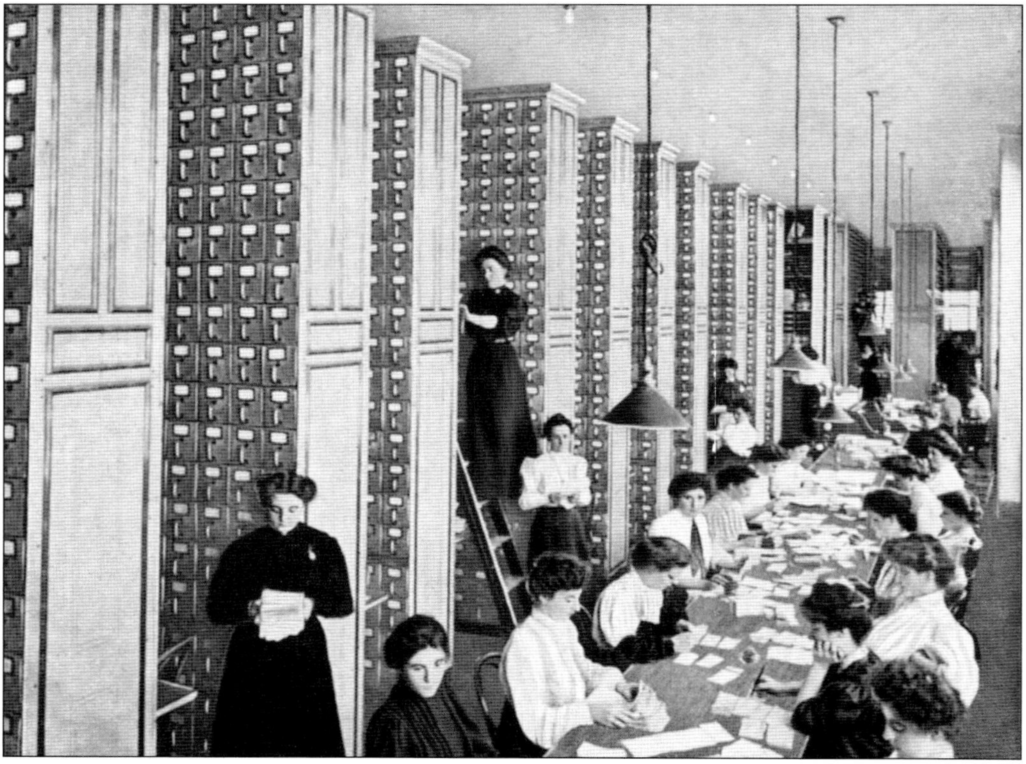

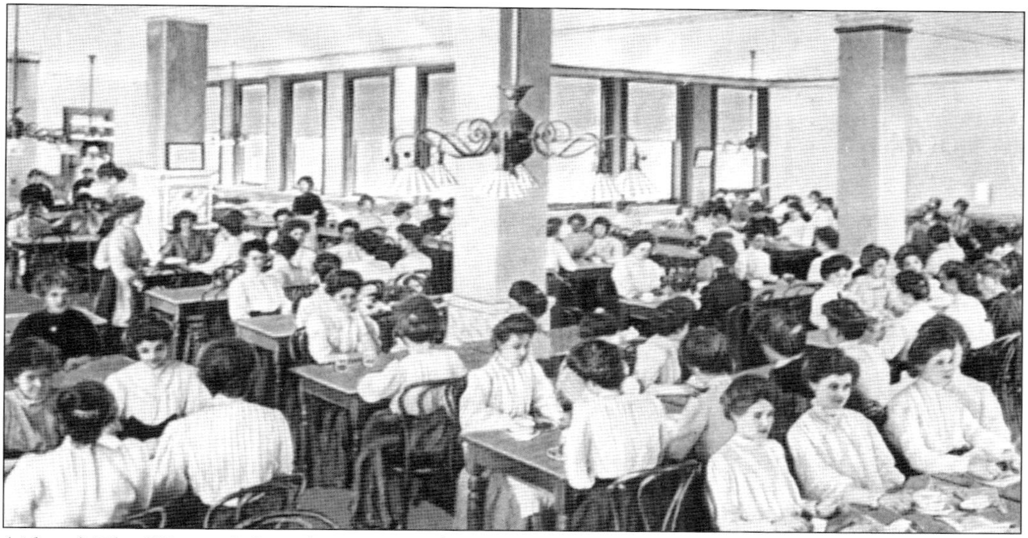

(*Above*) The Women's Lunch Room at the Metropolitan Life Insurance Building. (*Below*) The building's elevator and electrical machinery.

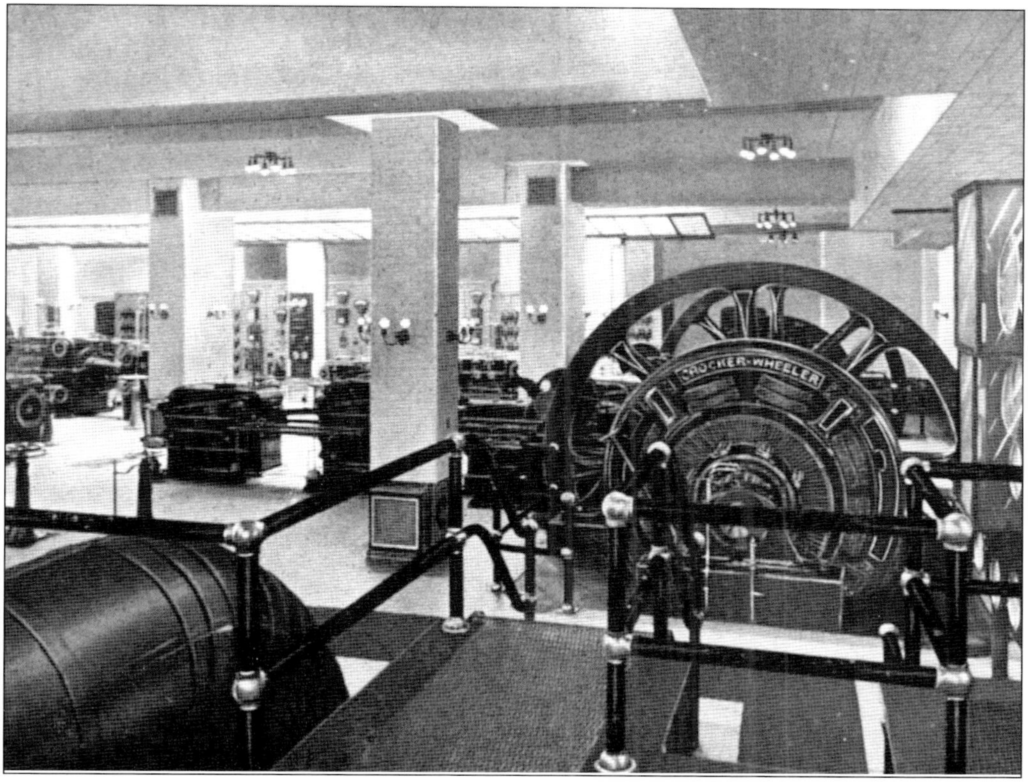

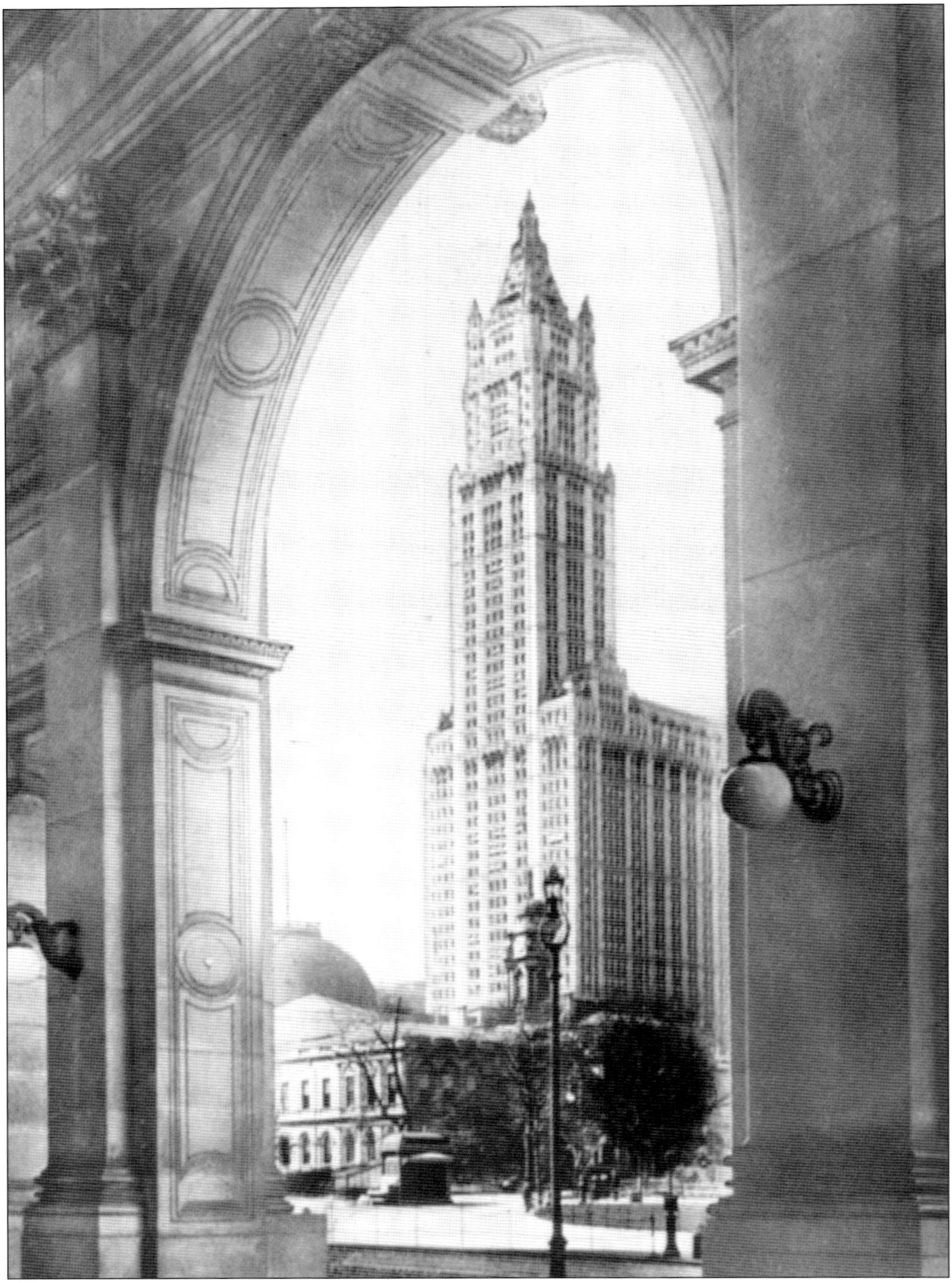

The Woolworth Building, Cass Gilbert's Gothic masterpiece, seen through a graceful arch of the Municipal Building. From 1913 to 1930, the Woolworth reigned as the world's tallest building. A curtain wall of ivory-colored terra-cotta clothes the steel skeleton in a soaring array of flamboyant Gothic tracery that rises nearly 800 feet above street level.

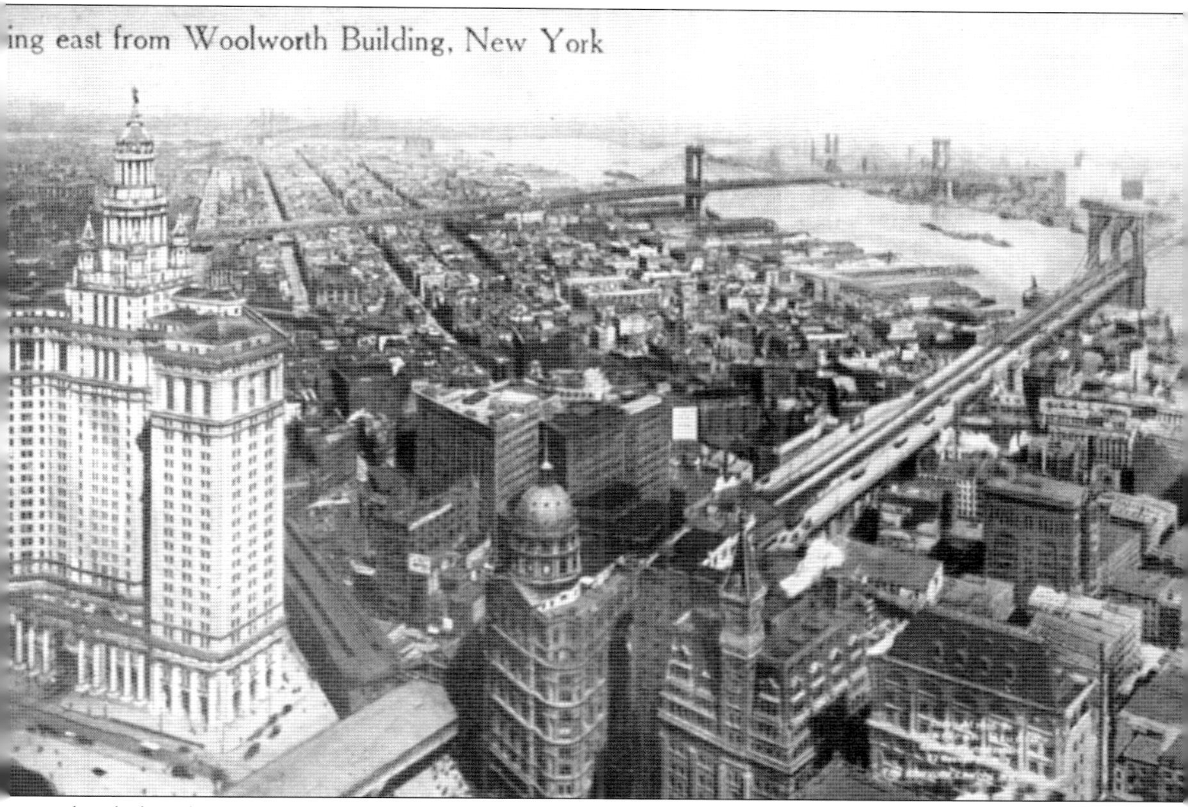

The skyline looking east from the Woolworth Building.

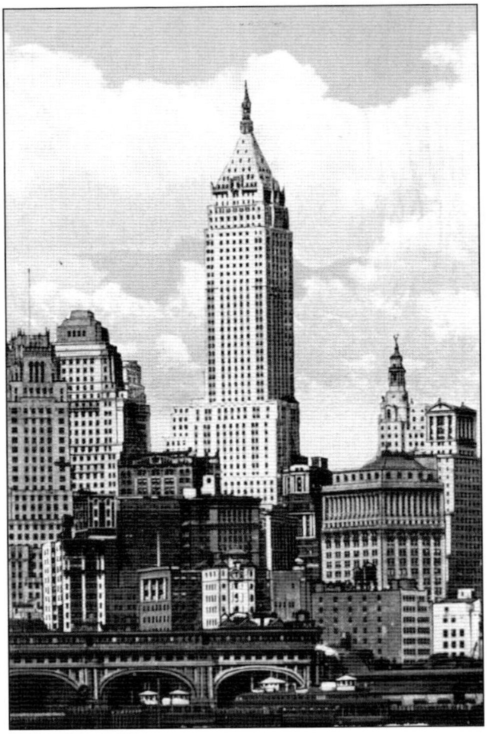

(*Left*) The Bank of Manhattan Company, a 70-story, 925-foot-high, post–World War I building located on the north side of Wall Street. (*Below*) The City Investing Building.

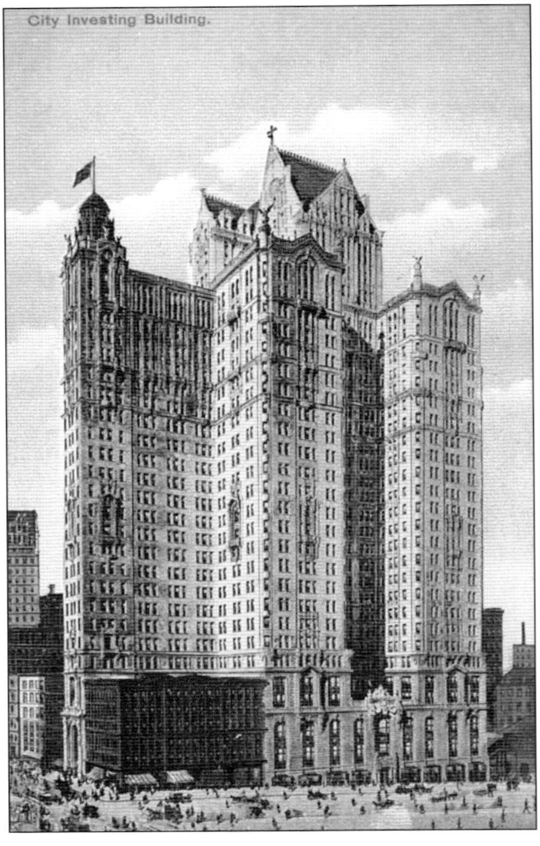

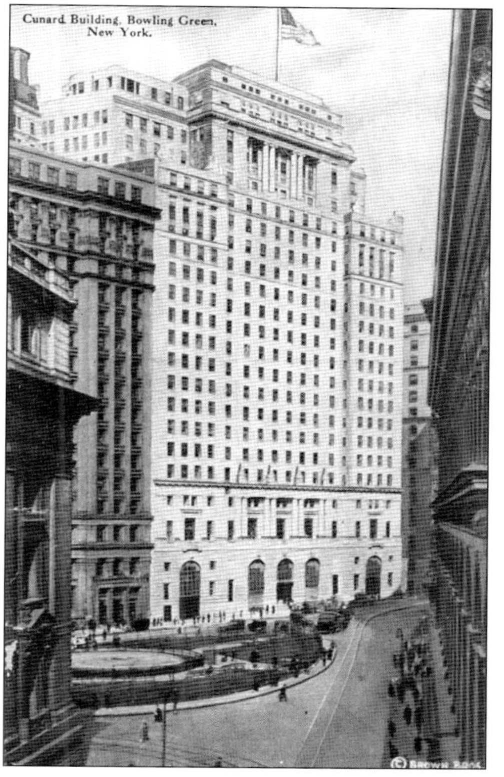

(*Right*) The Cunard Building, 25 Broadway, famous for the exceptional murals on the ceilings of the entrance hall. The 25-story steamship line headquarters was built at a cost of just $13,250,000. (*Below*) The New York Life Insurance Building.

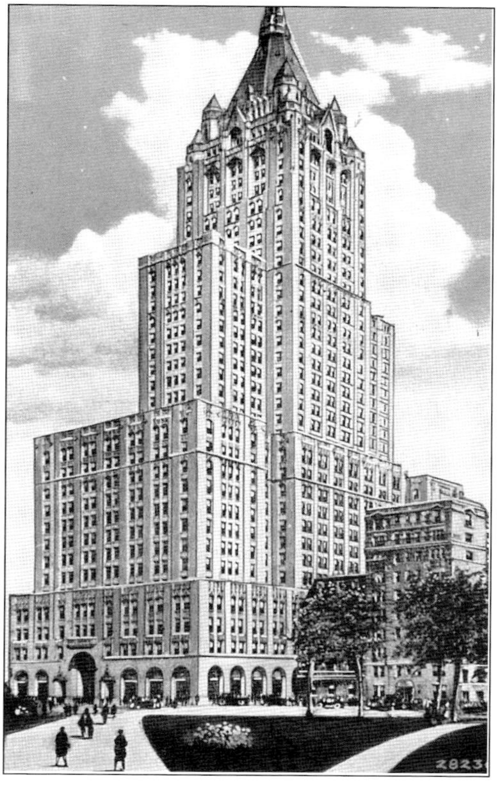

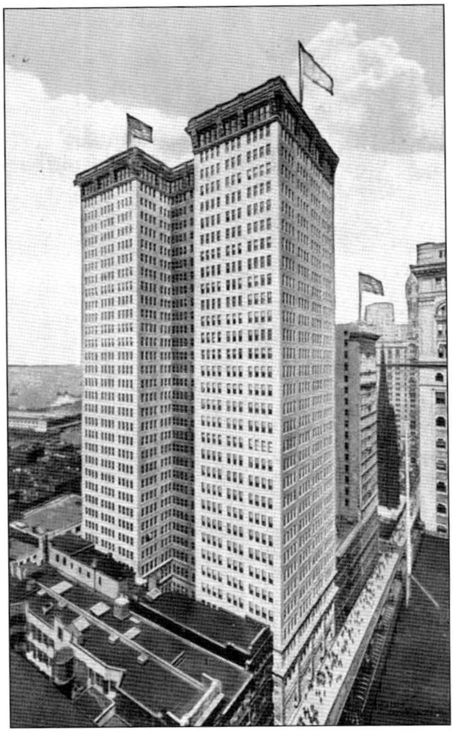

(*Left*) The Adams Express Building, 61 Broadway. (*Below*) The neo-Italian Renaissance-style Standard Oil Building at 26 Broadway near Bowling Green.

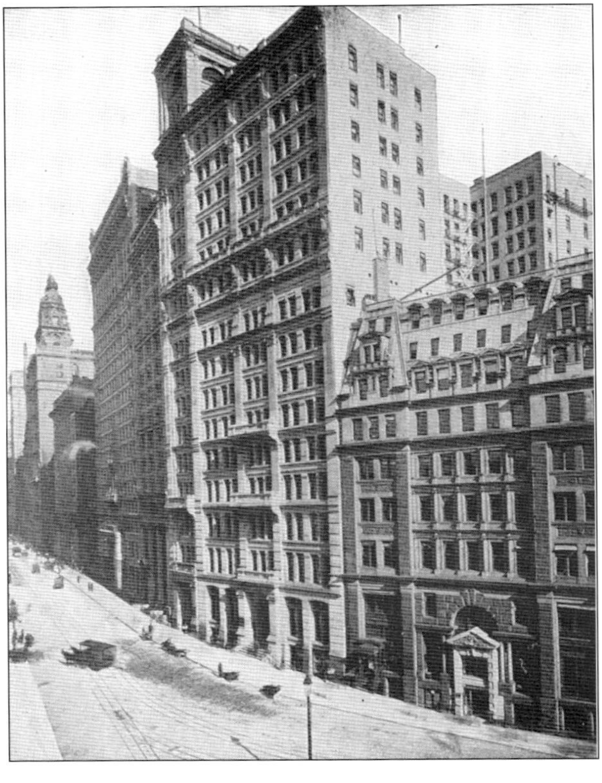

(*Right*) The 23-story Manhattan Life Insurance Building. At the turn of the century, the 361-foot-high tower was one of Manhattan's tallest. (*Below*) The Williamsburg Bridge approach at Delancy Street. It was the second span across the East River, built in hopes of relieving congestion on the Brooklyn Bridge, and was completed in December 1903.

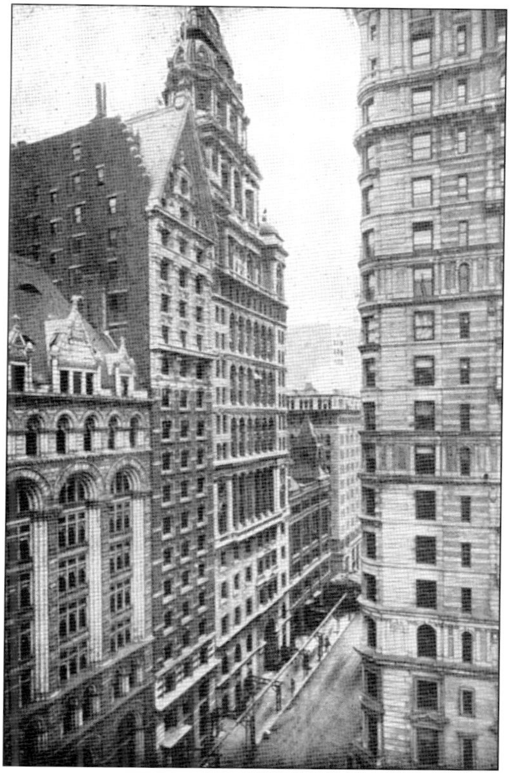

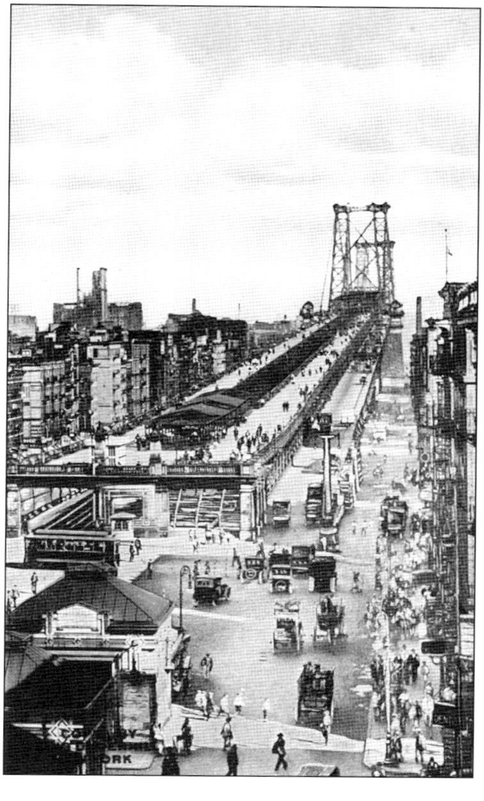

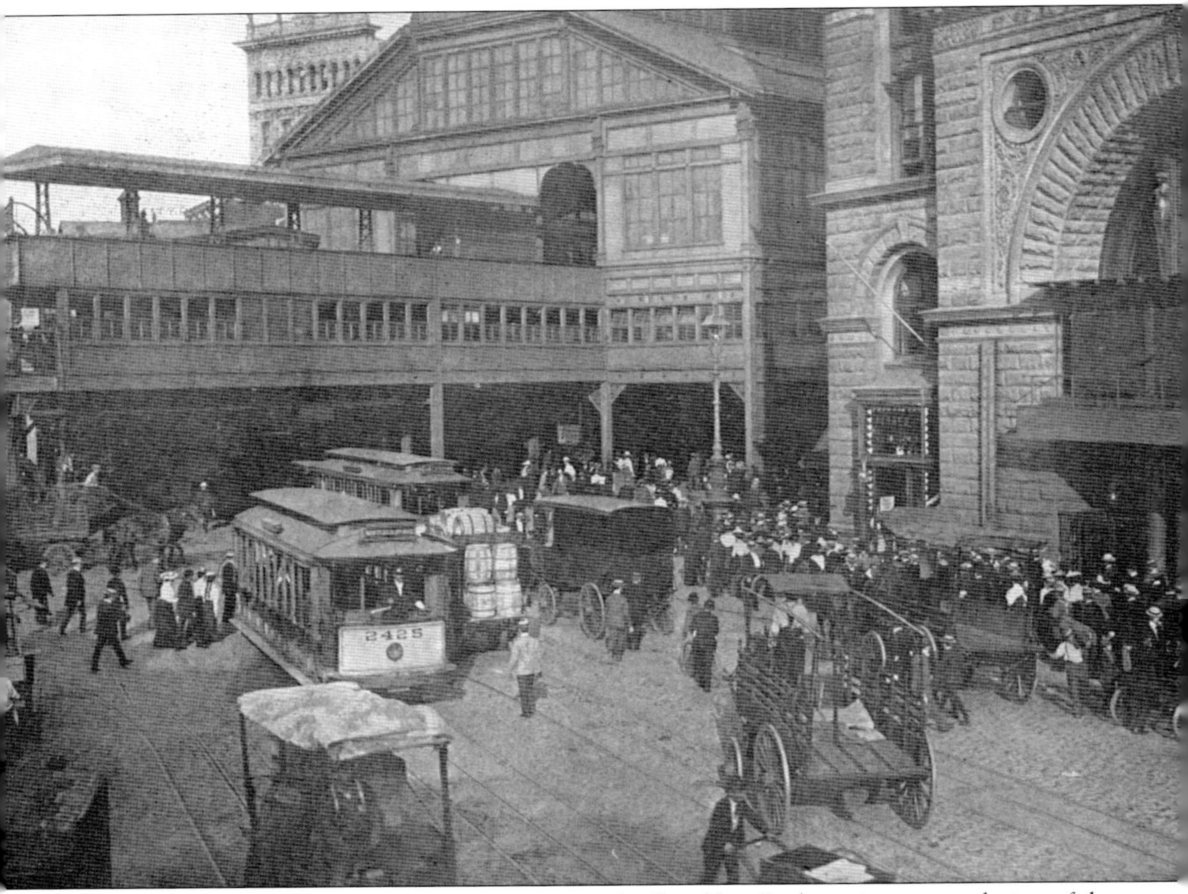

Heavy congestion at the Park Row entrance to the Brooklyn Bridge prior to completion of the East River Bridge.

Seven

Open Spaces

The famous master grid plan of 1811 mandated a host of squares and vest-pocket parks throughout Manhattan. By mid-century, there was wide agreement that something more was needed to accommodate the island's blossoming population.

In 1857, the Central Park Commission held a contest for the design of what was to be the first landscaped public park in the United States. The winning entry for the 843-acre park was submitted by Frederick Law Olmstead and Calvert Vaux. The plan called for a combination of rolling meadows, rambles, and formal areas such as the Promenade or Bethesda Fountain.

Thousands of shanty town residents were dispossessed, including the African Americans of Seneca Village, German gardeners, and Irish pig farmers. The project was one of the largest public works projects undertaken in the city during the 19th century. Nearly 20,000 workers were employed to do extensive blasting, plant more than a 250,000 trees and shrubs, and remove nearly 3 million cubic yards of soil.

In the early years, the park was the exclusive domain of the rich. By the 1880s, it was open to a much wider audience and Sunday concerts were held for workers. In the early 20th century, the park gradually began to cater to the immigrant communities that had settled on some of its borders. In 1927, August Heckscher donated the park's first equipped playground.

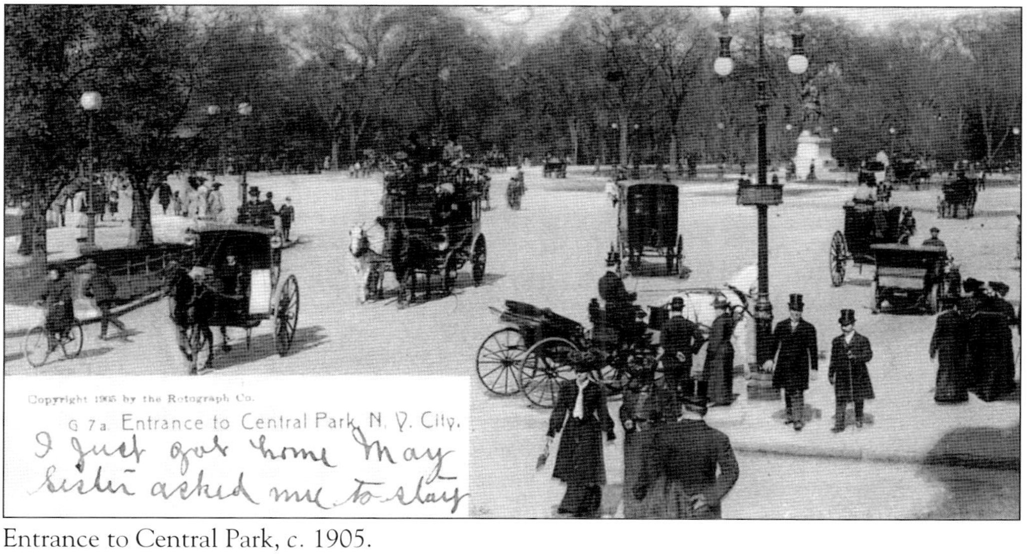

Entrance to Central Park, c. 1905.

1857. CITY OF NEW YORK. 1896.

DEPARTMENT OF

PUBLIC PARKS

Central ◇ Park.

FOUNDED 1857.

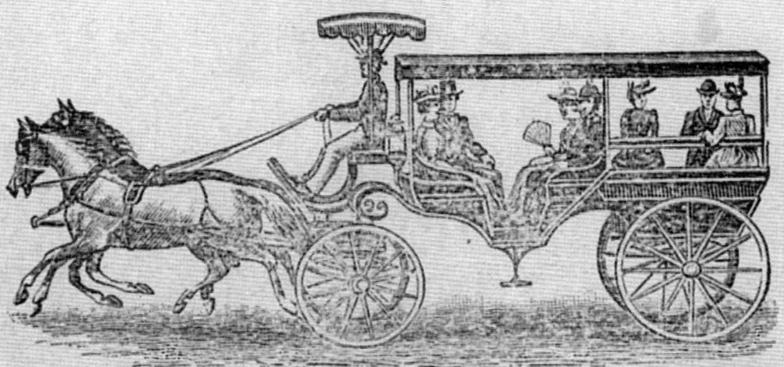

CENTRAL PARK CARRIAGE SERVICE, ORGANIZED 1869.

Carriages will leave the Scholars' Gate, 59th Street and Fifth Avenue, and the Merchants' Gate, 59th Street and Eighth Avenue, making the circuit of the Park, at brief intervals, and MAY BE TAKEN ANYWHERE on the road.

Fare for Each Passenger for the round trip, **25** cents. Tickets must be purchased of the Starter, and they entitle passengers to be put down and taken up at the Museum of Natural History, Mt. St. Vincent, Museum of Art and the Terrace Bridge.

Carriages in going take the West Drive, in returning the East Drive, thus making the tour of the Park. In going, you are driven past the Museum of Natural History in Manhattan Square, and the great Croton Reservoirs. The tower at the lower Reservoir is the Belvedere, from which a fine view of the Park and the surrounding city may be obtained. In returning, carriages stop at Mt. St. Vincent, Museum of Art and the Terrace Bridge.

Carriage rides through Central Park. This activity was as popular in the 19th century as it is today. In 1896, the department of public parks advertised complete circuits of the park, departing from various locations, for just 25¢.

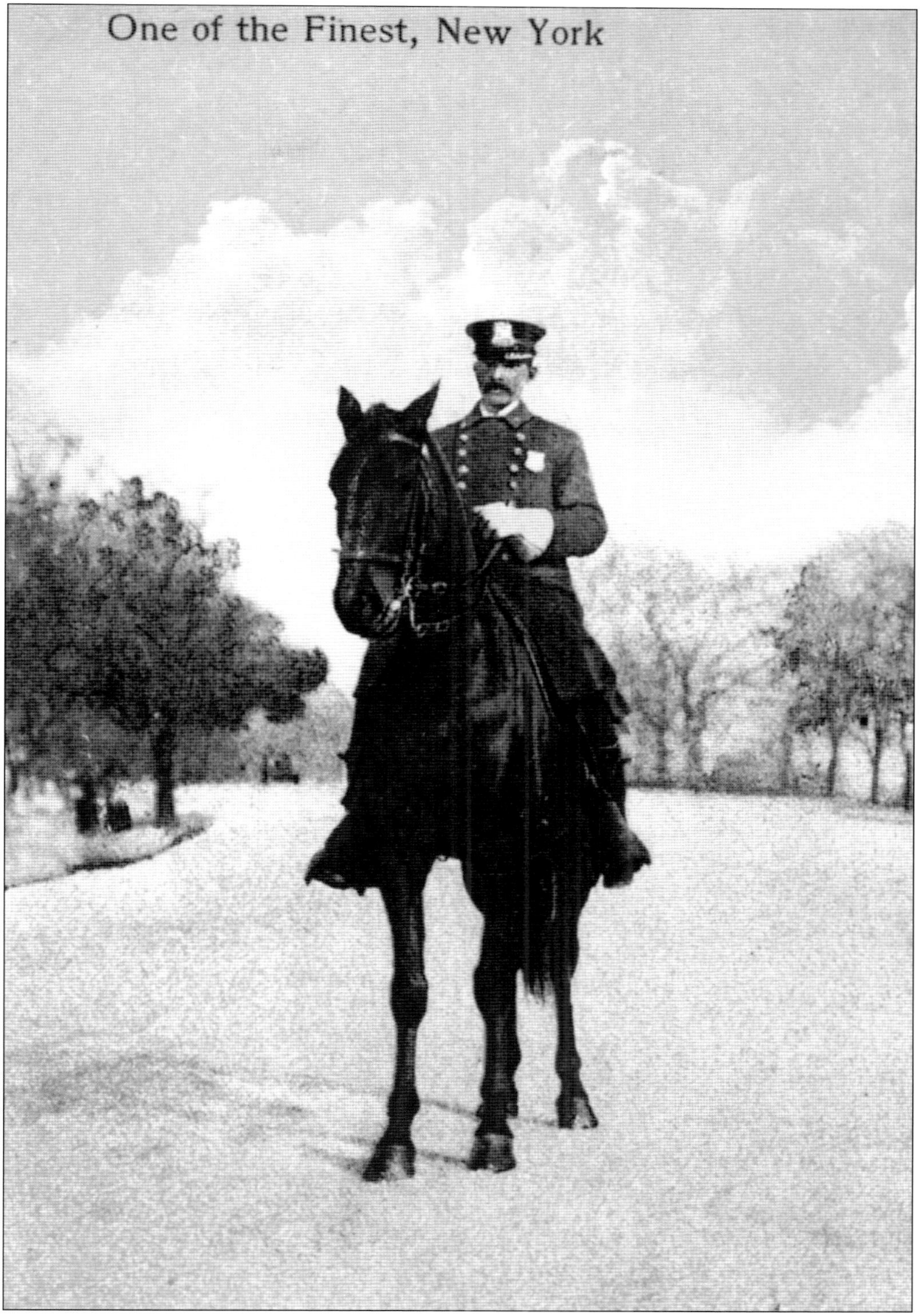

One of New York's Finest patrolling the park at the turn of the century.

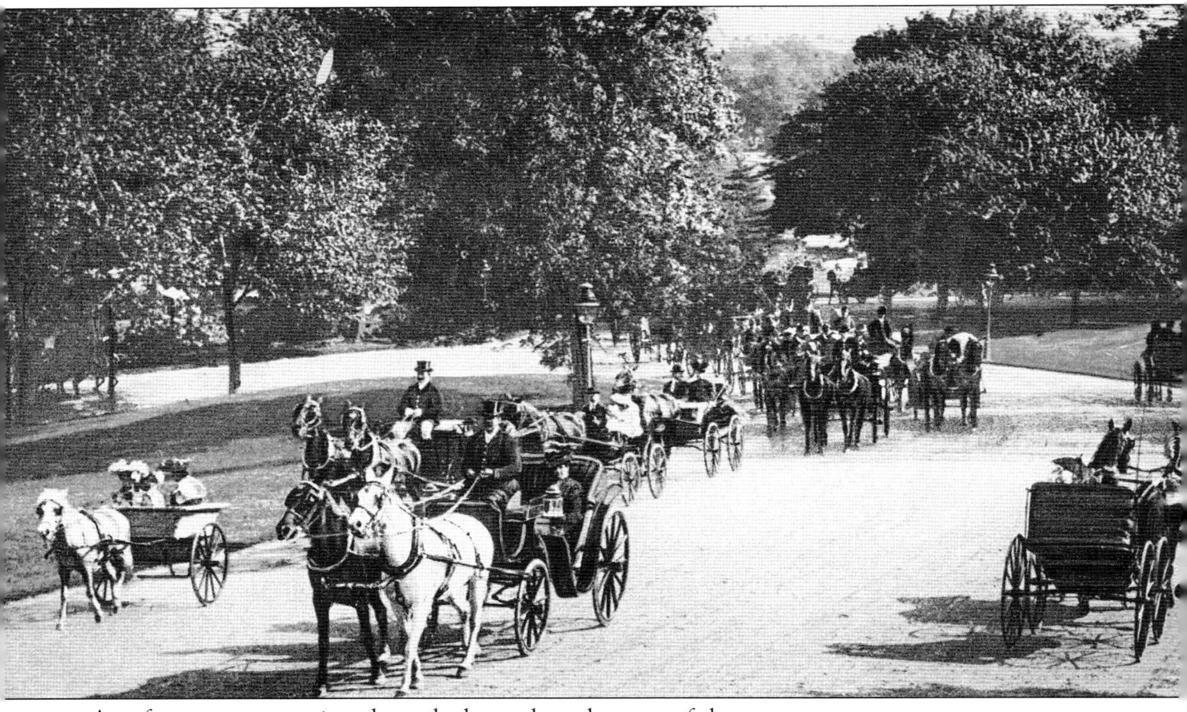

An afternoon procession through the park at the turn of the century.

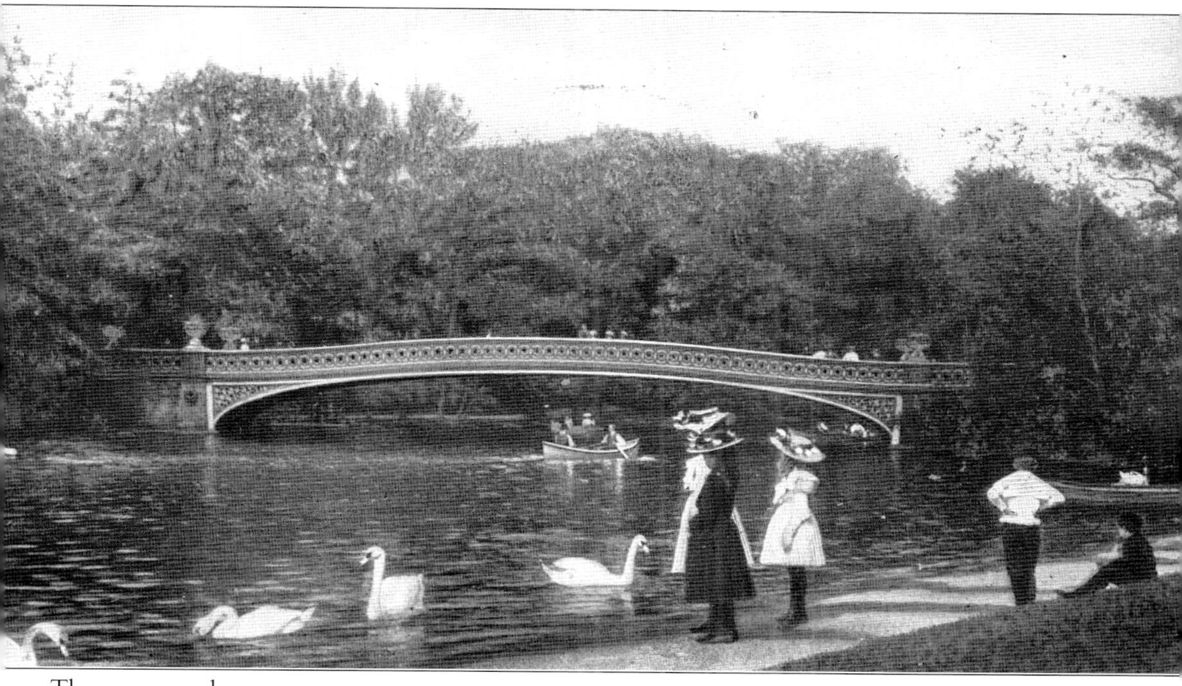
The swan pond.

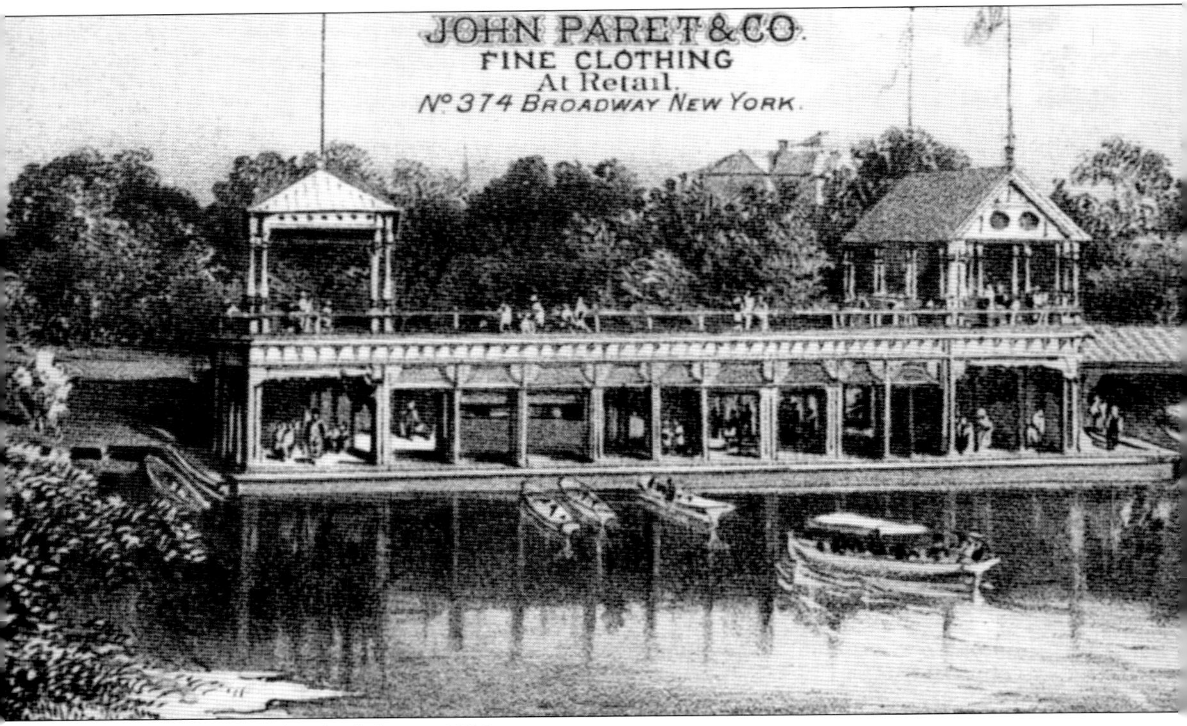

The boathouse by the lake, *c.* 1890.

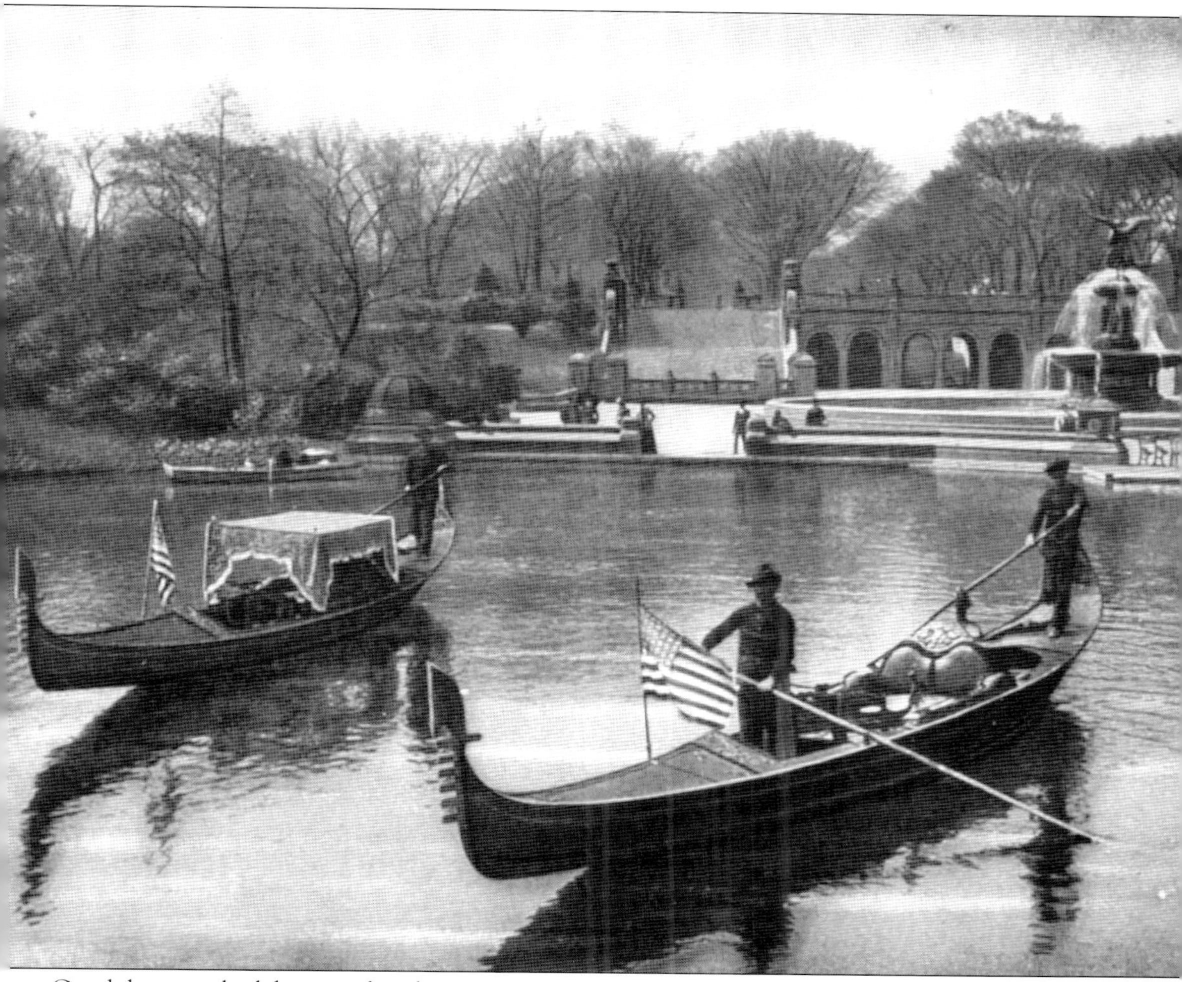

Gondoliers on the lake just after the turn of the century.

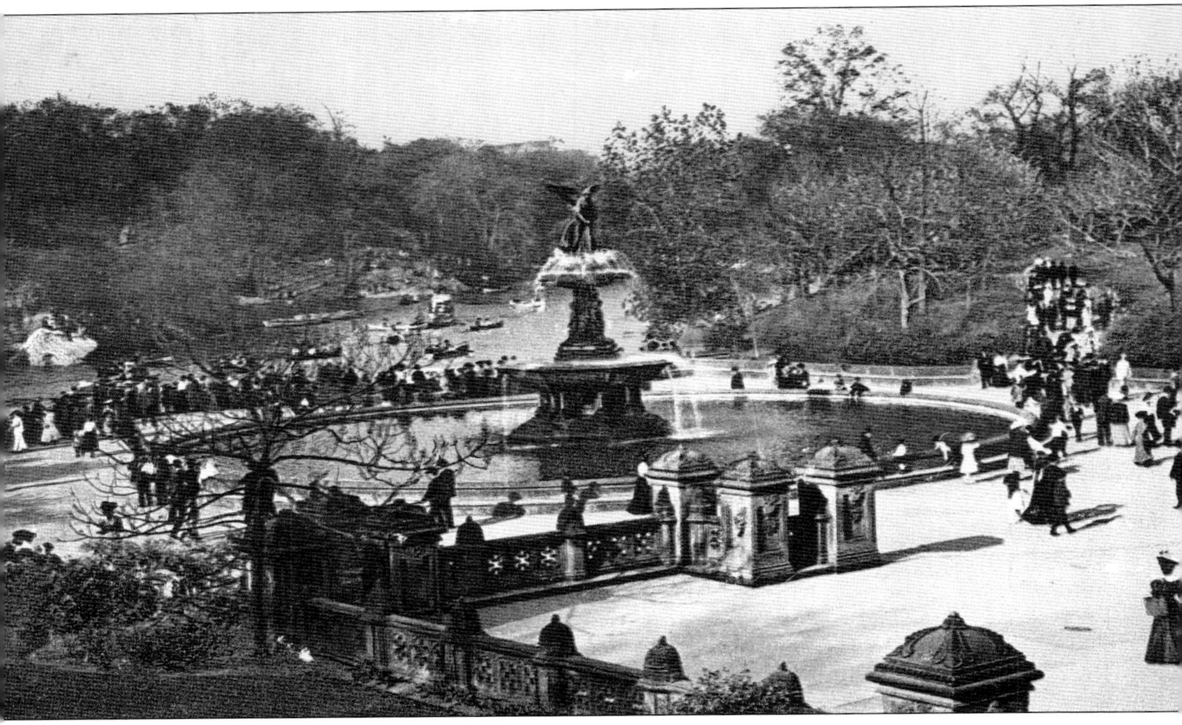

The lake and terrace.

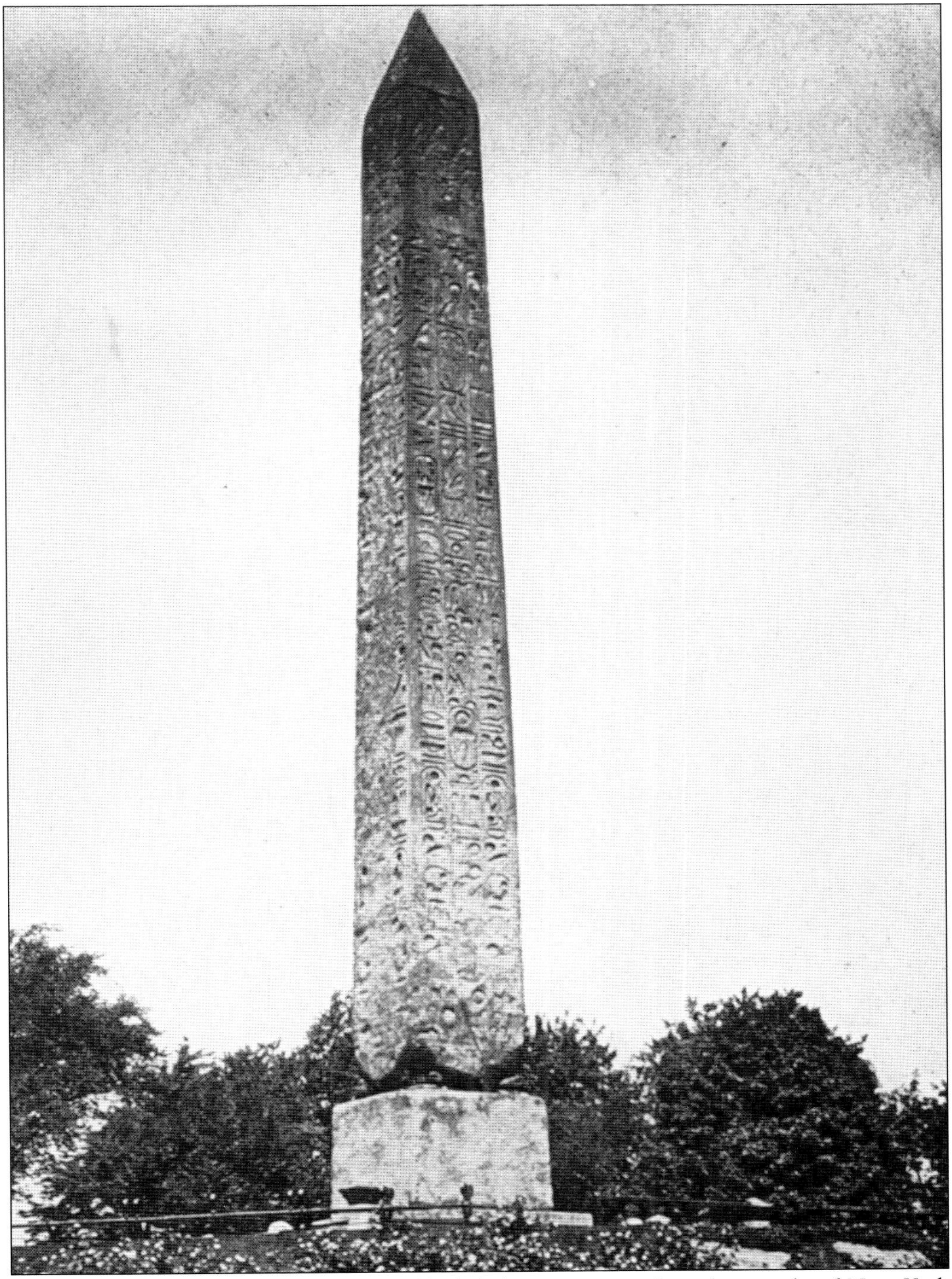

“Cleopatra’s Needle.” This 3,500-year-old obelisk was presented to the people of New York in 1877 by Ismail Pasha, Khedive of Egypt. William Vanderbilt picked up the tab for floating the 69-foot 2-inch granite monolith 6,400 miles to Manhattan, dragging it halfway across the island, and erecting it in the park.

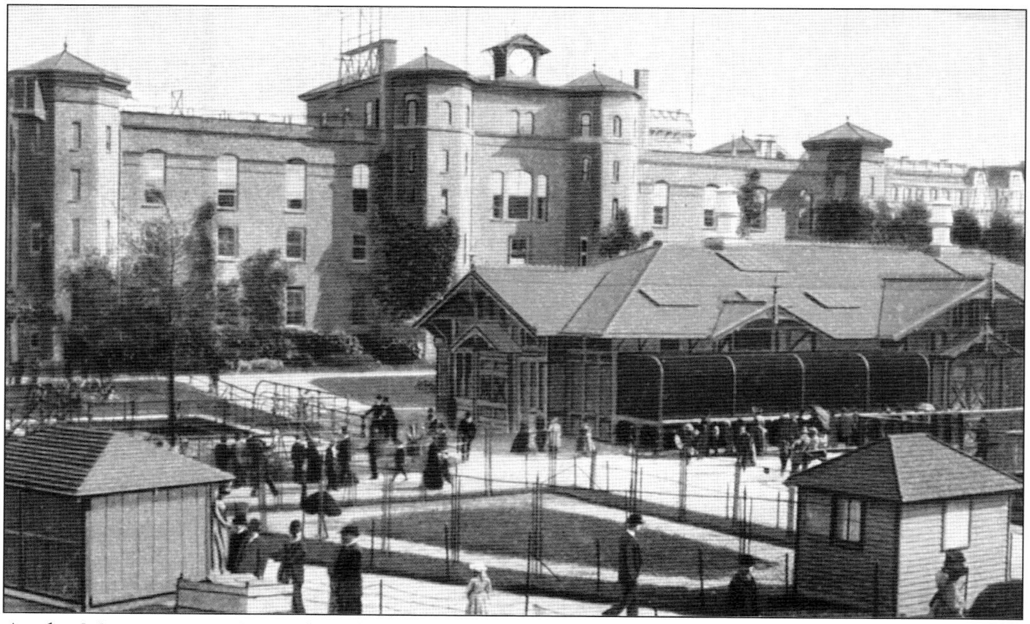

At the Menagerie in Central Park.

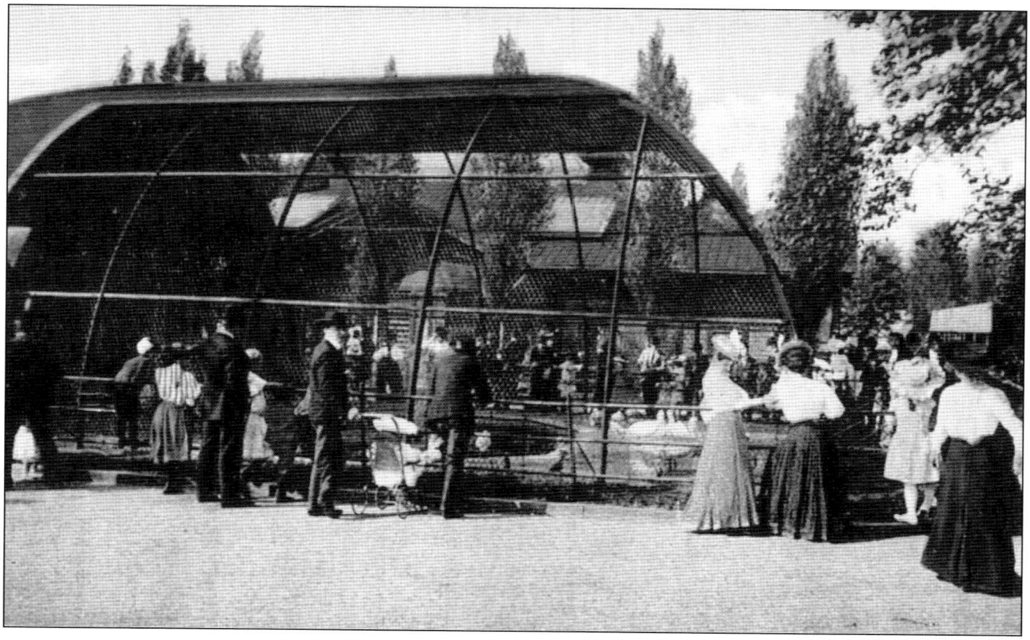

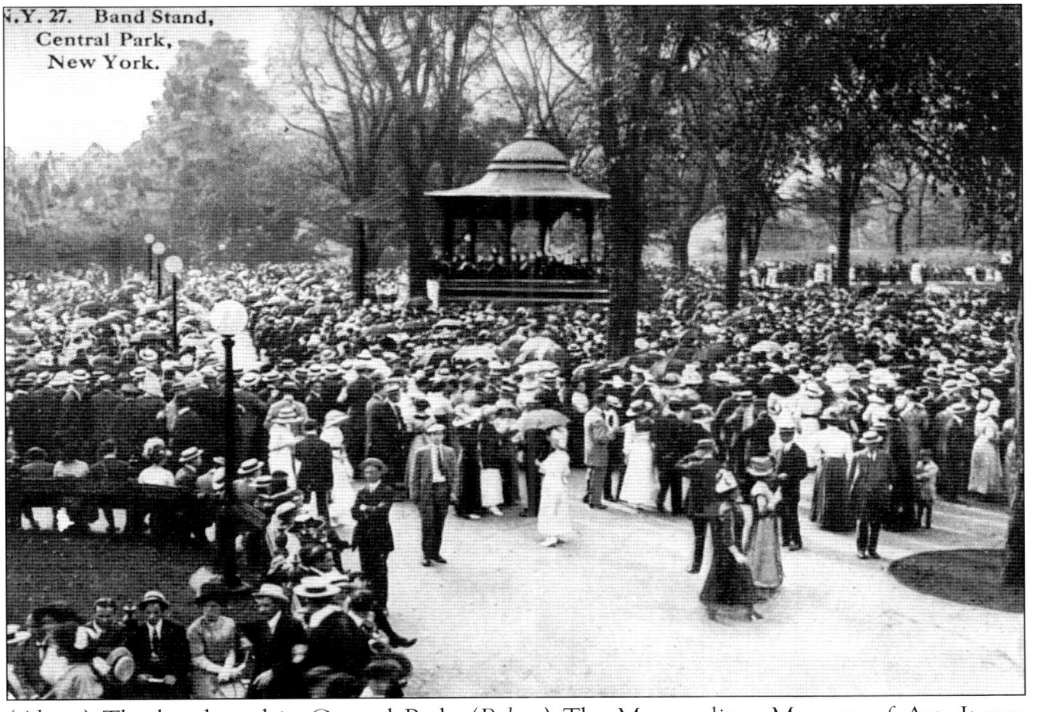

(*Above*) The bandstand in Central Park. (*Below*) The Metropolitan Museum of Art. It was formed in the 1870s by members of the Union League.

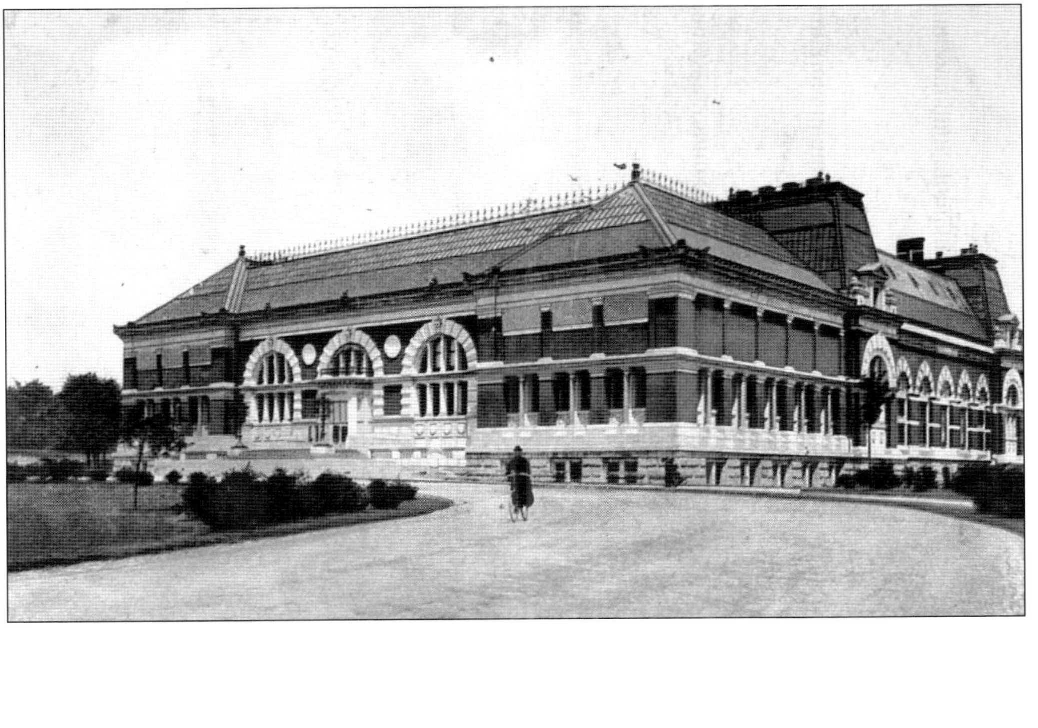

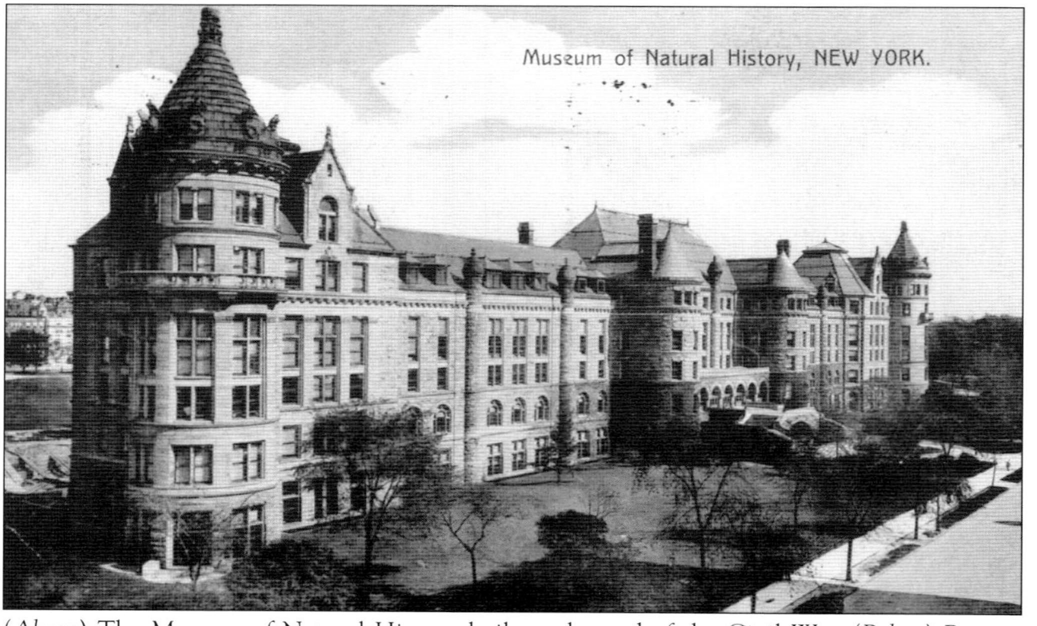

(*Above*) The Museum of Natural History, built at the end of the Civil War. (*Below*) Battery Park.

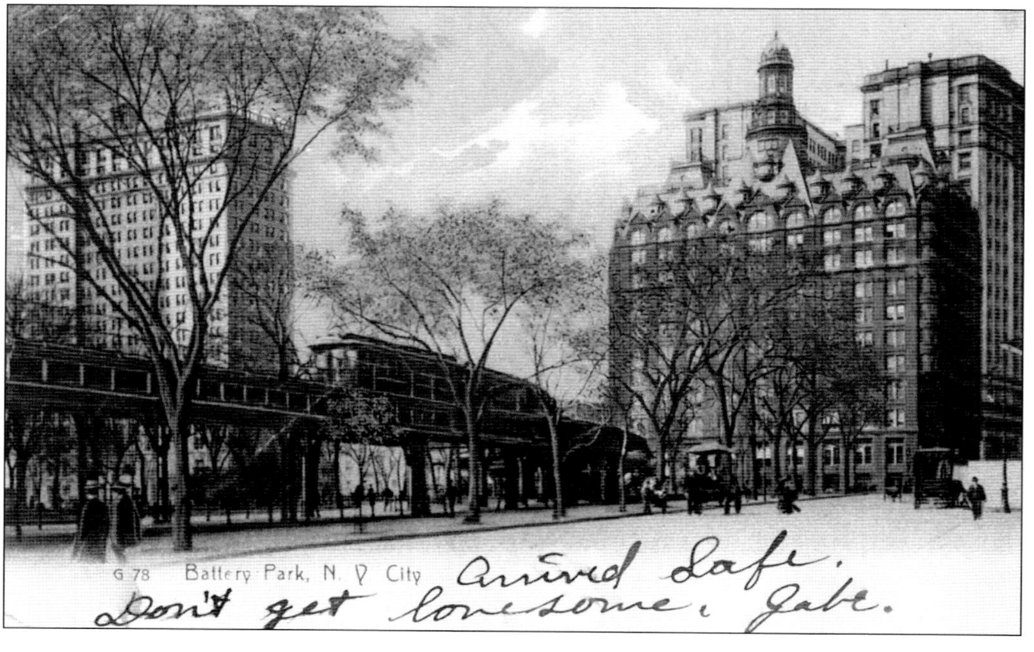

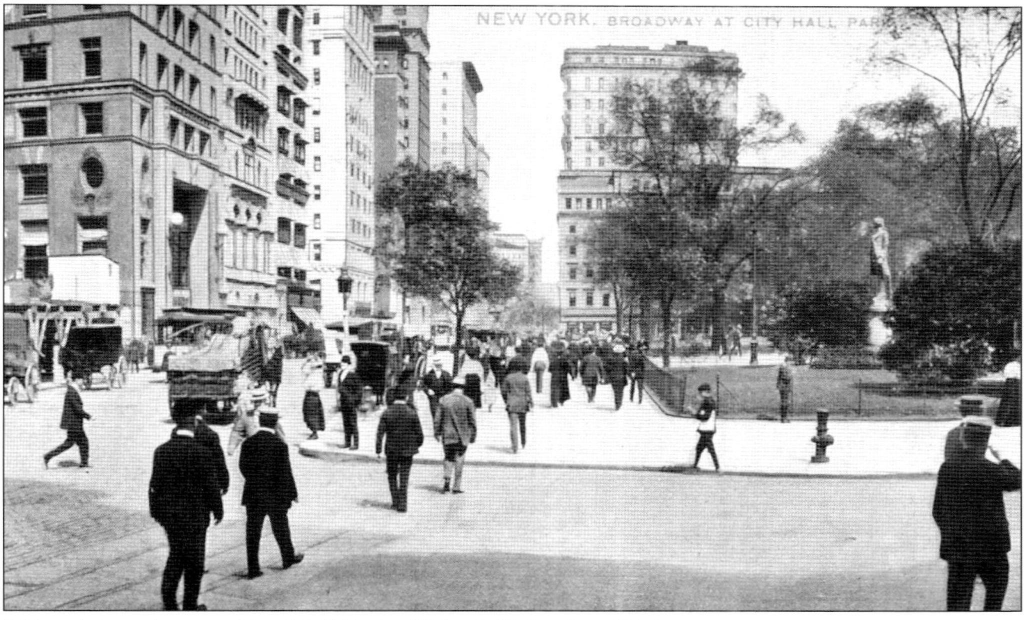

(*Above*) Broadway at City Hall Park. (*Below*) Columbus Circle.

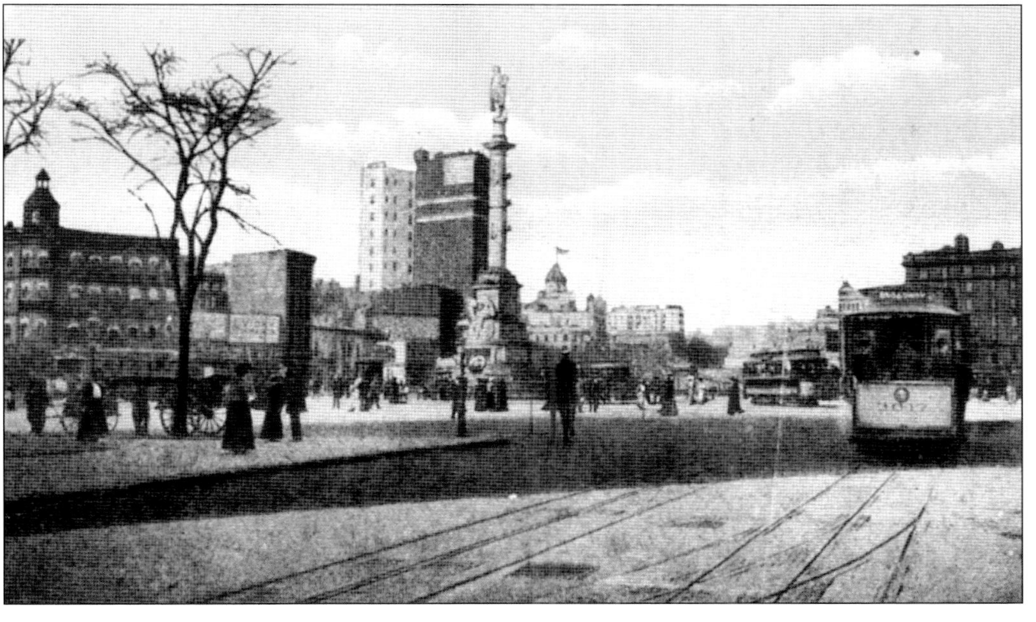

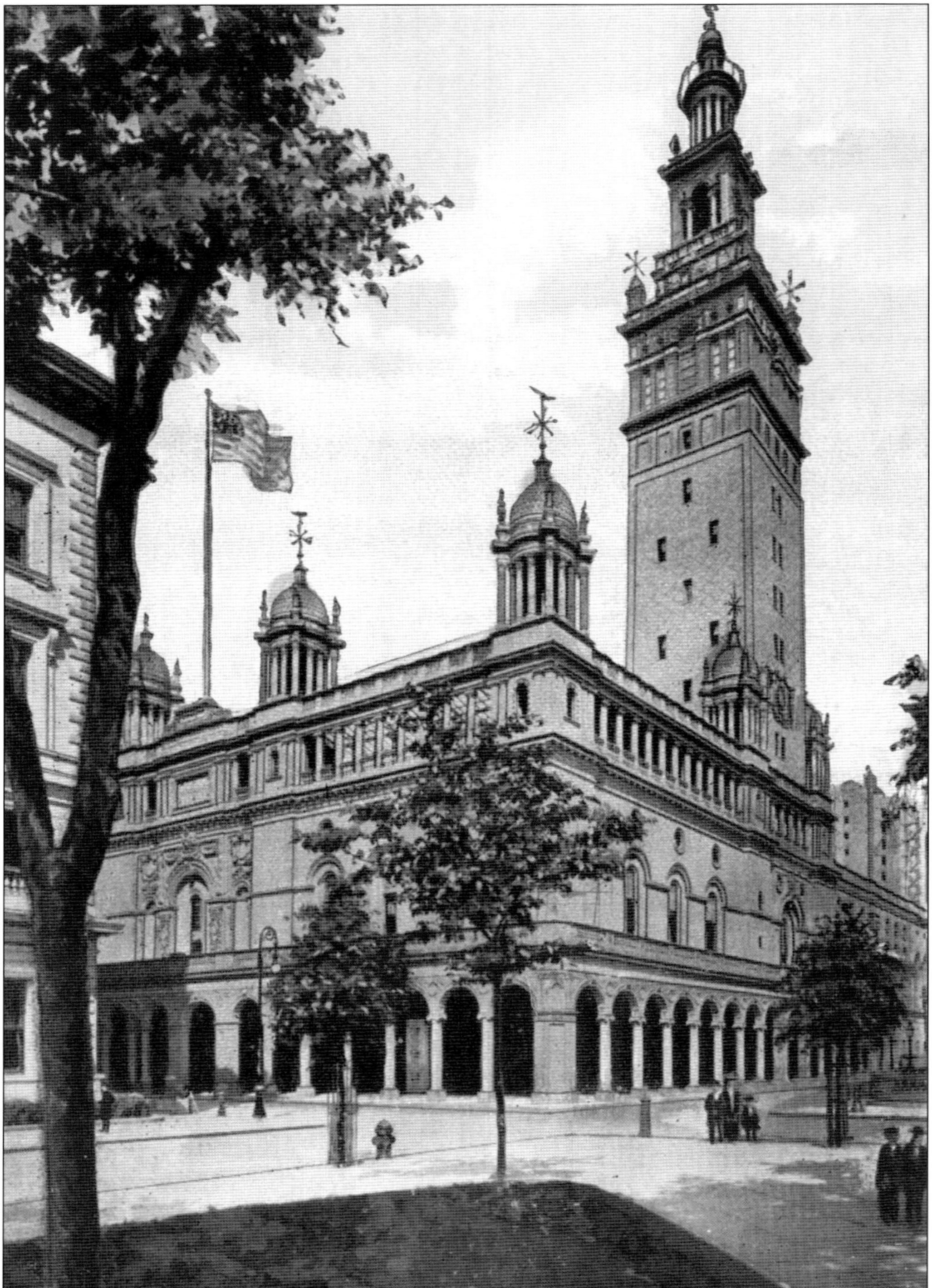

Madison Square Garden. The Giralda tower is on the right.

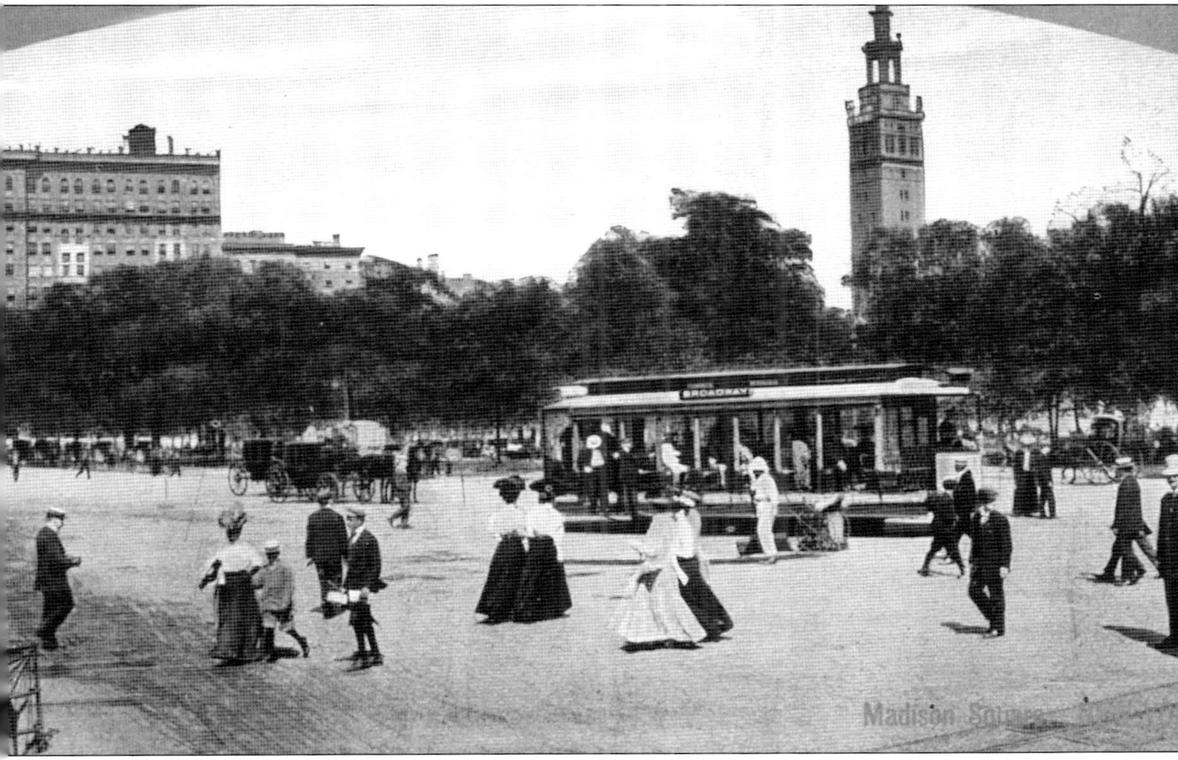

Madison Square with an open-air trolley.

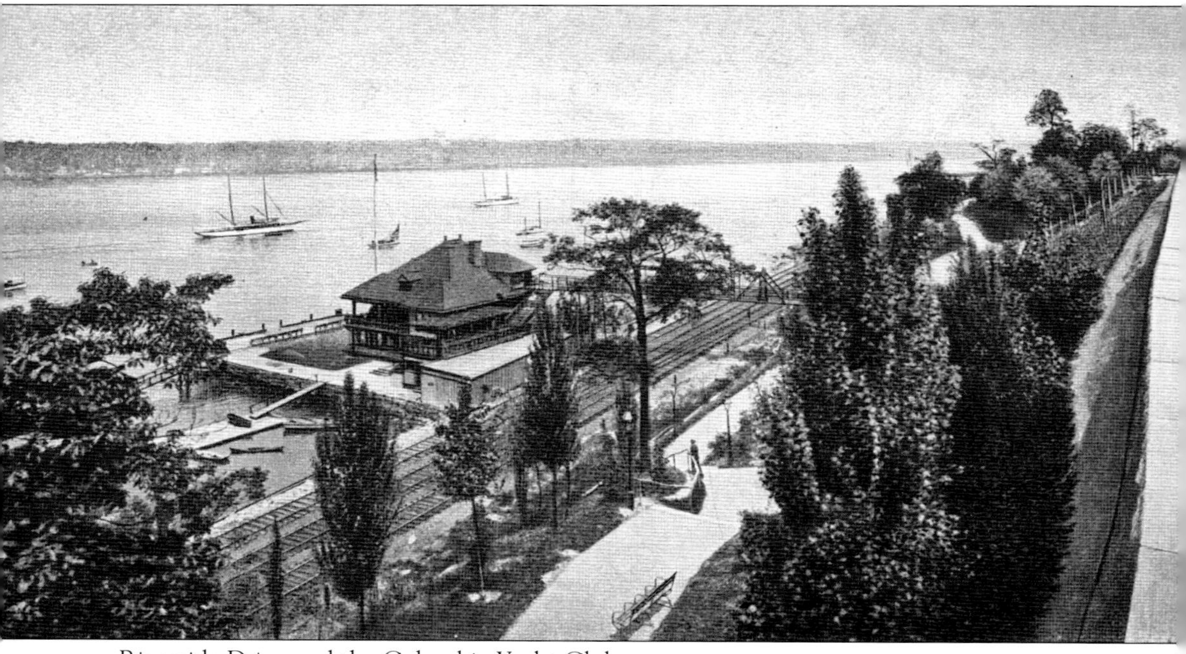

Riverside Drive and the Columbia Yacht Club.

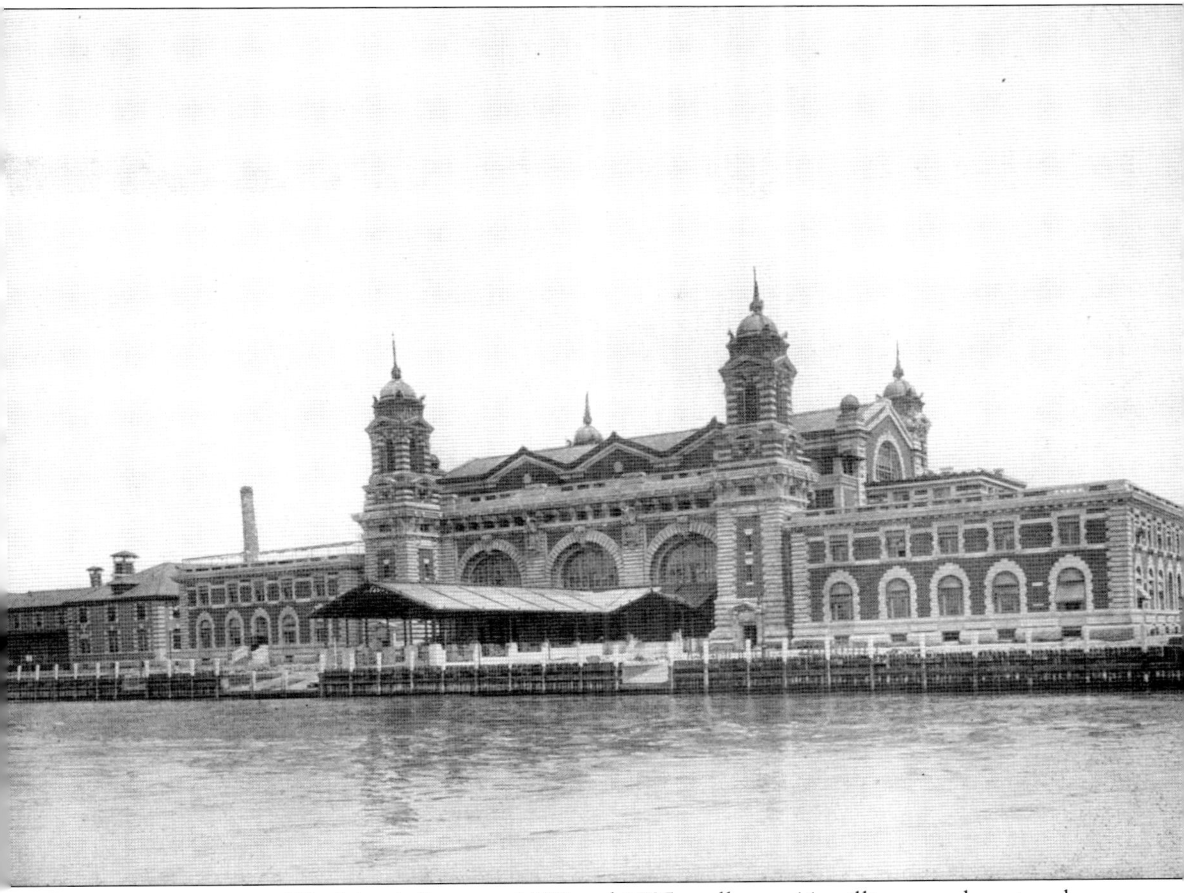

Immigrant station on Ellis Island. Between 1880 and 1905, well over 11 million people entered the country through Ellis Island.

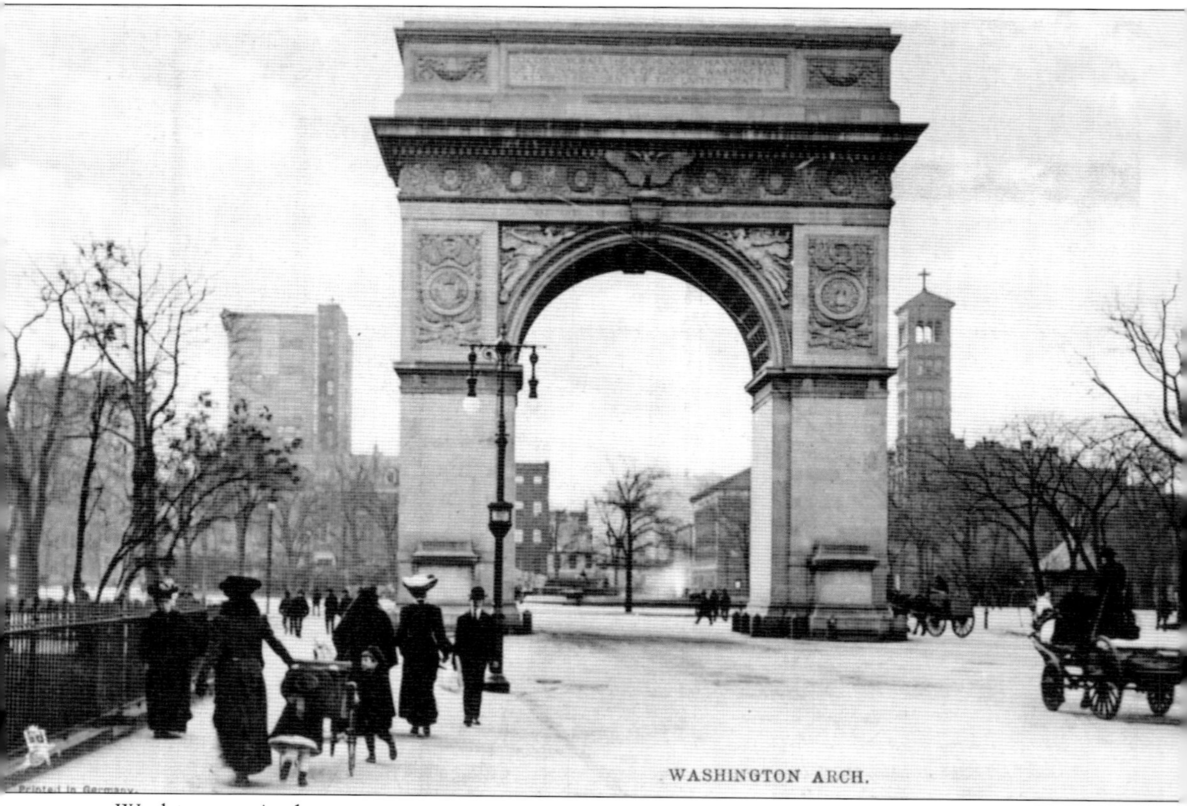

Washington Arch.

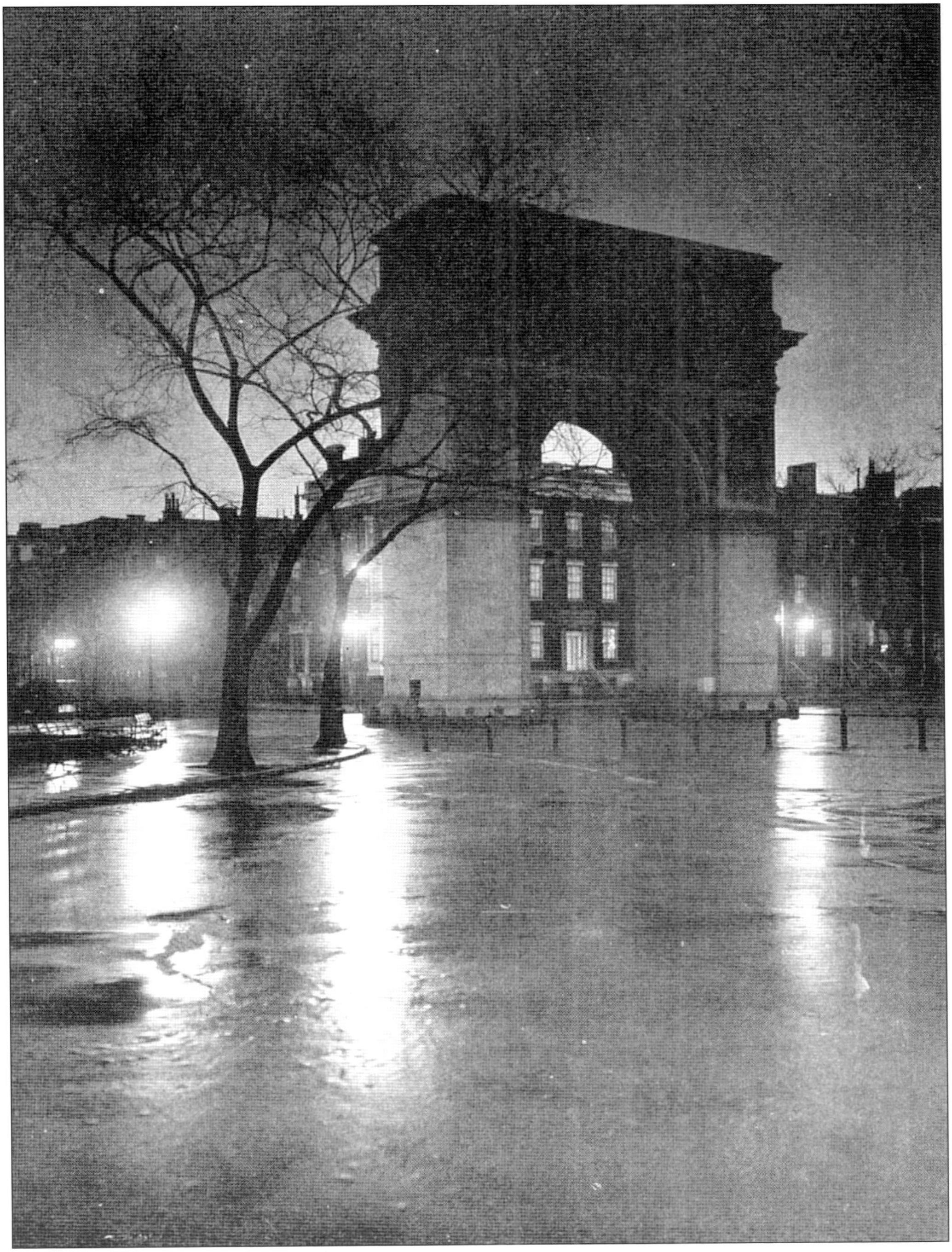

Washington Square Park at night.

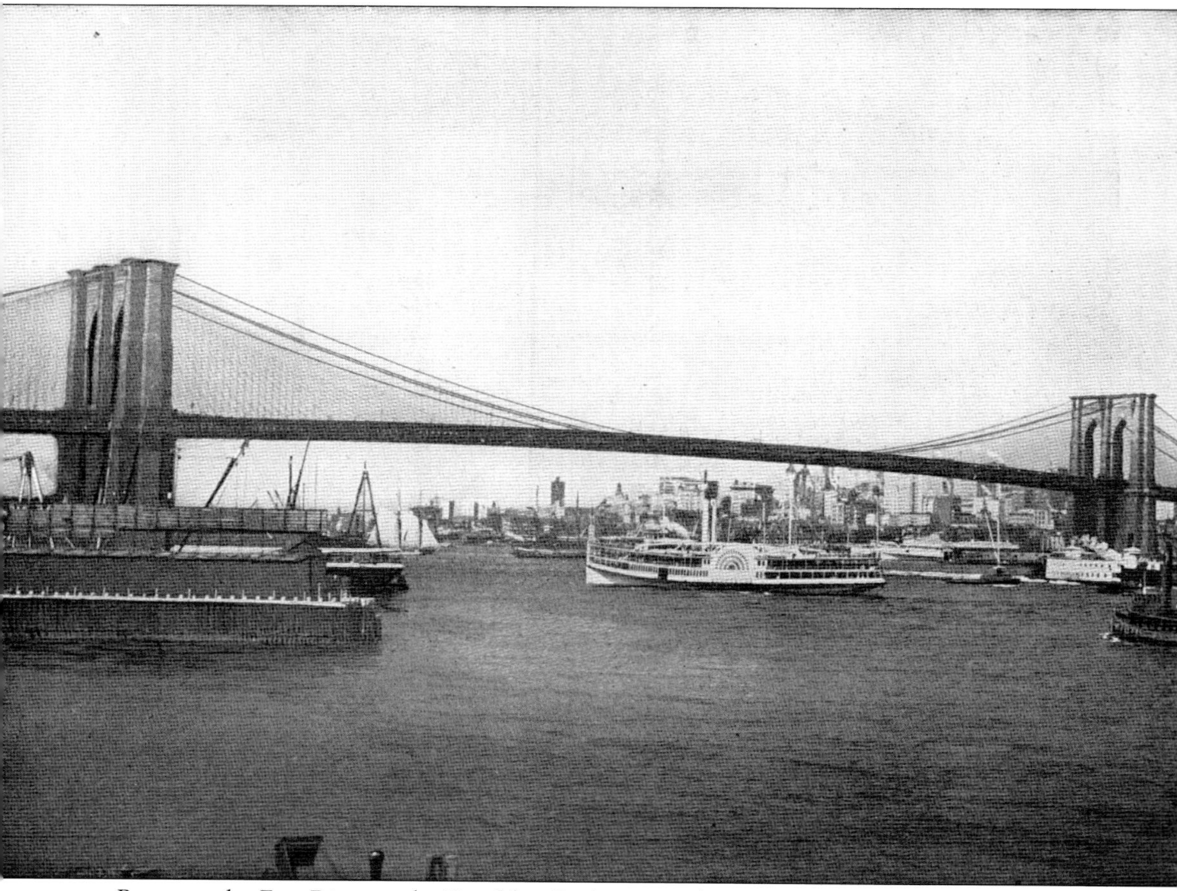

Boats on the East River at the Brooklyn Bridge around 1904.

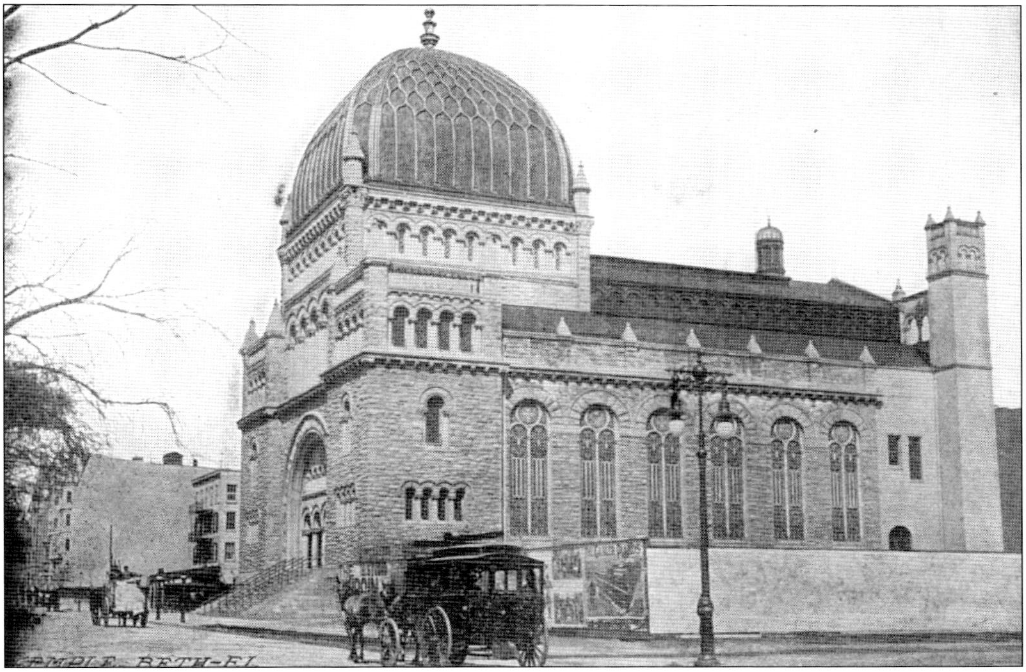

(*Above*) Temple Beth El on Fifth Avenue near Seventy-Eighth Street. (*Below*) The Church of the Transfiguration, popularly known as the Little Church Around the Corner.

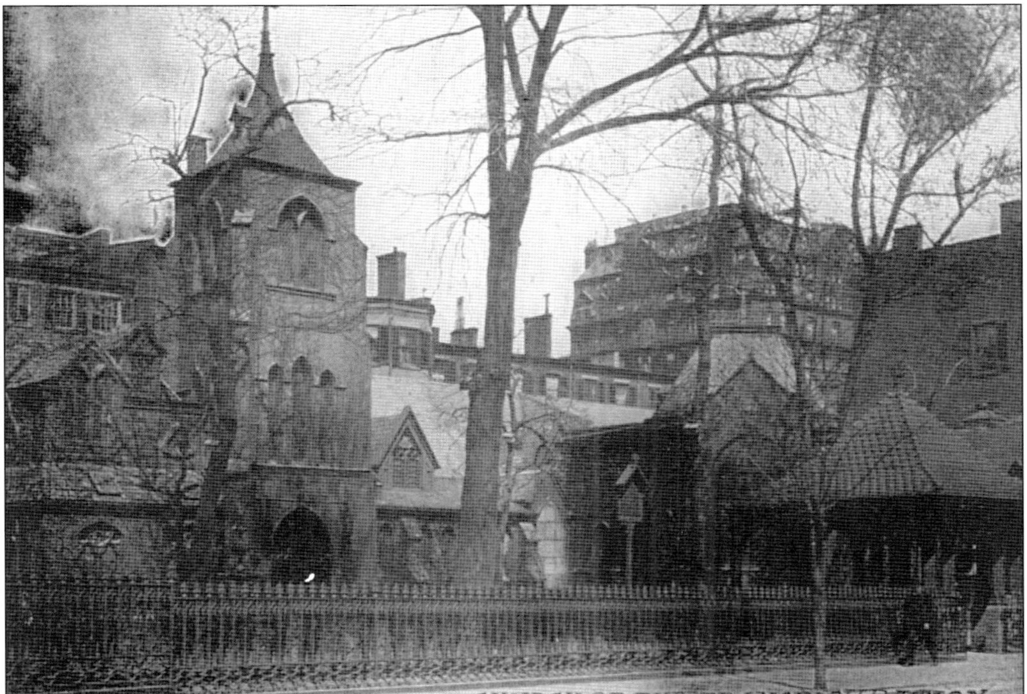

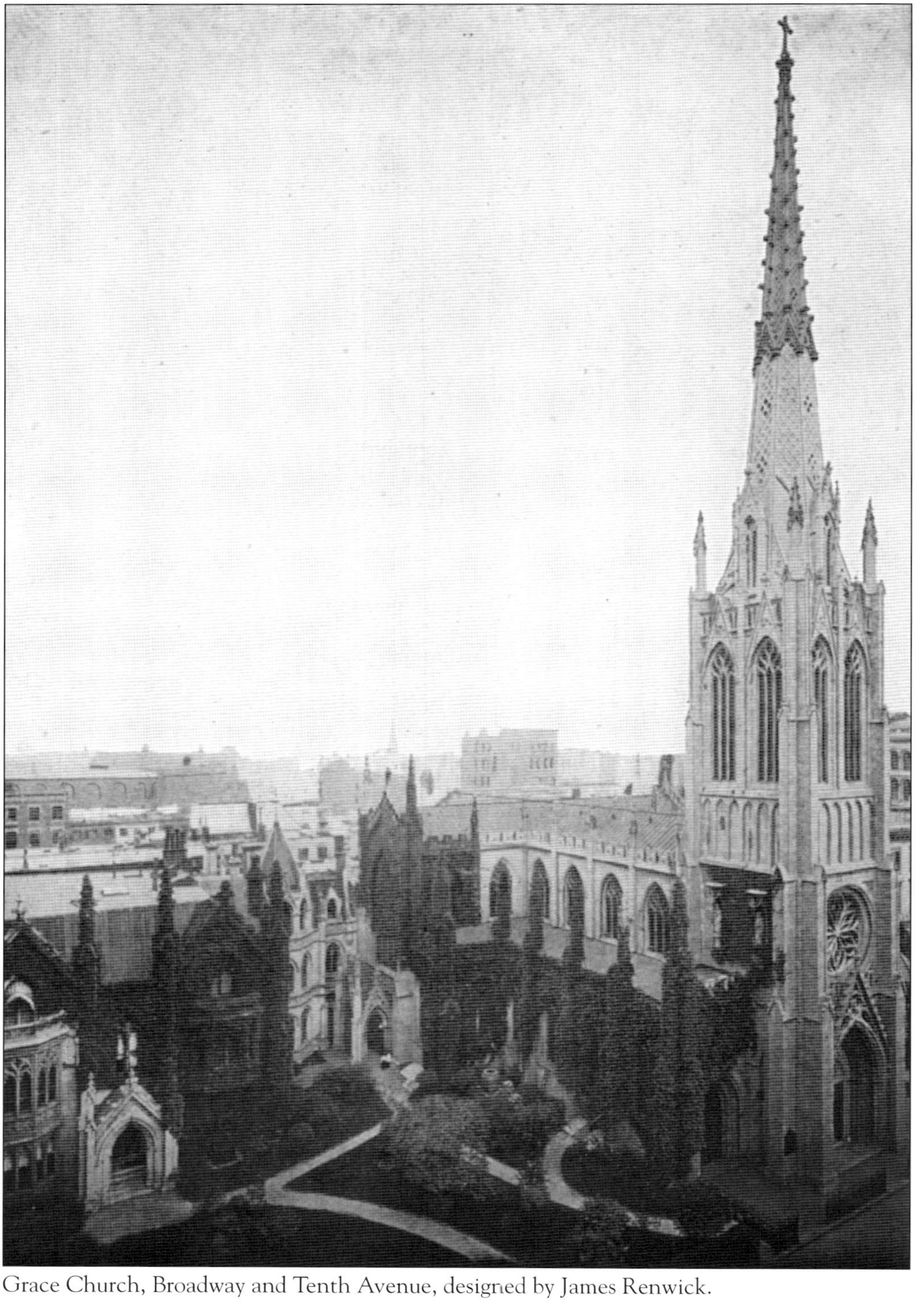

Grace Church, Broadway and Tenth Avenue, designed by James Renwick.

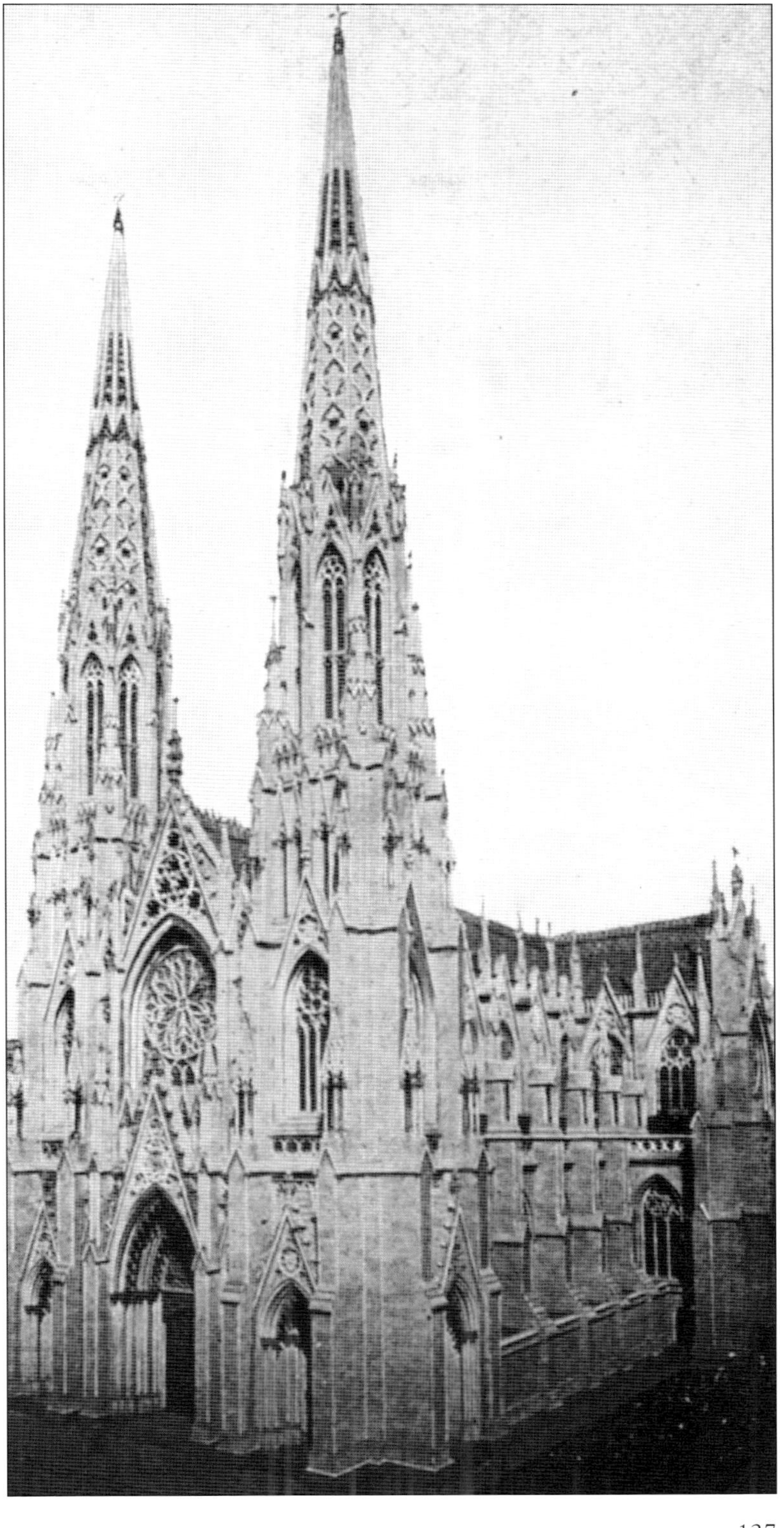

St. Patrick's Cathedral, designed by James Renwick and built over an eight-year period beginning in 1859.

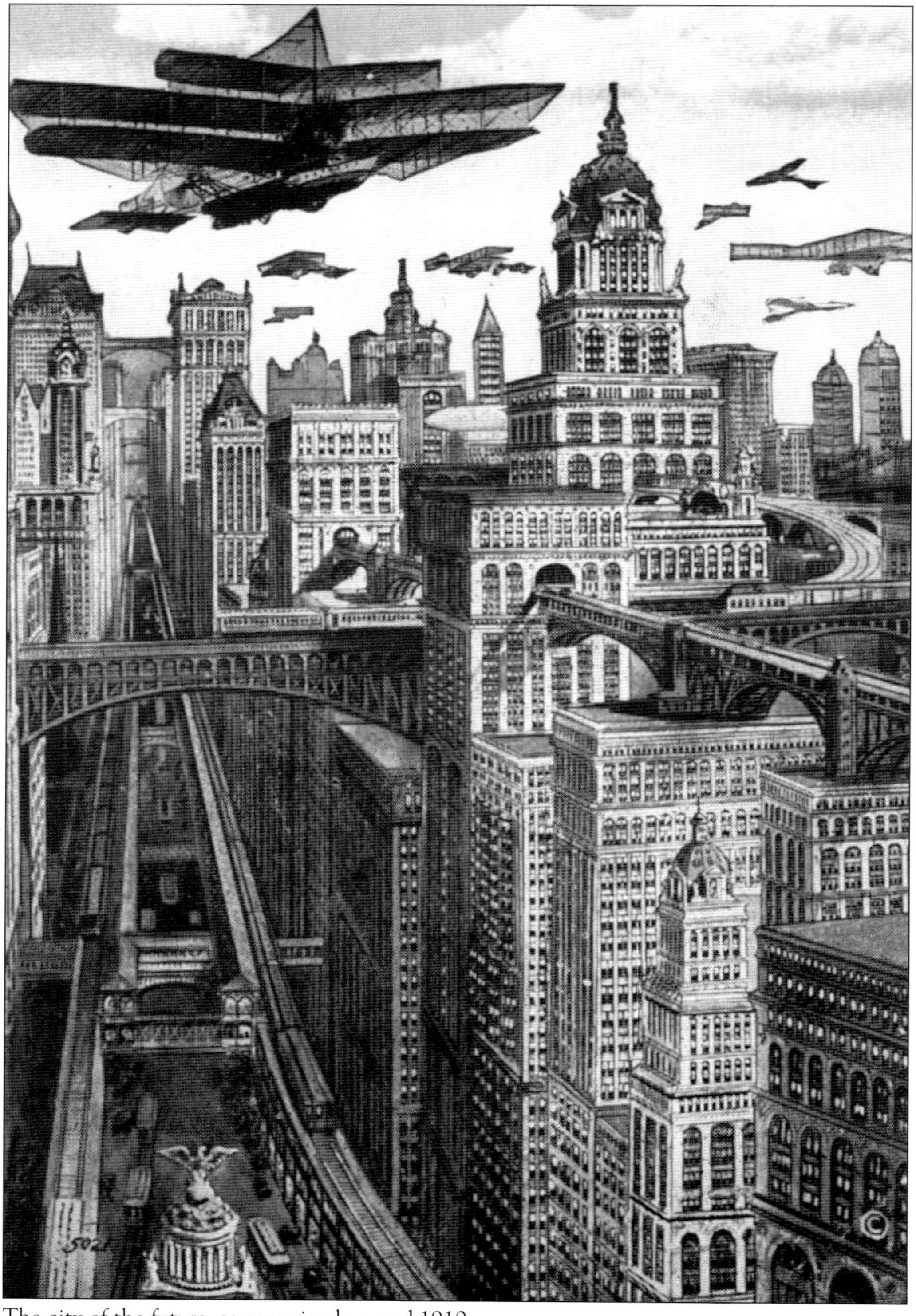

The city of the future, as conceived around 1910.